TOMORROW BY DESIGN

THE WILEY SERIES IN SUSTAINABLE DESIGN

The Wiley Series in Sustainable Design has been created for professionals responsible for, and individuals interested in, the design and construction of the built environment. The series is dedicated to the advancement of knowledge in design and construction that serves to sustain the natural environment. Titles in the series cover innovative and emerging topics related to the design and development of the human community, within the context of preserving and enhancing the quality of the natural world. Consistent with their content, books in the series are produced with care taken in the selection of recycled and non–polluting materials.

Gray World, Green Heart
Technology, Nature and the Sustainable Landscape
Robert J. Thayer, University of California, Davis

Regenerative Design for Sustainable Development
John T. Lyle, California State Polytechnic University, Pomona

Audubon House
Building the Environmentally Responsible, Energy-Efficient Office
National Audubon Society
Croxton Collaborative, Architects

Design with Nature
Ian L. McHarg

Wind Energy Comes of Age
Paul Gipe

Tomorrow By Design
Philip H. Lewis, Jr.

TOMORROW BY DESIGN

A Regional Design Process for Sustainability

PHILIP H. LEWIS, JR.

John Wiley & Sons, Inc.

New York • Chichester • Brisbane • Toronto • Singapore

Copyright © 1996 by Philip H. Lewis, Jr. and John Wiley & Sons, Inc.
Published by John Wiley & Sons, Inc.

Library of Congress Cataloging in Publication Data:

Lewis, Philip H.
    Tomorrow by design : a regional design process for
sustainability / Philip H. Lewis Jr.
        p.   cm. — (Wiley series in sustainable design)
    Includes bibliographical references and index.
    ISBN 0-471-10935-5 (acid-free paper)
    1. Regional planning—Environmental aspects—United States.
2. Land use—United States.   3. Sustainable development—United
States.   4. Environmental protection—United States.   I. Title.
II. Series.
HT392.L49   1996
307.1'2'0973—dc20   95-43871

Printed in the United States of America

10 9 8 7 6 5 4 3 2 1

This book was supported by a grant from the Graham Foundation
for Advanced Studies in the Fine Arts
and by Florence Lewis

ACKNOWLEDGMENTS

Indispensable collaborators have been Charles Holzbog, whose many sketches over the years buttress and strengthen the argument for sustainable design, Lester Doré and Heather Putnam for aiding in organization of graphics and the first-draft text, John Wiley & Sons editor Dan Sayre, the Graham Foundation for the grant that paid for the staff to prepare the materials for this book, and Dean Don Field of the School of Natural Resources, the College of Agriculture, the University of Wisconsin for encouraging and aiding in my obtaining a sabbatical leave during which to write this book. A lifetime endeavor is aided and supported by students, friends, and associates—far too many to name. As a token list, I mention my parents, Florence and Philip Lewis, who first nurtured and encouraged me. My professional education was strongly influenced by Professors Hideo Sasaki, Stanley White, Karl Lohman, Florence B. Robinson, Walter Chambers, Norman Newton, Lester Collins, Charles Eliot, and Charles Kneir in the areas of landscape architecture, design, and regional planning. Architects and architectural historians Walter Creese, Paul Spreiregan, Andrew Euston, Fumihiko Maki, Richard Rogers, Moshe Safdie, Walter Gropius, Richard Williams, John Replinger, Ed Deem, Philip Horvath, and Mary Rathbun were important to the formation of the ideas in this book. Soil scientists Minott Silliman, J. L. Bartelli, and R. W. Oertel had an early influence. Contemporaries Charles Harris, Robert Goetz, Patrick Horsbrugh, Lewis Clarke, Jaime Bellalta, and Esmee Krome in the same arena and the same time were important throughout the years as personal and professional friends. University colleagues Allen Corey, Jake Beuscher, Jerry Rohlich, Carl Runge, Ray Penn, Harold Jordahl, Stephen Born, Jerold Kaufman, Richard Andrews, Steven Smith, Ben Niemann, Bruce Murray, Dennis Wilkenson, Tom Lamm, Atef Sharkawy, Peter Olin, Bob Sykes, Roger Martin, Ayse Somersan, Marvin Beatty, John Ross, Wolfgang Hoffman, Dean Proctor, Chuang-Chung Chiang, and the University of Wisconsin Department of Landscape Architecture faculty were all important and influential over the years. Research support came from the Marshall Erdman family, the Koval families, Timothy Radelet, Clyde Engel, and the National Endowment for the Arts, among others. At various times authors and editors Dennis Moore, Carole Neckar, Mik Dirks, Grady Clay, Charles Little, and Tony Hiss worked with me and on my behalf. Important governmental figures were Gaylord Nelson, David Carley, Stuart Udall, Conrad Wirth, Theodore Sudia, Hodge Hanson, Frank Einsweiler, and Marty Rayala. Dr. Tom Kirkwood and, in recent years, Drs. Louis Berhardt, Janet Johansson, Paul Simenstad, and Robert Henderson have been largely responsible for my continued state of health and productivity.

To my wife, Elizabeth, for collaboration, editing skills, and patience;
and above all faith and encouragement that have endured for forty-two years.

CONTENTS

CONTENTS

« xi »

FOREWORD

The first Earth Day, in 1970, was a nationwide expression of our concern for our environment: our resources, our physical and spiritual well-being.

Wisconsin, at the beginning of the decade of the sixties, undertook an inventory of its physical and cultural resources as described in the following pages. The method and approach were developed and applied by Professor Philip Lewis to establish priorities for the development of our $50 million Outdoor Recreation Act Program for Wisconsin. A part-time staff of 30 worked under his direction over a period of a year and a half. The Wisconsin inventory and analysis, plus similar studies done under Professor Lewis's direction of the Great Lakes basin, the Upper Mississippi valley, and the states of Illinois and Alaska which were supported by the National Park Service, the U.S. Corps of Engineers, the Illinois State Housing Board, and the U.S. Land Law Review Commission, are a core prototype of a national inventory and analysis.

This task has still not been accomplished for the United States on a uniform scale to establish a framework for national, state, regional, and local land-use decisions. Immediate use for recreation and tourism alone would be served, and it would serve also as a tool for protecting threatened natural resources, for protecting and enhancing water resource quality, and for guiding transportation planning and other ongoing land and resource uses. The broad-brush survey and inventory are amenable to the addition of more detailed information when and as it becomes available. When millions are being spent for long-term specific ecological studies, the first step should be to compile and graphically standardize existing data and establish priorities to fill in the gaps where data are most obviously needed. Using data already at hand should be the first priority. We know a lot of resource measurements that should be put to wider use to make better decisions for economic, social, and environmental reasons. We are all members of the global ecosystem. Readers of this book can assimilate and adopt what has been practiced and taught in Wisconsin and elsewhere by the author and like-minded regional design practitioners.

We must continue to respond to the desire of Americans to foster and protect the means of survival. The economy is a wholly owned subsidiary of the environment. That applies equally in all places. We can't afford to pay the rent by selling the store.

The application of simple analytical methods and an interdisciplinary approach can yield the means of identifying for every state and region the range of resource priorities and the most immediate threats to those resources. In the vast reaches of our mountains, forests, plains, deserts, wetlands, lakes, and waterways, in constricted ranges of endangered habitats, and in the tiny crevices in the mud where frogs winter is the source of our country's future life.

Gaylord Nelson
May 26, 1995

INTRODUCTION

This book is for everyone who is interested in exploring an alternative process for reconciling explosive urban growth with our regional natural and cultural landscape features. I know that many people are concerned about current trends and want change but feel that they do not have much power to effect change. My 42 years of applied research in the upper midwest landscape have taught me that every person can indeed make a difference. If you want to take an active part in your own regional growth patterns, this book is for you.

I am concerned about many of the changes I see around me (Fig. I.1). I want to make a difference, and so for 42 years I have applied my efforts to finding answers through absorbing explorations of the *sustainable*★ features of the natural and cultural world (those resources that are renewable or that can be replenished or restored, for which adequate substitutes can be found, or which can be left alone without great detriment to either humanity or its surroundings).

We know that the natural world is essential to life, that we are unquestionably tied to it, but we

cannot just determine to preserve everything that is natural because everything we do has some impact on the land. The key to *sustainability* is to understand the nature of the impact and its implications to the total natural and cultural system. Before we can do anything, we must understand what comprises the landscape continuum and how critical each resource and pattern of its occurrence is. Once we recognize where all the known resources in a region are, we can see the patterns in which they occur. These patterns can guide how and where future growth can be placed to avoid destroying the essential resources that sustain life (Fig. I.2).

Ultimately, we need studies to support long-range models of the human and natural resource relationships necessary for a sustainable future. (However, while these extensive studies are under way, we cannot afford to have this be our single path of action.) Present decisions need to be based on present knowledge and data. Ingenuity can extrapolate and evaluate what we now know so that we can make better and less destructive broadscale decisions. For example, by combining knowledge of critical water, wetlands, steep topography, and *aquifer recharge patterns* (the

★ Terms that appear in italics are defined in the glossary.

(a)

(b)

(c)

(d)

(e)

(f)

Figure I.1 The rapidly changing landscape.

areas in which water enters the groundwater system from the atmosphere and surface of the earth), we can easily identify *environmental corridors* (combined water, wetland, and steep topographic patterns), which encompass 85 to 90 percent of the natural and cultural resources in need of protection. Much of the current environmental change currently causing concern, such as the draining of marshes and destructive development on shorelines and steep topography, is centered in this pattern. Nearly all of this information is already available on U.S. Geological Survey (USGS) maps.

In addition to being direct, simple to implement, and financially reasonable; identifying environmental corridors quickly leads us to the most critical lands to preserve, providing a sound basis on which to make basic decisions about where to build, where not to build, and how to build. Once these fundamental decisions are made, critical and sensitive areas should be earmarked for future evaluation. The key, I believe, is a structured but flexible approach that can be altered as new and more comprehensive data and techniques evolve.

We tend to approach the environmental movement by breaking it down into discussions

Figure I.2 Regional landscape resource patterns (underground, on the surface, above the surface).

about such issues as population, pollution, transportation, energy, food, and biodiversity. Recommendations for the future are often found within the context of a particular issue, but when considered as a whole the suggestions tend to become diffuse and incomplete. All of these issues have a common theme that is not much talked about: guiding human growth to minimize impact on key land and cultural patterns (Fig. I.3).

We can make much progress toward sustainability if we recognize this theme as a unifying framework that provides an opportunity for a common discussion of all the issues together. From here it then becomes possible to suggest a comprehensive process that takes all these issues into account. In searching for solutions to problems, it is natural to want to understand the source of various problems. So the origin of awareness of the crisis and the environmental movement is of interest. A commonly accepted benchmark is 1964, when Silent Spring, by Rachel Carson, was published, focusing public attention on the lethal impacts of pesticides, especially DDT. Personally, I would date the start of the current environmental movement a bit earlier, to the 1955 conference at Princeton Uni-

Above the Surface

On the Surface

Underground

Figure I.3 Guiding human growth patterns, utilizing landscape patterns as form determinants.

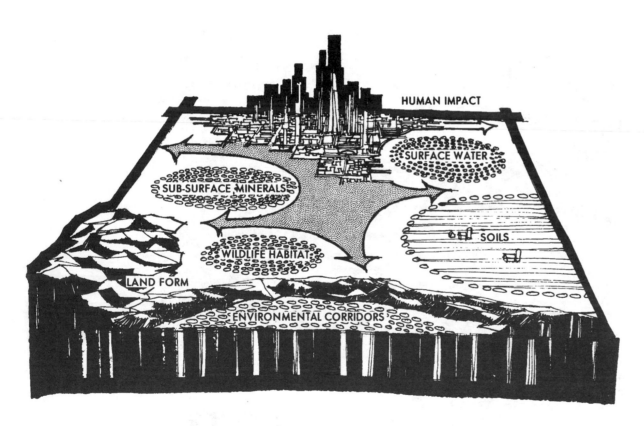

versity and its resulting publication, entitled *Man's Role in Changing the Face of the Earth*.[1] The conference brought together many people from diverse backgrounds to learn what others were thinking and to keep abreast of all the means at man's disposal to affect deliberately or unconsciously the course of his own evolution; in this case, what man has done and is doing to change his physical–biological environment on the earth.[2]

We must, of course, also recognize that this is certainly not the first time we have faced a need to adjust our relationship with our environment. In Rome at the beginning of the third century A.D., the founder of Christian Latin literature, Tertullian, observed:

There are few places now that are not accessible; few, unknown; few, unopened to commerce. Beautiful farms now cover what were trackless wastes, the forests have given way before the plow, cattle have driven off beasts of the jungle, the sands of the desert bear fruit and crops, the rocks have been ploughed under, the marshes have been drained of their water, and where once there was but a settler's cabin, great cities are now to be seen. . . . Everywhere we see houses, people . . . the vast population of the earth to which we are a burden and she can scarcely provide for our needs; as our demands grow stronger, our complaints against nature's inadequacy are heard by all. The scourges of pestilence, famine, wars, and earthquakes have come to be regarded as a blessing to overcrowded nations, since they serve to prune away the luxuriance of the human race.[3]

Many rulers and powers, ancient and modern, stripped the hills bare of timber for armadas, mined the soil for crops, enslaved nations for labor, and commandeered artisans and precious materials to glorify their presence among humankind as we have continued to do to the present day. Tertullian wrote at a time when Roman methods, tools, and plants were dispersed to an area extending from the British Isles through northern Europe, Scandinavia, and eastern Europe to western Siberia and the eastern and western coasts of Africa, north Africa, and points eastward.[4]

No matter how we believe we came to inherit the benefits of the earth and its resources, we have a responsibility to humanity (family and friends, on an extended scale), present and future, or risk being cast out of the social contract: "Do unto others as you would have others do unto you." Will we deny our place as both the instrument of change and the subject of change until it is beyond our power to steer the process? Since the scale of modification of the landscape is now so much broader than in Roman times, are we facing potential destruction of our species and not just the dispersal and reduction of dominant nations? I believe it behooves us to act immediately to change our course; extinction need not be our fate. Until the basic nature of our situation, not to mention knowledge of the intimate details, are widely understood, we stand absolutely no chance of reversing the march toward environmental crisis. We must take into account the basic components of the forces at work and we must understand the rules governing their interaction.

The three major interrelated factors that determine environmental change, as identified by the *Man's Role in Changing the Face of the Earth* conference, are:

1. The earth's resources
2. The numerical pressure of population upon, and sustained by, the resources
3. The differing human cultures, or ways of life[5]

Interactions among these elements can be viewed as the result of many opposing factors. It is easier to provide solutions concerned with analysis and recommendations for a single element of a situation than to treat the dynamics of all the elements and the range and magnitude of effects that might be produced in the three sectors outlined above. One-faceted plans might seem beneficial in the short term but cause more harm than good in the long term. A global perspective of the unprecedented rapid increase in population is required, and far-reaching changes in our global physical home, as well as technological, intellectual, and social changes, need to be made. Priorities must be reviewed and sorted.

We must act on the premise that all is not hopeless and that there are options other than to continue on our clearly ill-fated path and to accept our demise. If we accept that the environmental crisis is serious, we also accept that we have an ongoing responsibility to be aware of what humankind has done, is doing, and might do to change the face of the earth. With a keen awareness of the impacts of our behaviors, combined with knowledge of how physical laws function, we can continually fine tune our actions to stay within appropriate limits to maintain the dynamic balance of our *life-support system*. There is really no place on earth unaffected by humankind, but a process of mutual evolution is under way, and we are capable of safeguarding our own best interests as the dominant species as long as we do not remove ourselves in some way from competition in the survival race.

One of the largest obstacles to adopting this sort of approach is human resistance to change. Cultures develop traditions and customs as a mechanism to ensure cultural survival. Then human identities are defined partly by their cultural matrix. Thus if a new way to approach the use of basic resources of land, air, and water is suggested, the new way means much more than simply changing rules governing behavior. It can mean a fundamental change in culture and traditions and therefore how we define who we are and how we create the *sense of place* that makes life meaningful. This implied change of identity is one of the major barriers to averting the environmental crisis because human identities are very closely intertwined with consumptive methods of resource use such as filling prime farmland with sprawling subdivisions that meet our single-family home expectations, or acceptance of the many environmental consequences of our cultural love affair with the internal combustion engine and automobiles.

Convenience has risen to a central position among American cultural priorities. The concept is an attractive and natural response to the availability of time-saving, comfort, and access to more goods and services. Any pioneer would have welcomed tools or processes to make dealing with everyday realities a little easier. How-

ever, with technological innovation, unforeseen corollary results are likely to occur. Now, with the leisure that comes with the degree of comfort we have achieved as a nation, we can attempt to calculate and recognize the undesirable consequences of any given present-day convenience and determine whether the long-run benefits outweigh the costs. If the environmental costs are identified and measured, some elements of "progress" may be less appealing. We are beginning to understand the nature and extent of the total costs of allowing unlimited sprawl and highway development when we recognize that serious deleterious environmental impacts result from this development. Regulation of any sort of development requires public understanding of the necessity of regulation. Human self-interest requires as complete a knowledge as possible of the effects of our actions. We have reached a point where there is no other reasonable choice. If we do not design change ourselves, we will be forcibly changed. We resist because we are afraid of losing control of our sense of place and self. What is not evident is that changes need not be so radical and ongoing that all identity is lost. Although pride in auto-

mobiles and other material possessions prevails, I believe it is possible that one day we might instead take pride in and ownership of the beauty of our environment (Fig. I.4).

Change is not easy, especially on the scale required to avert environmental crises. In part, the required changes are resisted because of the difficulty in envisioning a *quality of life* (our degree of satisfaction with our surroundings) that is actually improved in both the long and short term by giving up or altering the very things that are so firmly believed to be necessary to a superior quality of life. However, many communities and cultures around the world have demonstrated that quality of life is not wholly related to consumption. Some new developments are beneficial, some are environmentally neutral, and some have significantly harmful effects. Whether the harm is basic to the technology, idea, or method or whether it can be made harmless is important, as is the relative value of the new idea to humanity as a whole. The Regional Design Process put forth here provides an alternative vision of the future concrete enough that the path toward sustainability is clear. To live sustainably, our present standard of living need not be diminished. The Regional Design Process is

Figure I.4 Observing our landscape as a collective work of art.

being stated so as to share the history of its development and the findings of its application so that it can be put into action by others. Part of that action is bound to include some redefinition of a desirable standard of living.

The process requires the use of terms that may be fairly new to the reader's vocabulary. With reference to problems, one encounters *population explosion, resource depletion, urban sprawl,* erosion, and environmental degradation; and in finding solutions, *resource inventories,* natural and cultural resources, resource *patterns,* environmental corridors, building higher livable *densities,* quality of life, *interdisciplinary imperative,* and *edu-*

cational tourism opportunities. The Regional Design Process provides a systematic and flexible way to guide land use, design, development, and *restoration.* It takes into account environmental problems such as population explosion, erosion, resource depletion, urban sprawl, and landscape degradation, and operates with an understanding of the relationships between people and nature to accommodate growth by determining where to build or rebuild and where not to build. The Regional Design Process for sustainable design provides a critical understanding of and access to regional values and visions. The method calls for the use of interdisciplinary teams imbued with an *integrated land and social ethic* to perform inventories of resources and provide options that:

• Sustain and restore our life-support system
• Enhance our quality of life
• Preserve and add to our sense of place
• Include an awareness of and respect for natural and cultural diversity
• Permit beneficial choices among alternatives
• Inform the discretion of the public by means of such tools as:
    • *E-Ways*
    • *Guideways*
    • *Awareness centers*
    • *Academies for sustainable design*

The Regional Design Process is intended to be a comprehensive process for design, development, and restoration. Application of the model at a variety of environmental scales is provided in the following chapters.

Notes

[1]Paul Fejos, in *Man's Role in Changing the Face of the Earth,* edited by William J. Thomas, The University of Chicago Press, Chicago, 1956, 1193 pp.

[2]Thomas, William J., op. cit.

[3]Tertullian (Quintus Septimus Florens Tertullianus), in "De Anima" ("On the Soul"), in *The Fathers of the Church,* Vol. 10, translated by Rudolph Arbesmann, Emily Joseph Daley, and Edwin A. Quain, Fathers of the Church, Inc., 1950.

[4]See Fritz M. Heichelheim, in Arbesmann et al., for more on classical period history.

[5]Thomas, op. cit.

PART I

NATIONAL OVERVIEW

Part I focuses on the purpose and application of the Regional Design Process at the national scale. We must have a national overview available that consolidates and presents in an easily read format the information available to all of us in order to guide the use of resources for planning, remediation, and restoration at the regional and local level. Local and regional land-use decisions are often made without an awareness of resource information available from federal agencies, although vast quantities of resource information on water, wetlands, geology, vegetation, weather, wildlife, soils, climate, crops, population, economics, manufacturing, and related subjects are available showing past, present, and trends for the future. These data can be shown as mapped resource patterns. Presently, a consistent, comprehensive process for gaining access to the pertinent information, organizing it, and relating it to regional and local design solutions is sadly lacking. In many cases it is apparent that the existence of

the needed data is unknown. In others, the state and regional agencies that had been available to coordinate and disseminate such knowledge, such as the Great Lakes Commission, the Ozarks Commission, and the New England Commission, have been dissolved because of lack of funding.

Understanding the usefulness and the necessity for a Regional Design Process is the first step toward establishing regional organizations and design programs that have the capacity to inventory, analyze, and synthesize national resource information, as such information would provide a comprehensive base for developing further regional and local planning and design concepts, in addition to making reasoned and logical land-use decisions at the present time.

Identification, assemblage, interpretation, and translation of national information into sustainable options for land use is only the beginning of a comprehensive growth strategy. A national design

program can have all the data possible and the best interpretation possible by creative staff, but these identified values and visions are meaningless unless a national effort to communicate these ethical options is made that operates successfully at the level of current entertainment and information technologies.

In the following four chapters we describe the necessity for a Regional Design Process, the integrated land and social ethic needed to guide such a process, a national growth strategy, and possible national programs to communicate sustainable design options for both the present generation and those of the future.

CHAPTER 1

NECESSITY FOR A REGIONAL DESIGN PROCESS

POPULATION PRESSURES

There are many pressures on the intricate dynamic balance of our planet. Perhaps the most immediate of these is the ever-growing human population. In 1993, world population swelled by about 90 million people[1]: 246,000 additional people every day. It appears certain that the total human population will eventually reach the earth's *carrying capacity*. The standard of living possible for such a rapidly increasing population is a matter of considerable debate, but it is clear that only a minority of the present world population enjoys the standard of living held to be basic by the industrialized countries. Sufficient food, clothing, and shelter as well as health care and available universal primary and secondary education are not even available to every sector of the industrialized nations. The best evidence now available indicates that if the present growth trends in world population continue and industrialization, pollution, food production, and resource depletion continue unchanged, the limits to growth on this planet will be reached sometime within the next 100 years. The many beneficial effects of technological developments will not allow us to escape this reality.

World population growth throughout history has been far from a linear process. It was only after several million years of growth that the human population approached 1 billion in about 1800.[2] In 1974, only 174 years later, the figure had ballooned to 4 billion. We have already reached the fifth billion (1988), and by 1998 we will have added yet another billion if the present rate of increase continues. The current rate of increase, 1.64 percent per year, means enormous actual numbers of people. To count to 5 billion at the rate of one per second would take 160 years. The daily rate of increase now is 246,670 per day. Where are we going to put 365 cities of about 250,000 each this year and every following year? Can you imagine 90 million new babies to be fed, clothed, sheltered, and cared for in one place—our earth? These ever-increasing needs are putting tremendous pressures on the earth's resources.

We can already see signs of a world bulging at the seams. Soil systems are being eroded, and are also being removed from production in favor of other uses. Land unsuitable for farming (such as drained wetlands, steep and easily eroded soils, and already contaminated land) is often utilized in addition to arable acres. Land is often cultivated too intensively and overtreated chemically. The number of acres available for cultivation is inadequate to produce enough for increasing numbers of people. Overgrazing means less pasturage and soil *erosion*. Acres of fertile farmland are lost to growing cities and their associated structures. Soil quality is diminished as animal wastes are burned for fuel rather than returned to the soil as fertilizer as was done for centuries. Topsoil exposed by agricultural practices is lost to wind and water erosion at a rate faster than it can be formed—on average it takes 100 years to form an inch of topsoil. Deforestation is a strain on resources. Fuel shortages and large-scale slash-and-burn agriculture make the local soil nutrient supply unavailable for future crops or replacement of tropical forests as well as depleting the number of plant and animal species in those tropical areas. Shrinking tree cover from commercial logging and large-scale farming as well as attempts to produce food on submarginal lands result in the loss of precious topsoil and siltation of waterways (Fig. 1.1). Depletion of wetlands diminishes filtration of the surface waters returning to rivers, lakes, and oceans. Water tables are lowered by large-scale irrigation that draws water from wells and returns it to other aquifers. Diets high in animal protein from sources high on the food chain require the use of many more acres than do simpler, more vegetarian diets. Intensive agriculture is dependent on petroleum products, which are a limited resource. This is merely the opening of a litany of the pressures brought about by increasing populations and rising expectations with respect to the basic standard of living. The creation of centers of population peripheral to our larger cities (continuous urbanization along American coastlines, expanding rings of new commercial and residential centers around our established large cities at *population densities* decreasing with distance from the city center) demands proportionally more land and other resources per person than in more central areas.

Proliferation of social problems is evidence of stress. People flock to the cities when agricultural workers are displaced because of technological improvements, increased size of farms, and decreased numbers of farms. They also leave rural areas when food production slumps due to the vagaries of weather and poor agricultural practices. There are population dislocations both within and across national borders caused by economic, political, social, and religious strife. Slums and squatter camps, and internment camps for refugees without adequate water and sanitation facilities proliferate as more people are dislocated and flee to find asylum of one sort or another. Despair, poverty, and poor living conditions perpetuate crime, malnutrition, and disease.

Extensive documentation of information on the population explosion and the consequences of such vast new numbers on global landscape resources (both natural and cultural) are presented daily in many forms. I have intentionally chosen to discuss these threats to our present and future only sparingly and to recommend strongly that the reader learn of such present and potential future disasters from the writings of others, such as Paul Ehrlich (particularly *The Population Bomb*), Paul Hawken (in his provocative national best-seller *The Ecology of Commerce*) and the yearly state-of-the-world publications of Lester Browne's Worldwatch Institute. This startling array of sobering facts touches on what's happening to our protective ozone shield, the loss of plant and animal species, vanishing world forests, the loss of productive soils, the warming of the earth's surface, the lack of food to sustain malnourished children, unclean water, pesticide poisoning, and all other forms of waste, pollution, and threats to human health.

Figure 1.1 Impacts on the land and landscape: (a) strip mining; (b) cultural impact; (c) erosion.

(a)

(b)

(c)

One does not begin to think about the importance of a Regional Design Process toward reversing such trends until the scale and rapidity of these changes are realized. The degree and scope of the degradation caused by them can be overwhelming and create a dangerous state of hopelessness and unwillingness to act, or simple abdication of responsibility in the face of seemingly inevitable change for the worse. Action, coupled with wisdom, is called for.

Instead of repeating in this book what so many have documented so well, I have chosen to record my 42 years of field experience in developing a Regional Design Process that can help protect, restore, and enhance what's left of our life-support system so as to offer the best possible options for society. Known pressures on the global system are increasingly severe, to the detriment of the human species, particularly in those parts of the world least able to meet the challenge.

We cannot deny that population is expanding rapidly. Even if current efforts to control population growth continue to be increasingly successful and the rate in increase levels off, human numbers will increase as longevity increases and expectations for a better standard of living increase the rate of resource utilization. The pop-

ulation will continue to grow for years into the future and will continue to have an increasing impact on the *environment*. We must plan now to guide human development so as to have the least possible impact on the dynamic balance of natural and cultural resources vital to our life-support system. This is the purpose and essential nature of the Regional Design Process. Applied on the national scale, it can establish a context in which regional and local plans can be made.

POPULATION AND RESOURCE DEPLETION

The present land-use crisis is due in large part to the present rate of change in land uses and the nature of those uses. Population is a controlling factor in global health because of its influence on resources, altering the dynamics of the life-support system on which we depend. There are very real concerns that go along with this kind of a population explosion and instability of political and economic structures. An early report produced for the President of the United States by the Council on Environmental Quality and the Department of State explains one such concern:

how much land is available to produce food for each person. Although the report came out in 1975, the concern is often reiterated, and what it says is still applicable today.

The world in 2000 will be different from the world today in important ways. There will be more people. For every two persons on the earth in 1975, there will be three in 2000. There will be fewer resources to go around. While on a worldwide average there was about four-tenths of a hectare of arable land per person in 1975, there will be only about one-quarter hectare per person in 2000. Environmental deterioration caused by large populations create living conditions that make reductions in fertility difficult to achieve; all the while, continuing population growth increases further the pressures on the environment and land. The declines in carrying capacity already being observed in scattered areas around the world point to a phenomenon that could easily be much more widespread by 2000. In fact, the best evidence now available—even allowing for the many beneficial effects of technological developments and adoptions suggests that by

2000 the world's human population may be within only a few generations of reaching the entire planet's carrying capacity.[3]

In 1993 there were 3.95 per hectare, virtually the predicted density for the year 2000. The projected population for the year 2010 is now 7,035,950,000.[4] To meet the needs of this ever-increasing population, there is a corresponding ever-increasing pressure to bring more land into food production and to increase crop yields, and to provide more housing, transportation capacity, and both raw materials and finished goods of all kinds. Under this pressure, land and other resources are yielded here and there, little by little, year by year. The changes are gradual, subtle, and little noticed from one year to the next, but the cumulative impact over the past three or four decades is altering the face of the landscape in significant and unwanted ways.

In much of the United States the need to preserve present resources diligently is not perceived, and as a result these areas are essentially being destroyed. Areas such as the national parks, national forests, wildlife refuges, Bureau of Land Management lands, and the wilderness areas within their borders have been set aside because

we agree that they need to be protected. However, despite this acknowledgment, even these areas are being compromised and degraded in manifold ways: by soil erosion, air pollution, water pollution, aircraft noise pollution, overuse by visitors, excessive road construction, excessive timbering, excessive grazing, stream siltation, overdevelopment, habitat destruction, scenic degradation, oil spills, and the decrease in biological diversity. We set a national goal of protecting these areas, but they are suffering many of the same ills as those of unprotected lands. Many areas are presently assumed to be protected and laws are being written to extend protection, but over time, small compromises are now manifesting themselves as big problems that threaten the survival of protected areas. Exceptions to environmental pollution standards, zoning regulations, and management plans exemplify dilutions of adopted policies.

Although people of many cultures agree that use of the land is a life-giving necessity, the meaning of "use" can vary dramatically. In many traditional cultures, the use of land incorporates the responsibility for preserving and sustaining it. Contemporary pressures to produce more and more commodities to satisfy more and more people result in exploitation of resources to the detriment of renewal and preservation of land. To cut trees, bring more land into production, to plant a new high-yielding variety of seed, to apply a newly developed fertilizer or to plant a monocrop to be able to increase production efficiency; to use nonrenewable resources such as oil, gas, and mined raw materials; to fish the sea relentlessly; and to dispose of waste products with insufficient treatment and attention to conservation and recycling is justified by short-term expediency. Individually, each practice seems to offer the promise of improving the quality of life. Unpredicted results occur when these practices are not controlled and they lead to the depletion and contamination of air, water, and soil that plague us today. The total of all their effects is also more than the sum of the individual effects due to interactions such as the effect of waste disposal into the sea on fish growth and reproduction, and thus on human nutrition and health and on economic stability.

An important lesson from observations about resource losses and environmental degradation in the last several decades is that human impacts on the land, air, and water include the expanding infrastructure of transportation facilities, urban services, and industrial and commercial development as well as resource depletion.

This impact is particularly evident in the United States, where although the 1993 population growth is less than 1 percent, the impact on the planet's resources is particularly significant.

According to *Wildlife Fund Atlas* figures, in 1987 the United States consumed 24 percent of the world's total commercially traded energy resources (oil, gas, coal, hydro, and nuclear), although it accounts for only 5 percent of the world's population.[5] Therefore, energy consumption is clearly not proportionate to either population size or growth rate, and even if population size and growth rates are low, the demands of a high material standard of living and industrialization are inordinately high.

As a result of its ready ability to buy virtually anything needed, the United States is exempt from some of the problems brought about by overpopulation and increased resource use in other countries. Crowding, disease, poverty, and warfare are not part of everyday life for most Americans. There is still plenty of open space, and the tradition of personal mobility persists, so that if we do not have enough elbow room, we can just move to a more sparsely populated part of the country.

But this notion of the ever-advancing American frontier is illusory. Interstate highways connect our ocean coastlines. Roads are being built through wilderness areas as we extract and exploit more major resources. Increasingly we experience overcrowding in our national parks, beaches, and other natural recreational areas. Hazardous wastes and agricultural chemicals poison groundwater and lakes and destroy the animal and plant life essential to a healthy ecosystem. By-products of industry, energy production, and automobiles pollute the air (with sulfur oxides, nitrogen oxides, other substances in the gaseous state and particulate matter) and destroy pristine lakes and buildings of historic importance. Such pollution increases the incidence of illnesses such as emphysema and cancer by the introduction of complex organic chemicals into the air, the water, and the food chain. In addition, the massive water requirements of modern agriculture, mining, and industry deplete readily available surface and groundwater supplies.

It may be difficult to imagine how the United States could possibly become so crowded as to be overpopulated in the near future, as most recent world population increase is occurring in the less developed countries. Overpopulation does not mean only that people are crowded together. It also exacerbates social inability to provide everyone with the means to obtain food, shelter, medical care, and education, so that some are forced to live without the means of meeting their basic needs. We can already see the strains that population expansion places on our society both here and abroad. On a daily basis, news reports vividly describe hunger, poverty, and joblessness in our nation, including a growing number of homeless men, women, and children.

We must fully understand that although the population in the United States is expanding more slowly than in many countries, the expansion is significant and it is something about which we need to be concerned. In my lifetime, the population of the United States has doubled. To understand the significance of both the U.S. and global population explosions, we need to understand it in greater depth than a flurry of statistics not presented in meaningful terms.

URBAN SPRAWL

The scale of global population growth, of course, must be seen in spatial as well as temporal terms.

In temporal terms, the global population continues to increase. In spatial terms, this same population growth means that more people need a place to live. Our current lack of long-term planning and design and our dependance on automobile transportation has led to sprawl.

Gaylord Nelson, governor of Wisconsin from 1959 to 1963 and father of Earth Day, aptly summarized the spatial implications of population explosion.

> Cities are rapidly becoming larger, busier, and more crowded. Population densities are increasing, traffic is growing, and satellite bedroom communities are eating up nearby countrysides. Country highways are becoming mere extensions of city streets, complete with second rate commercial slums, traffic signs, and one billboard after another. The great outdoors is shrinking.[6]

As the cities expand, problems are magnified. Communities become overcrowded. Toxic waste, ozone levels, poverty, and hunger all increase. In addition, social chasms grow between the haves and the have-nots, between urban and rural interests, and between environmentalists and developers.

Sprawl has other side effects, including disproportionate increase in the infrastructure required to serve these expanding urban areas. Doubling the human population of a community multiplies by several more times the distances in the web of services such as communication, transportation, utilities, shopping, and governance, which in turn have multiple impacts on the lives of the people who are served. Also, as demands for services multiply, the services themselves become more complex technologically.

The rapid rate of technological change demonstrates that environmental problems can expand faster than population. Many small changes can have a far-reaching collective impact. Aerial photographs taken at night indicate, through patterns of light signifying human habitation, the density of human population on earth. Big cities show up as large spots of light, and even the interstate highway system is visible, dividing the landscape into a grid system. Considering such an image of the United States suggests the complexity of fostering the kind of awareness that we need to promote (Fig. 1.2).

Obvious questions are illustrated by viewing urbanization from a satellite. There is a great deal of uninhabited space in the picture. Why can't

Figure 1.2 Photographs of
the United States at night
emphasize the spatial extent
of human impact on the
land. (Courtesy of Argonaut
Press.)

that be settled? Most people live where there is employment and where human services are available. There is some crowding, but where there is crowding there is also convenience. Why give up convenience? Why can't technology ameliorate crowding? Even supposing that crowding is a serious issue, isn't it far less important than, say, poverty and hunger around the world?

When important matters are at issue, the Regional Design Process *can* provide an element of awareness that must be communicated through explanation, demonstration, and persuasive education. In the case of the population explosion and the resulting resource depletion and urban sprawl, we must become aware of the magnitude of population growth, its relation to urbanization, the lack of overall design and planning to guide urban sprawl, the impingement of such sprawl on food and other natural resources, and the consequent damage to quality of life for all of us. (Figs. 1.3 and 1.4).

Our increasing numbers take a toll on the quality of life as well. With economic affluence, some of us can abandon our inner cities for a cleaner and safer existence on the urban fringe. Many properties in our urban cores become inadequately cared for or underutilized. Mean-

while, residential and commercial development sprawls into our prime agricultural and recreational lands. The costs of capital services soar while we lose the unique character of our towns and city cores as well as open space.

RELATIONSHIPS BETWEEN PEOPLE AND NATURE

Most Americans today live at a distance from nature. We take devices such as cars, refrigerators, and light bulbs for granted and are glad that we have "progressed" beyond living like the pioneers of this country, who spent most of their time trying to subdue the wilderness and survive. Pioneer travel was either on foot, by boat, or by horse, all of which were slow and exposed the traveler to the natural elements. The early settlers obtained food by hunting, gathering, and subsistence farming—much as the indigenous people had done—and they had to build their own shelters and gather their own fuel from the resources immediately at hand.

The land of this country was used ever more intensively to support an increasing population with more goods. Industrialization required

fewer people to produce the necessary products from the land and added manufacture and commerce to our stock in trade. In winning the battle with the wilderness, new technologies were used, new kinds of plants and animals were raised, and new raw materials were mined. They were combined with an organization of production and finance into an economy highly efficient at extracting natural resources and utilizing them to solve the problems presented by human needs and desires. Throughout the years, this attitude has become deeply embedded in our value systems, and even today we continue to distance ourselves even further from the natural world and create tools that multiply the physical and intellectual effort of which one person is capable.

Today, with our choice of fast and convenient modes of travel, how far we want to go and what the weather is outside are of no great concern. Our automobiles are motorized minienvironments. As we whiz down the highway the interior temperature is maintained by heating and air-conditioning at a constant, comfortable level, the soundscape provided by the audio system is of our choosing, and the landscape goes by in a blur. No longer do we feel the sun beating down on our backs, or hear the birds singing in the

Figure 1.3 Urban sprawl. In 1993, in the United States alone, 2 million acres of cropland were lost to urbanization. (Courtesy of Dane County Regional Planning Commission.)

thickets, or smell the heavy perfume of freshly mown hay.

As we develop more and more technologies, we become less and less aware of our remaining connections with the natural world. Schoolchildren in cities can believe that milk and apples originate in grocery stores, unaware of the connection between milk and the cows that produced it or between apples and the trees on which they grow. Further, we take for granted the electricity that allows us to turn on the lights, watch television, and refrigerate our food. In addition, we give little thought to the energy required to produce that electricity.

We tend to think that our modern conveniences are benefits that make our life better and more fulfilling. Rarely do we step back and look at the bigger picture. Most people would agree that we benefit from being able to enjoy leisure-time instead of doing physical labor all day. But what is the price we pay, and is it worth it?

In the United States, in 1992, the number of deaths due to motor-vehicle accidents was 36,411.[7] "A recent study for the U.S. Federal Highway Administration included estimates of the monetary worth of pain, suffering, and lost quality of life in its tally of the costs of U.S. road

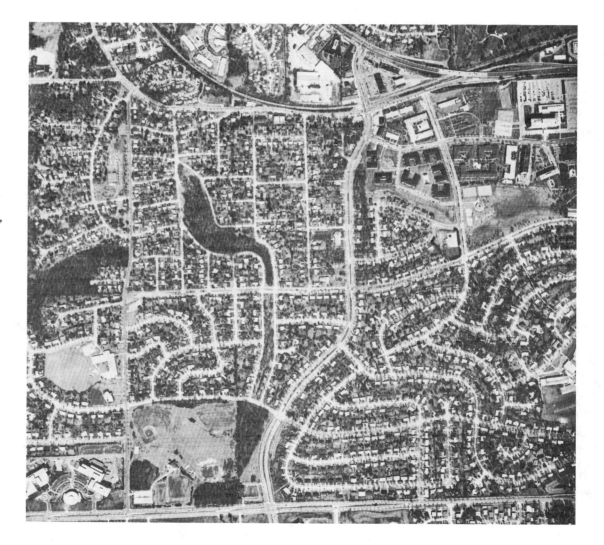

Figure 1.4 World lights at night. (a) Asia at night, February 1979. The light areas represent not only urbanization, but the burning of forests to make new cropland.

(b) South America at night, February 1979. As in the satellite photo of Asia, we see that major impacts are occurring in developing countries as well. It suggests that the concept of development itself needs rethinking. (Courtesy of Defense Military Satellite Program (DMSP).)

(a)

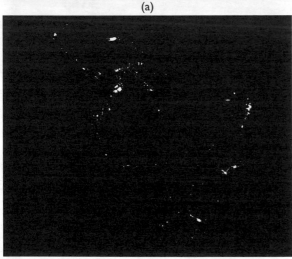

(b)

accidents in 1988. It arrived at a total of $358 billion, 8% of GNP."[8]

Aside from a financial burden, each of these tragedies affects the lives of families, friends, co-workers, and neighbors. Motor-vehicle related deaths, accidents, and illnesses can be reduced by reducing reliance on road-based transportation in favor of other safer, more efficient modes of transportation of which rail is the pre-eminent candidate for expansion. "Passenger rail is 18 times as safe as private car travel, with 0.4 deaths per 1 billion passenger-kilometers, compared with 7 deaths for private automobiles."[9] Even though car and road safety improvements are being made, community designs and the lack of alternatives require driving further and more frequently. This drives up the death, injury, and disability rates as well as increasing urban air pollution in spite of increased fuel efficiency and emissions controls. Worldwide, increases in motor-vehicle use will increase risks to health from degradation of environmental degradation directly (engine emissions, brake and tire break-down products, oil and grease, disoposal of old vehicles), and indirectly (by-products of vehicle and petroleum product production, highway construction, loss of food productivity, and many auxiliary processes).

We have to reestablish awareness of humanity's ecological niche if we are to be successful in our efforts to preserve and enhance the natural beauty of the earth for ourselves and our progeny. It seems clear that current global trends are unsustainable. The human population cannot expand without increasing limitations being imposed by the natural system to the degree that further existence is impossible for some or all of the population. We cannot consume our natural resources at ever-increasing rates indefinitely and change the conditions of life so that our basic requirements are met with conditions increasingly different from the optimum conditions for life. Uncontaminated air, water, food, clothing, and shelter are the obvious parameters of human requirements for life. Sprawl cannot solve our space problems and the price we must pay for the lack of identification with our place in nature is too great. The forces of nature are implacable, so we must adapt in order to continue our membership in the global ecosystem. We need a flexible, systematic, comprehensive approach to analyzing the landscape and guiding human growth to minimize human impact on the land. Such an approach must facilitate consistent, informed decisions about our future. The Regional Design Process involves taking into account natural features and human requirements in relation to them, and designing to maximize the long-term health of both in tandem and guiding human growth to minimize its impact on our critical resources. My applied research of 42 years has resulted in the development of this Regional Design Process.

Basically, the process identifies these resource patterns that we cherish and wish to pass on to future generations, utilizing these value patterns as form determinants to guide new and sustainable development. The process then proceeds to inform the public in creative ways of these values and new development options that are available today.

If we preserve and enhance critical natural and cultural resources, we can provide for both the planet and a number of people consistent with the extent of the global environmental system at the same time. The goal is a national or continental overview context in which the process applied to regional or local design studies is consistent with the overview at each scale of application. Additional data can be included where pertinent and necessary.

Identifying and protecting critical natural and cultural resources is the crux of analyzing the urban and rural landscapes as a single continuum and therefore the crux to sustainability. These resources are not only the basis of our life-support system and our economic well-being but are also the basis for quality of life, sense of place, diversity, and options of choice. Because of this, we should focus our efforts on keeping these resource patterns for future generations.

Once a resource pattern has been protected, it is possible to enhance that pattern so that the area in which it occurs is improved. This might involve the aesthetic value of the resource, whether urban or nonurban, by restoring and maintaining historical buildings, creating pleasing three-dimensional spaces, and designing pathways to incorporate maximum diversity. Enhancement might also involve improving the quality of an ecosystem by restoring vegetation or a wetland, protecting surface and subsurface waters from pollution, or improving the safety of an area by ensuring that it is accessible to the elderly and disabled. In such cases care must be given to controlling and diverting increased traffic from fragile areas. Urbanized areas can incorporate much of the regional character of the landscapes by emphasizing those features and designing them and views of them into cities and towns.

Notes

[1]Population Reference Bureau, Inc., Washington D.C., in the *Encyclopaedia Britannica Book of the Year, 1994,* Encyclopaedia Britannica, Inc., Chicago.

[2]Special Report, "World Population Year," in the *Encyclopaedia Britannica Book of the Year, 1975,* Encyclopaedia Britannica, Inc., Chicago.

[3]Warren S. Thompson, "The Spiral of Population," in *Man's Role in Changing the Face of the Earth,* edited by William J. Thomas, The University of Chicago Press, Chicago, 1956, 1193 pp.

[4]*The Global 2000 Report to the President of the United States: A Report Prepared by the Council on Environmental Quality and the Department of State,* U.S. Government Printing Office, Washington, D.C., 1975.

[5]Geoffrey Lean, Don Hinrichsen, and Adam Markham, *The Wildlife Fund Atlas of the Environment,* Prentice Hall, Englewood Cliffs, N.J., 1990.

[6]Philip H. Lewis, in the *Wisconsin Recreation Plan,* 1962.

[7]Population Reference Bureau, *Encyclopaedia Brittanica Book of the Year, 1994.*

[8]Marcia D. Lowe, "Rediscovering Rail" in *State of the World, 1993 (A Worldwatch Institue Report on Progress Toward a Sustainable Society)* Lester R. Brown, 1993, W.W. Norton & Co., New York, London. The U.S. estimate for 1989 is from The Urban Institute, *The Costs of Highway Crashes* (Washington, D.C., 1991). The accident rate figures are for 1989 from National Safety Council, *Accident Facts, 1991 Edition* (Chicago, Illinois, 1991).

[9]Population Reference Bureau, *Encyclopaedia Brittanica Book of the Year, 1994.*

CHAPTER 2

AN INTEGRATED
ETHIC

The Regional Design Process needs an ethical foundation that integrates a land ethic with a social ethic. The criteria for decisions about resource use today are codified in laws and regulations that are subject to change over time. Because land-use controls are far from permanent, preservation of our critical natural and cultural resources must become more deeply rooted not just in our laws but in our culture and ethics. Like laws, cultures change over time, but cultural changes are slow and gradual in nature. Minimizing the impact of future developments on the land will be more successful if a unified natural and social ethic becomes prevalent than if we depend solely on laws and regulations to guide our consciences.

Ethical issues always underlie human behavior. Generally accepted standards about how we should treat each other arise from widely accepted social ethics. Aldo Leopold articulated a land ethic to guide our relationship with the land that is widely known and respected. A further step is necessary to adopt an ethic that integrates our relationships with each other and the land into a single system. By articulating the relationships among people and those between

society and individuals and the system that supports our life and livelihood a consistent ethical fabric for contemporary life can be formed. In this chapter we comment briefly on social and land ethics and then outline an integrated ethic for sustainability that encompasses our life-support system, quality of life, interactions between art and life, sense of place, diversity, and the available range of choices among all the actions possible in a democracy.

SOCIAL AND LAND ETHICS

Social ethics, which encompass respect for human rights to fulfill basic needs, including housing, food, and health care, are widely held to be valid, although we still struggle with the details. Many questions about resource allocation remain the subject of fierce ongoing debates. Technology has often been the tool for meeting the goals of the social ethic, but the results have not always been promising. Even in prosperous nations, efforts to provide housing, food, and health care have often failed to ensure adequate resources for all.

Aldo Leopold wrote extensively about his homeland in Wisconsin's sand country. His deep sense of respect for the land and his sense of right and wrong is expressed elegantly and simply in his land ethic essay.

> There is as yet no ethic dealing with man's relation to the land and to the animals and plants which grow upon it. . . . The land relation is still strictly economic, entailing privileges but no obligations.
>
> The land ethic simply enlarges the boundaries of the community to include soils, waters, plants and animals, or collectively: the land.
>
> A land ethic, then, reflects the existence of an ecological conscience, and this in turn reflects a conviction of individual responsibility for the health of the land. Health is the capacity of the land for self-renewal.
>
> The "key-log" which must be moved to release the evolutionary process for an ethic is simply this; quit thinking about decent land-use as solely an economic problem. Examine each question in terms of what is ethically and aesthetically right as well as what is economically expedient. A thing is right when it tends to preserve the integrity, stability, and beauty of the biotic community. It is wrong when it tends otherwise.[1]

Just as social ethics say that we should treat people and cultural artifacts with respect, Leopold's land ethic suggests that we must have reverence for the land and treat it with respect. His land ethic provides guidance for identifying, protecting, and enhancing our life-sustaining resources to assure clean air, clean water, productive soils, and preservation of biological diversity and the beauty of the land. The land ethic is involved in discussions about contour farming, reforestation, saving the rain forests and other imperiled biotic communities, recognizing the importance of soil organisms, preserving biodiversity, protecting waterways and wetlands, and the entire range of biological issues, as well as saving scenic landscapes and the qualities that make them scenic. Joining social and land ethics is called for because human and natural habitats are part of a continuous system. Resources critical to both must be the determinants of the form of human growth patterns. An integrated ethic is a solid foundation for how to approach in word and deed both people and the land that supports the life-support system.

LIFE-SUPPORT SYSTEM

Our life-support system is complex, involving many components and forces, great and small. We can consider water or air within this system and follow the molecular and atomic components through different forms and physical phases. Many familiar phenomena indicate our unfortunate influence on the cycles of air and water: smog, acid rain, diminished fisheries, increased rates of lung disease, wetland destruction, carbon dioxide levels in air, and perhaps global warming or cooling. We are closely connected mentally and spiritually to the natural world in which we are embedded. The late Joseph Wood Krutch, educator, biographer, and naturalist-philosopher, touched on the meaning of this connection and our need for a varied rural–regional landscape when he wrote:

> We need some contact with the thing we sprang from. We need Nature at least as a part of the context of our lives. . . . Without

Figure 2.1 We need some contact with the thing from which we sprang.

Nature, without wilderness even, we are compelled to renounce an important part of our heritage. . . . On some summer vacation or some country weekend we realize that what we are experiencing is more than merely a relief from the pressures of city life; that we have not merely escaped from something but have also entered into something; that we have joined the greatest of all communities, which is not that of men alone but of everything which shares, with man, the great adventure of being alive.[2]

This something, then, this natural context, is an essential factor for well-being and happiness as well as our physical existence. If we compromise our life-support system, we will lose out in both mind and body. Understanding our earthly home in the broadest sense possible will give us the greatest rewards (Fig. 2.1).

QUALITY OF LIFE

Huge prairies once covered much of the central plains, stretching as far as the eye could see. The vast areas of tall grasses provided unique habitats for wildlife and also led to a distinctive way of life for the settlers. A. W. Herre's recollections of the Illinois prairies reflect the effect these prairies had on him and how they enhanced his quality of life.

> One of the most marvelous sights of my whole life, unsurpassed in my travels in nearly all parts of the world, was that of the Illinois prairie in the spring. Unfading are my memories of that waning rippling sea of wild sweet william. It stretched away in the distance farther than the eye could reach. And as the sea of phlox faded it was succeeded by another marvelous flower bed of nature's planting, and instead of a single mass of color there was a vast garden of purple cone flowers, black-eyed susans, rosinweeds, blazing stars, asters, golden rods, and others. Every spring and fall the prairie was covered with water so that the whole countryside was a great lake. All day long swarms of water birds filled the air, and far into the night their cries sounded overhead. At the first gleam of dawn vast flights of ducks dashed to and fro and great flocks of wild geese sped swiftly across the sky.[3] (Fig. 2.2)

Figure 2.2 The Illinois garden: a vast garden of purple cone flowers, black-eyed susans, blazing star, and others.

Today farming, hunting, and other human activities have taken their toll on these awe-inspiring sights (Fig. 2.3). Tiling drained the fields that replaced the prairie in Illinois. The ducks and geese stopped coming for lack of water and food to attract them. The frogs disappeared and the prairie chickens were destroyed by the combined efforts of the plow and shotgun. The original plant and animal life of the prairies had disappeared. A way of life was gone. What a tragedy that more of it could not have been preserved so that those born later could freely enjoy its beauty.

Acting in accord with an ethic that gives the highest value to preserving our life-support system in order that life may continue as we know it, or in fuller abundance, would take into account the full effect of the changes that human activity causes.

ART, NATURE, AND LIFE

Destroying the natural landscape diminishes not only our physical resources but also the physical and aesthetic enjoyment of its many sensory aspects and the opportunities it affords for recreation of all kinds. Why do so many people lack a sense of preserving the landscape? Do they not understand the implications of their actions? Do they not understand that our life-support system and the source of joy and well-being is being destroyed? The answers lie in the separation of art from life and the division of daily life from the natural world.

My studies of the rural and urban landscapes suggest that if we are to attain sustainability, we must recognize that art and life are part of the same whole and that therefore we must see the landscape as a work of art to protect and enhance rather than exploit and use up. Sustainability depends on understanding the rules that govern nature. In understanding the natural landscape come the benefits of sensible land-use decisions as well as personally and socially rewarding benefits of enjoyment of our surroundings and the satisfaction of greater understanding of an incredibly complex, dynamic, and beautiful whole.

The artistic and aesthetic aspects of our lives are not a high priority with everyone. As John Biggs of Kansas State University explains:

Many of those who share this attitude are not really against the arts—they simply think that, on the continuum of human need, the arts come last. Somewhat like frosting on the cake, they view the arts as the proverbial 'sweet decoration' of life.

Such a notion obscures the true role the arts play in our personal lives and in society at large. For the arts are not merely superficial activities of amusement and entertainment, activities we pursue after the important things have been done. Rather,

Figure 2.3 The diversity of prairie grasses and forbs has given way to monocultures such as corn.

the arts are languages of communication, expressing what it truly means to be human.

It's axiomatic that science offers us languages of measurement such as mathematics or chemistry whereby we come to better understand the external world we live in. Similarly, the arts are languages of measurement too; languages whereby we come to better understand and communicate the inner world experience. When all is said and done, it is that relatively uncharted inner realm that contains the faith, love, hope, joy, and sorrow that is the essence of our lives. The value we ascribe to our inner life is, of course, a matter of personal choice or awareness. Regardless of the decision we make, our inner lives are hardly the stuff of frivolity.[4]

The division of soul from body may seem to have very little to do with the landscape. But on closer examination, soul and body have everything in common. How we perceive the integration or separation of art and life has a direct impact on how we perceive and use the landscape and its component resources. Too often the landscape is perceived as a vast supply of resources to be harvested and used for human

benefit. The relationship with the land is all take and no give; survival is not regarded as dependent on the land remaining intact, both ecologically and aesthetically.

On the other hand, recognizing art and life as two aspects of the same whole suggests a very different way to interpret the landscape. This acknowledgment suggests that instead of perceiving the landscape as a commodity to be exploited, landscapes should be perceived in the same way as works of art and cherished and treated with respect. Integrating art and life implies a reciprocal relationship with the land: that when we take something from the land, we must give something back.

If we were to truly connect art and life, we would recognize that there is a shared identity between art in the realm of painting, drawing, sculpture, and so on; music, drama, dance, and related art forms (works created in recognition of and with a goal of some sort of beauty, as well as unconsciously artful compositions) and the art in landscape art (both compositions contrived to have a particular effect and those that reflect harmony and beauty in their natural state or their pleasing or impressive reflection of human uses). We would recognize that our minds and souls gain much nourishment from the landscape, but that to truly benefit in more than an ephemeral way, we must ensure that the landscape remains intact and functioning. If we destroy either the aesthetic beauty or the ecological stability of the landscape, we also destroy an essential source of sustenance for our minds and souls to lead fulfilling lives in which purpose is present.

SENSE OF PLACE

Sense of place reflects our appreciation of the design elements, style, colors, textures, patterns, odors, and sounds of a given place that differentiates it from any other. Variety in the scale of the spaces we inhabit, spatial diversity, stimulates our imaginations and thus contributes to the quality of our lives. We can be dominated by monumental spaces, feel at home in spaces that are just adequate to accommodate our movements, and feel playful or amusingly in command overlooking doll-sized spaces. We can often feel comfortable in places that remind us of those places we have loved in the past.

In addition, the balance between public and private space contributes to sense of place.

Although residential neighborhoods once included small local shops and restaurants, in many communities zoning now strictly divides commercial and residential spaces. Community businesses are superseded by shopping malls at the edge of town. This trend has resulted in homogeneous neighborhoods that are almost completely composed of exclusively private spaces, with very few public spaces to accommodate social interaction. When connections to neighbors are lacking, community cohesiveness, a sense of place, and quality of life are lessened.

The scale of spaces, spatial diversity, and the balance between public and private space are all relationships that determine the total impression that an environment makes. Recognizing how important sense of place is to quality of life and how sense of place is created suggests that we must see our surroundings as a system (Fig. 2.4) rather than as a collection of individual objects. A series of objects are seen when we look around, and it is in these objects that we find meaning. Also, we see patterns, so that our definition of who we are and how we fit into our surroundings is derived from the spaces formed by individual objects.

Buildings, for example, can be seen as objects or as components in a system. They function as design elements as well as serving local neighborhood or wider needs. Quality of life and sense of place are increased if public and private spaces are well designed and reflect the character and needs of the communities in which they occur, and daily needs can be met within walking distance. Convenience in obtaining goods and services, and access to transportation to destinations that draw their constituency from a wider area, are also important.

DIVERSITY

It is obvious that some settings and views are more interesting and enjoyable than others. Endless fields of corn or wheat pall quickly. The pedestrian in a district of diverse buildings or homes is more engaged in the surrounding scene than is the pedestrian in a suburban subdivision composed solely of houses of the same style. Leisure travel is often centered on experiencing new, exciting, diverse, and beautiful places. This is a matter of general agreement. Diversity is stimulating and monotony boring in both the social and biological senses (Fig. 2.5). Analyzing the nature of diversity and classifying its range to

Figure 2.4 What makes this place so special? (a) Seasons; (b) grandparents.

take advantage of it are matters of some complexity, however. Here is where the skill, training, and experience of the designer comes into play. For a designed space to be valuable and attractive, it must recognize the diversity of its setting and include diversity as a component of design.

PRESERVING OPTIONS PROVIDES CHOICES

As dull urban sprawl swallows up towns and prime farmland, the range of options of many sorts is diminished. As dwellings and commercial enterprises are thrust heedlessly into areas of natural beauty, the array of possibilities is diminished. As unsustainable agriculture and improper resource extraction defile the land, and economic worth is defined by technologically defined and manufactured possessions, as inner cities are rendered hostile by the failure of employment opportunities to keep pace with the expansion of the workforce, options are limited. As remnants of our early history are torn down and covered over, and decisions affecting our future are consolidated into fewer and fewer hands, the range

of choices is smaller and the desirable options fewer in number. Thus freedom of choice is lost. As our formerly agricultural nation is actively farmed by only a small percentage of the population, our changing economy and society still require clean water, air, and land as well as a continuing resource base of raw materials, energy, and a harmonious fabric of countryside and development.

Without freedom of choice, democracy is limited and life is duller. Life with few choices is simple, but without diversity future possibilities will dwindle, dreariness will set in, cultural and biological stability will be destroyed, and quality of life will be diminished. The basis for the future is widest when the number of options that are cut off is minimized. Rather than reducing the number of options from which to choose, using design skills and processes can achieve harmony among them. Only with a basis for comparison can we hope to allow for a future in which there is freedom of choice. The best solution to any land-use decision is the choice least destructive to the resource base and its inherent multiplicity of values and choices.

An integrated ethic requires the preservation and enhancement among natural and cultural

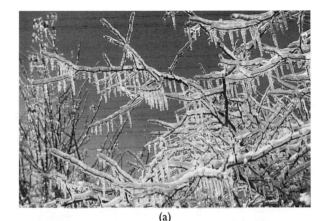
(a)

(b)

Figure 2.5 Monotony versus
diversity. (a) Monotony;
(b) or fitting the road to
the land.

(a)

(b)

choices for ourselves and our environment. It implies honoring our past, including the lessons of errors and omissions, which is embedded in the present time. Its goal is to ensure a future in which the wisdom of our successors has as much latitude in which to operate as we can provide.

An acceptable social ethical standard is more often met when we have a life-support system that assures us of the basis for life, beautiful surroundings that enhance our behavior, a sense of place that provides comfort, and a rich and diverse environment where we have the freedom to be selective in our choices. Wars, slums, inadequate food, and health problems can all be the by-products of a failed land ethic and diminish the opportunities of any constructive social ethic.

Notes

[1]Aldo Leopold, *A Sand County Almanac: with Essays on Conservation from Found River,* Ballantine Books, New York, 1970.

[2]Joseph Krutch, *LIFE,* December 22, 1961.

[3]Philip H. Lewis, *Recreation and Open Space in Illinois,* State Housing Board and U.S. Housing and Home Finance Agency, Springfield, Ill., 1962.

[4]John Biggs, the Art Department Newsletter, Kansas State University, Kansas City, Mo., 1991.

CHAPTER 3

URBAN CONSTELLATIONS: THE REGIONAL DESIGN PROCESS AT THE NATIONAL SCALE

To proceed in an ethical, aesthetically satisfying, and economically rewarding way, guidelines for the process are essential. Forming a theoretical description of the regional design process is a stimulating exercise, but to be effective such descriptions must be translated into practical realities. The first step in this translation is recognition of the breadth of the spectrum of ways that land can be used: urban core, central business district, suburbia, productive farmland, forest, wilderness fringe, wilderness, and all the variations among these uses (Fig. 3.1). Application of the regional design process involves identifying current land uses and then using design process principles to suggest how the land might be used sustainably so as to preserve as many options of use as possible for the future.

There are a mass of individual decisions involved in planning for the projected effects of our actions. How can we best transport goods and people between cities? How can we provide for people's recreational needs and desires without destroying the landscape? Should the major highway coming into town be expanded? Should a new shopping mall be constructed at the edge of town? How should erosion be controlled? Should a particular forest be logged? Should building in the floodplain be permitted? Although the questions appear complex and often overwhelming, the regional design process offers a logical and systematic way to tackle many of these issues in order to make positive strides toward sustainability. The sum of local decisions in a region determines the character of that

Figure 3.1 Ways land can be used.

WILDERNESS   FRINGE   FARMLAND   SUBURBIA   MIDTOWN   DOWNTOWN

(a)

(b)

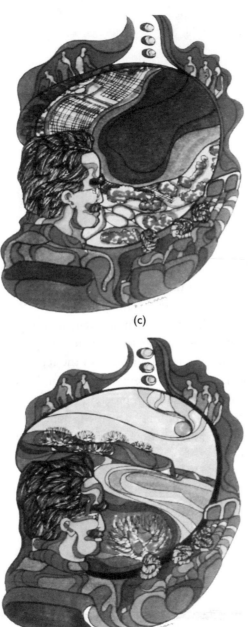

(c)

(d)

Figure 3.2 Scale of patterns:
(a) global; (b) national; (c)
regional; (d) local.

region and how much freedom of choice and flexibility remain for the future.

The process of regional design suggests three broad frames of reference within which to operate. The first scale at which any regional design process should be applied is the national pattern of urban and rural resources that identifies areas in which future urban growth should be maintained and areas that should be preserved as land for farm and other production, wilderness fringe, or wilderness. The other two major frames of reference are the regional and local scales. In this chapter we explore how the regional design process is applied at the national scale, in constellations (Fig. 3.2).

URBAN CONSTELLATIONS

Problems such as urban sprawl and environmental degradation can be staggering, and designing sustainable alternative paths can prove to be even more so. Modeling and visualization provide a tool for imaginative design to help us see the way things are and the way things might be. While searching for solutions to the urban threat to our natural and cultural resources, a marvelous

Figure 3.3 The United States at night. Courtesy of Argonaut Press, Madison, Wis.

computer-enhanced satellite photo of the United States at night came to my attention (Fig. 3.3). The concentrations of city lights reminded me of stars, which in turn brought to mind the constellations that had helped me to memorize 300 stars by which I had learned to navigate in the Army Air Corps.

Somewhere in our distant past, constellations were identified as a means of organizing and communicating knowledge of the location and size of the stars and the changes in the night sky. That same technique can be used to illustrate rampant urban sprawl and the threat to critical life-sustaining resources. By identifying the earthly lights that show human habitation on the major resource patterns of the country, it is readily apparent where local resources (based in land, water, and air) are most subject to immediate destruction or alteration and which areas should receive top priority for protection.

Figure 3.4 Key resources as form determinants: (a) surface water; (b) aquifers; (c) forests and farmland; (d) historic sites; (e) mineral deposits; (f) mountains and steep topography; (g) public lands.

RESOURCE PATTERNS AS FORM DETERMINANTS

Although global in application, the first practical use occurred at the national scale. Working with a group of graduate students, the first step in identifying the constellations was to gather available information and to plot nationwide patterns of water/wetland systems, class A agricultural soils, major topographic features, forests, mineral resources, aquifers, outstanding scenic diversity, historically significant buildings and sites, and publicly owned land (Fig. 3.4). This inventory identified on a preliminary basis the value patterns of cherished and essential resources that should be protected and enhanced if we are to attain sustainability.

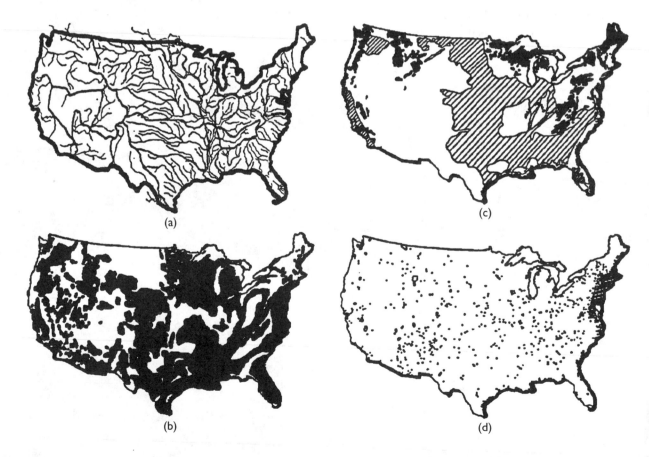

(a)

(b)

(c)

(d)

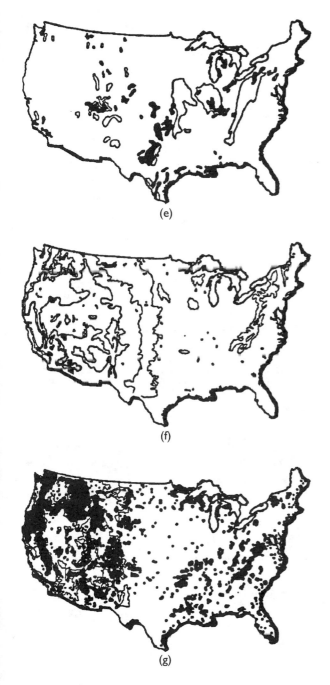

(e)

(f)

(g)

We then superimposed the pattern of cities and city clusters of 20,000 or more people onto the value pattern map. Recognizing that these bright urban stars were certain to grow brighter, we looked at how to guide growth connecting the urban areas so as to make the least impact on critical resources, using the value patterns as a form determinant. The result was a pattern of 23 constellations spread across the United States (Fig. 3.5).

Constellations outline high-density populations that either surround or are surrounded by the natural and cultural resources necessary to sustain them. Guiding the growth of these urbanizing systems, in harmony with the preservation of their life-sustaining natural resources, can offer quality of life, sense of place, diversity, and design options by manipulation of densities, characteristics, and balances of the human species in nature. Successful utilization of the constellation concept can achieve a far better alternative to the expanding homogenized landscape of uncontrolled and poorly designed urbanization that will continue to cover substantial portions of the United States if unchecked.

Eighty-five percent of the country's population lives within the boundaries of the constellation patterns (Fig. 3.6). If growth is to be guided toward sustainability, these are the areas into which future growth should be directed to minimize human impact on the land. But this does not mean that the whole constellation should be one giant city. Beginning with the rehabilitation of core areas within the existing cities along the constellation corridor, a new integrated transit, utility, and communication system must be developed first to encourage infill and then be extended to provide economically feasible services between the cities. Growth would then naturally occur along these arteries of growth and fill in the constellation form, while the parklike hole in the doughnut would retain its rural character with economically healthy small towns and natural recreational areas within easy reach of the urban population.

By this carefully managed process, the whole of each constellation would not become a great, high-density megalopolis but would retain its cities of high density while encouraging medium- and smaller-sized cities to grow along the integrated arteries. Through maintenance of a wide range of urban and rural diversity, constellation dwellers would continue to enjoy quality of life, a satisfying sense of place, and a range of options and freedom of choice in as many ways as possible.

Figure 3.5 Twenty-three constellations in the lower 48 states of the United States.

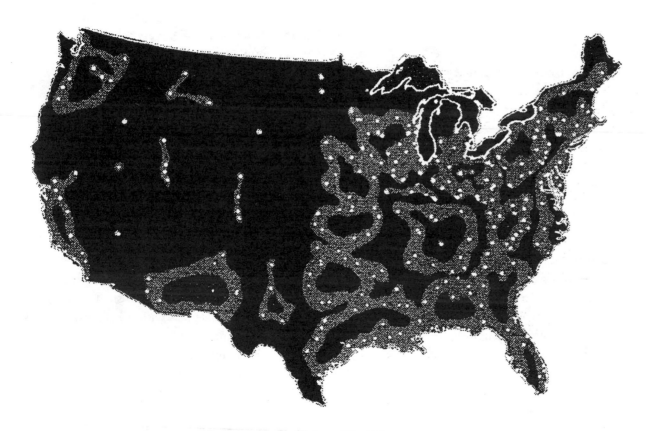

various components of urban megasystems. Therefore, guiding growth is a complex challenge composed of a mixture of rural and urban issues, interrelated and intertwined.

The vitality of rural areas depends on a diverse set of factors. Pressure to develop agricultural land (and other rural land) for suburban home sites, the toil and risks involved in modern agricultural businesses, the pollution of water and wetlands and groundwater, the need for costly urban service improvements in small towns, and the demand for recreational areas for urban dwellers are among the issues that most affect rural land-use policy. The challenge for rural areas is to maintain an economic base and agricultural production while preserving and enhancing the aesthetic, ecological, and recreational resources of the area.

The challenge in urban areas is to provide adequate housing and economic opportunity to support all members of the income spectrum and the necessary infrastructure and social services. For cities, higher *livable densities,* including ample recreation, natural beauty, and transportation mobility, are at the top of a needs pyramid, the base of which is seldom fully supplied with services.

Constellations suggest criteria for guiding growth on a national and regional scale to meet

SYSTEMS OF CITIES INSTEAD OF SINGLE CITIES

By portraying national growth patterns as a constellation system, it becomes clear that we must

view our local actions within a regional context. On this scale we can see the requirements for guiding growth within urban constellation boundaries. Meaningful growth strategies for constellation fringe and core areas involve the

Figure 3.6 Eighty-five percent of the country's
population live within
the boundaries of 23
constellations.

the rural and urban challenges. By outlining areas in which urban growth should occur in order to preserve critical rural and urban landscape patterns, looking at constellations provides an important framework for planning for biological and cultural sustainability and providing a vision for the future. They enable us to go beyond identifying problems to identify a sustainable alternative. By examining each regional constellation in detail, we can identify regional characteristics such as unique landscapes, regional foodsheds, distinctive building materials, a skilled labor force, transportation options, available capital, ethnic concentrations, and other regional characteristics that will more accurately define needed changes within these urbanizing patterns.

Constellation patterns also suggest directions for future transportation developments. Rather than cutting across the constellation's central core, introducing destructive impacts on the landscape system, rapid transportation corridors can be directed to connect the outer part of the constellation into a single urbanizing system. Further, constellation patterns provide a mechanism for guiding future growth dependent on the carrying capacity of the region, that is, the ability

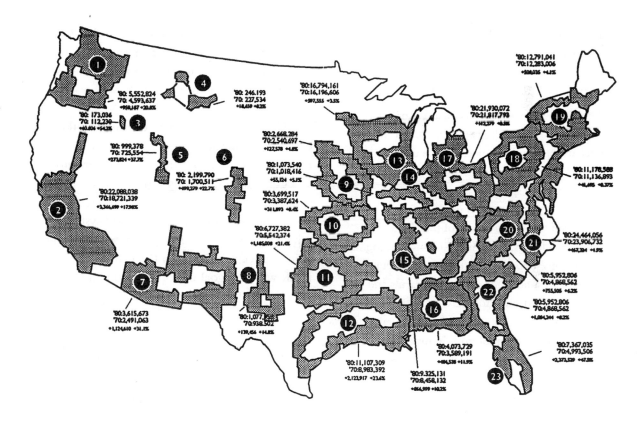

of a place to support population without sacrificing the resources of future generations.

This view of our urban systems has greatly altered our view of how these systems should be perceived, managed, and designed. Constellations offer discrete, logical units for national and regional focus and action and a significant key to fostering public and professional understanding of the region as a primary working scale. Containing, as they do, 85 percent of the population, constellations identify the most urbanized areas and the places where human impact on the land and landscape is greatest.

Charles E. Little, has observed:

> The city . . . need not be seen as centrifugal in its growth, sprawling amoeba-like from a nucleus, but could be perceived as many cities, large and small, which together surround an open space. In a stroke, [the constellation concept] turned urban theory inside out, for at the center of the city are not tall buildings, honking taxis, and surging crowds of shoppers and office workers, but more likely a bucolic landscape of farms and woodlands and small towns. Groups of cities are like doughnuts whose "hole" is a rural resource area—often of great beauty, agricultural importance, and recreational value— that the surrounding cities have in common.[1]

In commenting on the Circle City constellation, Robert Sykes noted:

> Circle City as a spatial design concept for our time bears a striking resemblance in scale and purpose to that proposed by Thomas Jefferson in the 1780's. The physical form and objectives of Jefferson's proposal are naturally different from . . . the constellation concept . . . but its role in history supports the appropriateness of Circle City to our times.[2]

Whereas Jefferson's grid encouraged the occupation and development of the country, the constellation concept offers a way to organize and guide now sprawling development in a country well past the stage of encouraging settlement. Furthermore, unlike the grid system, which was based on mere geometry, the constellation concept is based on the nature of the land itself, with the goal of conservation and reconstruction rather than exploitation.

Notes

[1] Charles E. Little, "Professor Lewis's Doughnuts," *Air and Space,* April/May 1986, published by the Smithsonian Institution.

[2] Robert D. Sykes, Professor of Landscape Architecture at the University of Minnesota, in *Agora, the Newsletter of the Landscape Architecture Foundation,* Autumn 1982.

CHAPTER 4

COMMUNICATING NATIONAL VALUES AND VISIONS

INFORMING THE PUBLIC DISCRETION

Recognizing urban constellation patterns is not sufficient in itself. Regional designs to guide growth can succeed only with public support. This requires effective communication to inform the public's discretion. Effectively disseminating information so that each citizen can make individual informed decisions about the future is essential. No plan to attain sustainability can succeed unless it is based solidly on democracy and informing people's discretion, because ultimately, sustainability depends on the collective impact of the actions and behaviors of many people. In this chapter we discuss communication and opportunities and concerns about combining *education and tourism*. The recent rapid population increase and increasingly complex national and global issues have induced a sense of powerlessness to change current trends. Inundated with statistics and random information, distracted by personal concerns, and seeing no place for themselves in the search for workable options, too many people abdicate their responsibility to leaders and lawmakers who are assumed to be more discerning and informed and thereby qualified to make crit-

ical decisions. The representatives of the people are subject to bias and sometimes beholden to special interests, sometimes ill-informed, and occasionally overcome by political expediency. This is not really news, but we must take these weaknesses into account.

If left to others, decisions will be made for us about how our land should be used, where our roads should be built, how our resources should be utilized, where our cities should grow, and how our environment should be protected. Instead of being provided with interdisciplinary, balanced options from which to choose, we are often presented with only a single option by policymakers. We wait for conditions around us to improve and grow disenchanted with our political system when conditions deteriorate. That is not the democracy envisioned by those who wrote our Constitution. In fact, Thomas Jefferson warned of the temptation to shift the decision-making process from the many to the few:

> I know of no safe depository of the ultimate powers of the society but the people themselves; and if we think them not enlightened enough to exercise their control with a wholesome discretion, the remedy is not to

take it from them, but to inform their discretion.[1]

The interests of the populace as a whole must enter into the process. But how are we to inform the entire population's discretion? Before informed decisions can be expected in the field of land use, an awareness of the natural and cultural values that characterize the national and regional landscapes must generally be acquired. Only when diversity and sense of place are cherished can long-range growth strategies be developed that will protect and enhance the dynamic balance of the natural world. Similarly, until a clear understanding of the problems and causal relationships of urbanization are disseminated, little progress will be made in guiding urban growth in harmony with our life-support system.

Informing the discretion of the people in these matters is a task that requires a concerted interdisciplinary effort to assure the free flow of relevant information. It is a crucial task that requires innovative communication programs to portray the urgency of mastering regional growth and change and to emphasize the critical value of our alarmingly finite resources. It is a task certainly as monumental as introducing to the world

an imaginary character named Mickey Mouse. The same sort of interest generated for our amusement by great entertainment giants such as Disney needs to be aroused to acquaint us with the nature of national and regional changes.

TOURISM POTENTIAL

Historically, attempts at broadscale change have been defeated due to lack of time, money, and personnel. However, rural and urban landscape studies by university students and staff have shown that we can remedy these deficiencies. This research shows that the tourism industry depends on the *same* resource patterns for its survival as those on which we depend for a satisfying quality of life and the stability of our life-support system. As the world's major industry, tourism is an invaluable mechanism for education, recreation, and economic stimulus. Natural and cultural values are the basis for this industry. If these resources are degraded and depleted, at the same time the world's largest industry will be destroyed. It is apparent that as the world's largest industry, tourism, could provide a percentage of the funds required to pro-

tect our critical resource patterns. In addition, because it is possible to learn while having fun, there is a natural opportunity to unite tourism and education in order to inform people's discretion.

The goal of tourism is to attract people to a particular area and to induce the expenditure of money once they are there. At the same time, attracting people to a region provides an opportunity to educate them about regional resources, thereby satisfying a natural curiosity and informing their discretion. However, tourism also presents the risk of promoting resource degradation. Unless careful design and planning are employed, attracting people to a region can destroy the very resources upon which the tourism industry depends for survival.

Applying the regional design process to inform and educate, as well as amuse, requires communication and transportation systems coordinated in a new way to bring about preservation and enhancement of natural and cultural resources while displaying the treasures of a region through tourism. One such tool is a national heritage rail spine that could link natural and cultural resources into a national tourism/education system. Branching off from such a large-scale pathway, *heritage necklaces* designed on national and regional scales as tourism travel loops would familiarize people with a region's diverse natural and cultural resources.

NATIONAL HERITAGE RAIL SPINE (FIG. 4.1)

Linking natural and cultural resources into creative alternative educational networks can inform people about environmental options as well as provide outstanding new opportunities for recreation and tourism. Examining the landscape continuum shows that we could identify existing highway, railway, and waterway networks linking the diverse natural and cultural resources into an exceptional human pathway offering a wide variety of recreational, tourism, and educational experiences (Fig. 4.2). As an education/tourism system, such a multimodal system can provide easy access to the significant natural and cultural resources of the region while highlighting the significance of these resources in order to give visitors a stake in preserving them for future generations. In this way the entire landscape is a teaching laboratory.

Railroad transportation costs for goods have been demonstrated to be less than costs for movement by highway or by air. It is interesting to note that since automobiles and fuel prices are likely only to increase in cost, a more economical and less energy consumptive recreational experience must soon be contemplated. Rehabilitation and reuse of principal and failing railroad networks offer exceptional opportunities for this purpose by providing passenger service with comfort, convenience, and cash savings as well as additional capacity for moving raw materials and manufactured goods.

Railroads also provide at least two attributes of sustainability. First, they are an economical and far less energy-consumptive mode of travel than most, and second, they offer a satisfactory way to control the impact of tourism on regional resources. By allowing trains to stop only at adequately designed facilities, scenic and recreational resources can be protected from becoming eroded and diminished by uncontrolled access at many points.

As demonstrated in resource inventories of the upper midwest (see Chapter 5) the majority of the outstanding natural and cultural resources of a region usually fall within water, wetland, and steep topography patterns. Coincidentally, it is in

the river valley patterns with slight topographic gradients that our early railroad networks were built. Wise planning and design should utilize the rehabilitation of rail systems to link key natural and cultural features. It is an outstanding opportunity to assure alternative transportation access to rural diversity by urban citizens and access to cities by rural citizens.

A national rail spine utilizing much of the country's first railroad, the Baltimore and Ohio, could stretch from Washington, D.C. to San Francisco by way of Harper's Ferry; Cincinnati, Ohio; Vincennes, Indiana; St. Louis, Missouri; Kansas City; and Denver, Colorado.

This system intersects most of the recognized national north–south trail systems and other outstanding linear corridor systems (topographical and human-made) of the United States. Tourists could travel from one coast to the other on the B&O railroad spine and auxiliary extensions across the nation's midregion. Along the way they could learn the history and potential of rail transportation. Tourists could also take side trips at leisure to explore the many significant north–south trails and resource systems that intersect this spine. Recently restored rail stations in Washington, Cincinnati, and St. Louis could

Figure 4.1 National Her-
itage Rail Spine.

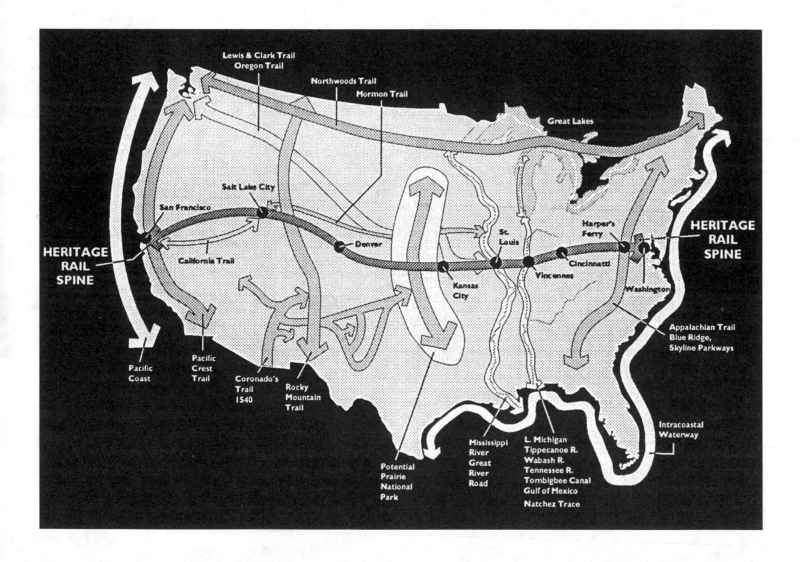

Figure 4.2 Environmental jewels on the landscape necklace. Linking natural and cultural resources into meaningful patterns provides the foundation for fostering a more holistic and comprehensive understanding of a region. Such comprehension is the precursor for sustainability, high quality of life, sense of place, integration of art and life, diversity and options from which to choose, and provides the basis for education and tourism.

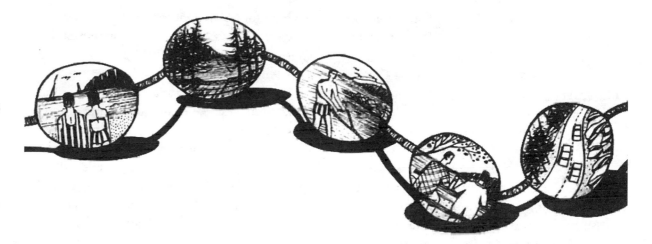

serve as regional discovery centers, portraying both educational and tourism options in their surrounding regions.

NATIONAL DISCOVERY CENTERS

Restoring major railroad stations as National and Regional Discovery Centers to provide information on regional resources would require an evaluation of past concepts and facilities that have combined education and tourism opportunities. Exhibits, displays, presentations, libraries, classes, activities for various groups, demonstrations, research facilities, archives, and collections can all be used to relate and explore natural and cultural features and values along the rail spine. Simulations portraying in three dimensions historical development and possible future aspects of our surroundings can use and demonstrate all degrees of technology. A "sense-of-place marketplace" keyed to the local region could make local arts and crafts as well as printed, sound, and video material available for purchase.

A similar example would be the Parkway Systems developed by the National Park Service, which offer an outstanding communication/education system linking some of the country's finest scenic and historic sites. Years of experience offer comprehensive guidelines for moving people through the countryside while imparting information about the nature and history of that countryside by means of signage compatible with the surroundings, interpretive centers, exhibits, simulation techniques, and historic interpretation by costumed guides trained in the crafts and customs of the place and period. The National Park Service has utilized and exemplified an exceptional array of communication tools.

WORLD'S FAIRS

Historically, world's fairs have exemplified interdisciplinary effort combining programming and display that dramatically portray national, regional, and local values and visions to the visiting public. This satisfies the Jeffersonian instruction to inform the discretion of the people in order for valid democratic decisions to be made while providing many opportunities to explore new and different experiences. Beginning in 1851 with London's Great Exhibition of All Nations, memorably housed in the Crystal

Palace, there have been 17 major authorized fairs, six of them in the United States. Recent world's fairs have varied in size in both physical scope and number of visitors. The 1933–1934 Century of Progress in Chicago, occupying 424 acres of land, attracted 48,769,227 visitors, while Montreal's Universal International Exhibition (Expo) in 1967 occupied 1000 acres and attracted 50,860,801 visitors. On a more modest scale, the Expo '74 World's Fair in Spokane was developed on 100 acres of land and attracted 5,100,000 people. Without exception, these fairs have affirmed technological progress and positive cultural quality of life, and they have helped to focus public and private action in the host city. Almost without exception, world's fairs have also been controversial enterprises. They require extensive planning and vast expenditure, and often they have run deficits in actual operation. But their environmental legacies have been substantial both in leaving behind physical facilities of benefit to the area where they occur and in providing new ideas in planning, design, and architecture.

In several cases—Paris's Eiffel Tower (1889) and Seattle's Space Needle (1962) come to mind—distinctive structures creating architectural identity for a fair have come to serve a similar function for the host city thereafter. Almost always there has been positive urban impact. In Chicago, the Columbian Exposition (1893) and the Century of Progress Exposition (1933) left the city with two major museums, an aquarium, a planetarium, a stadium, and substantial areas of improved landscape. Expo '67 in Montreal provided the impetus for a new subway system and highway expansion. The cluster of buildings designed for Seattle's Century 21 Expo (1962) has remained to house a cultural/commercial district that is still an active part of Seattle's community life. World's fairs have repeatedly demonstrated the possibilities of entertaining and educating vast numbers of casual visitors through visual display. They have also served to inspire professional designers. A famous instance is the General Motors' Futurama exhibit at the 1939 New York World's Fair, featuring a Norman Bel Geddes model for 100-mile-an-hour limited-access highways that influenced generations of transport specialists. More recently, the U.S. exhibit at Expo '67 resulted in widespread interest in Buckminster Fuller's geodesic domes and Moshe Safdie's innovative Habitat structure for living.

One of the interesting developments in world's fairs has been their gradual shift away from material display to a more direct emphasis on human issues. The Paris fair of 1989, for example, focused on the concept of liberty. This shift reflects both an admission that material advances are no longer the news they once were, and a sense that it is our relationship to those advances that count most.

World's fairs are comprehensive efforts and they are community intensive, but although they are typically more than 10 years in the making, each is ultimately a temporary phenomenon. In addition to festive surroundings and amusements, there are centers for display and research that are more permanent, and one category is well established. Its prototype was Chicago's Museum of Science and Industry (originally designed for the 1893 Columbian Exposition and improved for the Century of Progress Exposition in 1933), where generations of schoolchildren and adult visitors have been introduced to the development and character of modern technology through interactive exhibits with buttons to push and interesting spaces to explore.

The museum set a standard not only for innovative national display but also for interdisciplinary, public/private cooperation in educating people about how things work. Smaller-scale versions of this theme could be seen in Copen-hagen's DenPermanent, a combined museum and retail facility featuring household products judged to be Denmark's finest, and in the permanent design collection of the Museum of Modern Art in New York. In these cases, respect for creativity, aesthetic excellence, and useful impact brings evaluators from divergent backgrounds together to consider a wide range of manufactured items, producing display results that are models of quality in material culture.

EPCOT, DISNEY WORLD

A new generation in this category was born in the early 1970s with Epcot Center, part of Walt Disney World near Orlando, Florida. The concept behind this "Experimental Prototype Community of Tomorrow" was Disney's own. Epcot would, Disney said,

> take its cue from the new ideas and new technologies that are now merging from the creative centers of American industry. It will be a community of tomorrow that will never be completed, but will always be introducing

and testing and demonstrating new materials and systems. And Epcot will be a *showcase to the world* for the ingenuity and imagination of American free enterprise.[2]

Epcot differs from the Museum of Science and Industry in several ways. Its larger scale allows visitors to relate more realistically to displays, and its emphasis on the notion of a future community promotes better integration of display elements. Like the museum and world's fairs generally, Epcot features exhibits sponsored by major corporate interests and several foreign countries, but its overall design and coordination have been firmly in the hands of WED, the Disney Productions division which oversees this kind of activity. WED has spared no expense in realizing imaginative, functional center design, and Epcot represents the most advanced instance to date of the kind of people-oriented centers that we need to increase awareness and improve our relationship to the national and global environment. Indeed, in Future World we see significant efforts in the environmental area. Kraft's 6-acre Land Pavilion, for example, provides visitors with an introduction to prehistorical climatology, futuristic agricultural developments, and

demonstrations of positive potential in the impact of technology on the physical world.

The Disney name is associated primarily with popular family entertainment, and the Epcot Center continues that tradition by providing advanced display technology and highly effective traffic control. But there has also been a good-faith attempt to incorporate interdisciplinary academic expertise. Kraft's exhibit was developed in consultation with Carl Hodges, director of the Environmental Research Laboratory of the University of Arizona, and there is some opportunity within the pavilion for applied agricultural research.

There is a significant future for a high-tech exposition center like Epcot, at least partly because communications is an area where high-tech skills shine. Such centers can be of various scales. One such center is located in the Gordon Bubolz Nature Center near Appleton, Wisconsin. This underground facility, which utilizes solar and wind power, has meeting rooms, exhibits on local flora and fauna, offices, and storage rooms and offers an outstanding educational center program supported by private funding. It is open to all schoolchildren and the public from the region.

Funding from Milwaukee County supported an Environmental Awareness Center design for the Havenwoods Nature Center on a former Nike missile site that was transferred from the county to the state Department of Natural Resources for the implementation of the Environmental Awareness Center plans and the construction of a major facility.

My 1994 visit to Taiwan included visits to two awareness facilities designed by the office of a former student, Albert Tsao. One is included in the new Taipei Zoo; a natural history facility displays local and regional information about animal populations and regional habitats designed to precede seeing live animals in the zoo. The other is the newly completed Transportation Museum in the heart of Taipei. After passing through introductory exhibits, the visitor enters a simulated future space vehicle, where by use of a revolving seating arrangement, the audience sees a robotic crew explaining blast-off procedures. The seats shudder and shake as if taking off, and three-dimensional modules appear showing, in turn, transportation situations of the past and future and then new housing and transit options come into view, all augmented by imaginative sound tracks, lighting, models, and dioramas. What must be built in the near future to accommodate a rapidly expanding population is portrayed.

A combination of parkways, railparks, waterparks, and Discovery Centers would give people much-needed relief from routine while stimulating their imaginations and pleasing them with new encounters in other regions or in their own region. The result would be a happier and better-informed citizenry, a livelier economy, and an increased awareness of the importance of maintaining our environmental connections in the years to come.

Notes

[1] Thomas Jefferson in letter to William Charles Jarvis, September 28, 1820.

[2] Christopher Finch, *The Art of Walt Disney,* Abradale Press, Harry N. Abrams, Inc., New York, 1973 (1983 edition).

PART II

REGIONAL APPLICATION OF THE PROCESS:
UPPER MIDWEST FOCUS

In Part II we outline the Regional Design Process on a regional level, following the basic principles of resource value inventory, creative analysis, synthesis of two- and three-dimensional design options, and a specific educational effort in this country and throughout the world to assure citizens a role in the decision-making process.

The brief overview in Chapters 1 to 3 presented the human threats to our life-support system, stressing the critical need for an integrated land/social ethic to protect and enhance present natural and cultural quality and suggesting the desirability of restorative efforts by limiting environmental stress. They included broad guidelines for giving form to sprawling cities by use of the constellation concept and proposed a popularly appealing educational network to inform the discretion of the public about these issues, to reverse environmentally degrading trends. In Chapter 4 some values and visions of a demo-

cratic society involving tourism and education on a national scale were considered.

In Chapter 5 we describe the evolution of the inventory process to identify the natural and cultural features remaining to be protected and enhanced. To protect, manage, enhance, link, and communicate the outstanding natural and cultural resources of a region requires a workable approach for identifying and inventorying these diverse resource patterns.

In Chapter 5 we develop such a workable approach through a chronological series of progressively larger scale studies. This inventory approach to the design process has evolved over a 42-year period, supported by integrated faculty efforts, work/study–funded students working under faculty direction, student classroom exercises, and graduate research assistants in the university system. Ample opportunities have also

been found while working with federal and state agencies and through a private firm founded to pursue inventory methods and techniques to design problems.

In Chapter 6 different sorts of pattern analyses are discussed together with some of their uses and their relationship to the design process. In Chapter 7 the relationships between resource patterns and terrestrial constellations are described.

Recognizing that resource inventories of national and regional values, and plans for their protection and enhancement, are meaningless unless a broader public is informed about their value, proposals for regional rail and water transportation corridors that are linked with the National Heritage Spine (described in Chapter 4) are proposed in Chapter 8.

These many real-life opportunities to pursue the evolution of the Regional Design Process have been funded by way of salaried positions in government, universities, and the professional office. Foundation grants, Wisconsin cigarette tax monies, Title V Rural Development Act grants, and contracts with cities, counties, and townships have all played a role in testing inventory techniques as a part of the overall Regional Design Process. Undocumented hours of volunteer help in the Environmental Awareness Center have also made a substantial contribution.

CHAPTER 5

APPLICATION AND EVOLUTION OF THE REGIONAL DESIGN PROCESS

REGIONAL LANDSCAPE STUDIES: THE BEGINNING (1951–1953)

During my spring semester at the Harvard Graduate School of Design in 1952, where the collaborative team method was taught under Walter Gropius and Charles Eliot, I became intrigued with expanding the idea that an interdisciplinary team of professionals, working with local people, could identify and inventory critical landscape patterns to be used as form determinants to guide patterns of physical development on the land. I had the opportunity to spend one summer during my graduate studies working for an agency that used interdisciplinary talent to look at large-scale regional landscape patterns. My job search that summer had led me to the National Park Service and Jack "Hodge" Hanson, chief of master planning in the Region 1 office of the National Park Service (NPS) at Richmond, Virginia. I was accepted as a student trainee in a program established to bring fresh design talent into the NPS. Because I was encouraged by the personnel there and found my work that summer to be rewarding and fascinating, I proposed a graduate-thesis topic that would show, for a spe-

cific national park the step-by-step process by which the NPS acquires land, analyzes it, designs for it to be built upon, works with private concessionaires, and handles visitors within that design. I would also select and design a site to house park visitors overnight (Fig. 5.1).

The response to my proposal was so encouraging that the Everglades National Park project was adopted as a student problem for the entire Harvard Graduate School of Design (GSD). To set an appropriate mood, we transformed the design lab into the Everglades complete with fishnets and student-designed fish. We needed information from many different fields to approach the project holistically, so we organized into interdisciplinary teams that took advantage of the diverse specialized knowledge of the students. The architecture classes researched Spanish architecture of the Caribbean and learned to put structures on stilts to diffuse the force of hurricane winds and waves, as well as devising alternative solutions (Fig. 5.2). They also studied how to deal with problems of rot and insects and to employ the Venturi principle to pull cool air in through the lowest level and release warm air from the topmost level of a building. The planning students did a demographic study to deter-

Figure 5.1 Flamingo
overnight facility site plan
designed as part of the
author's thesis.

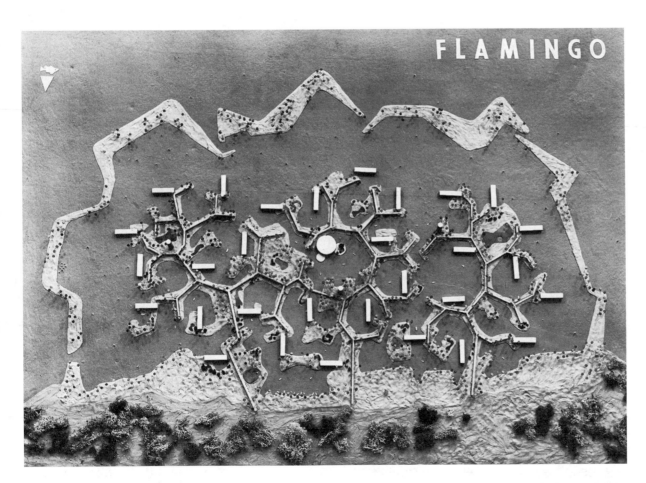

FLAMINGO

mine how many visitors to expect and how many rooms would be needed for housing them. Finally, the landscape architecture students inventoried the geology, hydrology, flora, fauna, climate and weather, roads and transportation, and site conditions in the park (Fig. 5.3).

We had access to the resources of the Harvard University Library as well as information from the National Park Service Library, which provided us invaluable information about many of the ecological characteristics of the area. In addition to understanding the ecological carrying capacities, we needed to know about the aesthetic characteristics of the Everglades, as I felt that only by combining both ecological and aesthetic inventories could we be able to design a facility in harmony with the site. Unable to take all the graduate students to the Everglades for firsthand inspection, I contacted Walt Disney to find out if we could use a film being made by a movie crew there. Mr. Disney kindly arranged to have the world premiere of *Prowlers of the Everglades* at the theater in Harvard Square. The film captured the colors, textures, patterns, and spatial qualities of the region and served as a surrogate visit.

The combined ecological and aesthetic data suggested Florida Bay at the southern tip of the

Figure 5.2 Floating overnight accommodations designed by Harvard architectural students.

Figure 5.3 Resource inventories of Everglades National Park conducted by Harvard Landscape Architecture students, 1952.

(a) Area of inventory.
(b) Visual aspect; this map delineates distinctive landscape types within the study area.

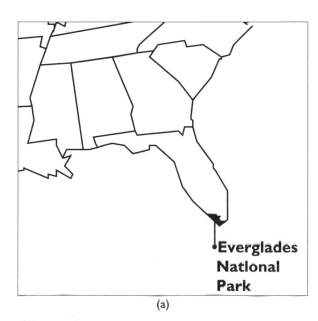

(a)

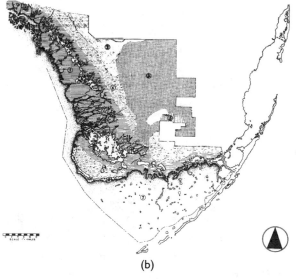

(b)

park for the visitor facility site at Flamingo. The site-selection method proved successful, and within a few years the Park Service built a visitor center there. However, the advice about building on stilts was ignored, and as a result the center was later destroyed by a hurricane while a nearby building on stilts was spared.

The Everglades experience demonstrated the need for comprehending regional context before giving form to smaller components such as cities, towns, and public facilities as well as determining land use and zoning. Interdisciplinary effort was also paramount in the regional approach to design, for if one sector of necessary knowledge and data is omitted, serious errors result. It seemed clear, evident, and basic to me; but at the time, the method was not in wide use outside the national parks or even common parlance among designers.

EMBARRAS RIVER VALLEY (1957)

Upon graduation from the Harvard GSD I took a position with the Bureau of Community Planning at the University of Illinois. My undergraduate and graduate training had taught me that to design for the future we must approach our urban and rural resources on a regional scale. The bureau was a fortuitous beginning for my professional career. It was established by Dean Rexford Newcomb of the School of Fine and Applied Arts, who, during the national planning days, worked with my former teacher at Harvard University, Charles Eliot. Dean Newcomb recognized in his own national planning work that the university possessed the broad range of professional disciplines necessary for comprehensive planning. His goal initially was to establish the bureau to coordinate and integrate such a range of professionals.

Like so many worthwhile efforts to coordinate the independent and applied research activities of a university with respect to a particular integrated focus, the goal was never attained. By the time I arrived, this interesting bureau, under the direction of Don Morgan, had reduced its agenda to the task of advising communities on the establishment of community planning programs and on the establishment of park districts throughout the state.

From the Bureau of Community Planning I moved to part-time and then to full-time teaching in the Department of Landscape Architecture, where I had received my undergraduate training. Both Dean Newcomb and the Landscape Architecture staff agreed that the scale of student problems, which up to then had never gone beyond consideration of anything larger than a state park, should include the scope I had been using in my graduate training and my work for the Bureau of Community Planning implementing planning programs in the state.

I hoped to use my position to demonstrate to other universities and governmental agencies that our only hope for the future was to begin looking at our landscape resources on a regional scale. I designed a student project for my class to study a region dear to my heart: the entire watershed of the Embarras River, which passes through the University of Illinois campus and the fertile cropland of Champaign County as a shallow tributary

in the prairie core, through my hometown of Lawrenceville, Illinois. From narrow pasturelands, through small woodlots, beneath iron trestles of the early twentieth century, it gains momentum through glacial moraines and flows into the Wabash River south of Vincennes, Indiana, between wooded bluffs that rise 20 feet above the floodplain (Figs. 5.4 and 5.5).

The goal was to study this region and use the information to suggest appropriate development strategies. One of the most important jobs for the landscape architect is to suggest design concepts for use of lands adjacent to corridors of outstanding diversity without destructive impact on those corridors—indeed, protecting and enhancing the landscape in the process.

The study began with looking at the river itself, since clean water is a resource crucial to life itself. We plotted the course of the river and its tributaries from U.S. Geological Survey (USGS) maps. The erosive action of water on the prairie over thousands of years has created many miles of steep topography along the river's course. This forms a three-dimensional space that provides a welcome relief from the wide-open spaces of the flat prairie. This steep topography is a cherished

resource because of this rare contrast. After plotting the river we plotted all topography with a slope of 12.5 percent or greater from the same USGS maps. This pattern was shown to enclose the floodplain, a poor choice for the site of human habitation. Siltation of these floodplains results in productive soils, but flooding presents the farmer with periodic losses (hence application of the name "Little Egypt" to southern Illinois, in recognition of the characteristic flooding, siltation, and a reference to the biblical allegory of seven poor years for every seven productive ones, as well as its reputation for producing good crops when productivity is poor in other areas).

By using information from existing USGS maps it was noted how easy it is to identify our critical waterways and the land adjacent to them. Without expending much time or effort, this method could be used to inventory critical patterns of water, floodplains and wetlands, and steep topography nationwide and identify top-priority areas for protection and management. We had found a shortcut to intensive and time-consuming analytical studies on the ground.

Vegetation, and archeological and historical sites, were added to these resource inventories.

Figure 5.4 Location of the
Embarras River Valley.

Figure 5.5 Landscape inventory of the Embarras River Valley features.

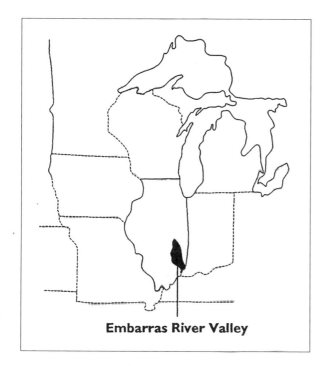

Embarras River Valley

Air photos were used to augment the vegetation patterns on the USGS maps and it was found that as with the steep topography patterns, the timber patterns also followed the waterways and their enclosing topography. This is because timber on steep banks is difficult to harvest. The timber-covered banks are vital sites of biological and scenic values and offer natural corridors for the movement of wildlife.

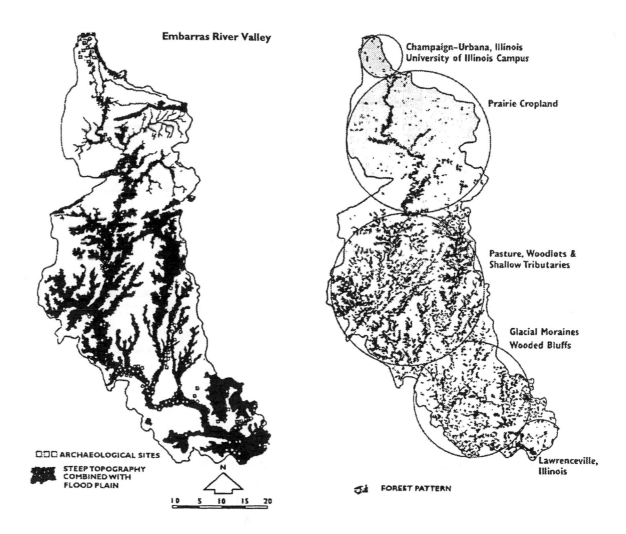

Embarras River Valley

Champaign–Urbana, Illinois
University of Illinois Campus

Prairie Cropland

Pasture, Woodlots &
Shallow Tributaries

Glacial Moraines
Wooded Bluffs

Lawrenceville,
Illinois

☐☐☐ ARCHAEOLOGICAL SITES

STEEP TOPOGRAPHY
COMBINED WITH
FLOOD PLAIN

N

10   5   10   15   20

FOREST PATTERN

Once the inventories were complete and the separate patterns overlaid to identify their congruence into corridors of diversity, it became visibly clear that protection of these corridors flowing through the landscape along water, wetland, and steep topographic patterns would ensure protection of the majority of the natural and cultural resources of the entire region. Using the inventoried information, each student then tackled a different design project connected with various human uses of the land, including farming, transportation, residential, industrial, commercial, and institutional construction as well as recreational uses. In developing creative designs for their projects, they focused on enhancing the health and beauty of the corridor fringe with its wealth of diversity as opposed to destroying the very values that attracted people there in the first place.

WABASH RIVER VALLEY (1958)

Convinced of the overriding importance of water, wetland, and steep topography and their relationships together with historical and archaeological features, we next sought to apply the knowledge on a larger scale. The Embarras River Valley was but a tributary of the Wabash River Valley, so the next step up in scale was to focus on the entire Wabash River Valley region (Fig. 5.6). The project demonstrated the use of concept and sketch plans and the importance of interdisciplinary teams, establishing short-term and long-term priorities, and the potential impacts of public education combined with citizen pressure.

The concept plan was based on what I had learned in studying the Embarras River and was revealed at a wild game feast in Mt. Carmel, Illinois, just south of my hometown. Mayor Roy Dee of Mt. Carmel was interested in cleaning up the town's waterfront. He had invited people from up and down the river to come to eat, socialize, and offer advice on the problem. Through a friend, Charles Hedde, who attended, I suggested that instead of looking only at the waterfront, the entire watershed be studied. This was agreed to and the Wabash River Valley study was under way. The next step was to pull together county-by-county data to develop a sketch plan to provide an approximation of the in-depth studies required to generate comprehensive options for a better future for the Wabash River Valley (Fig. 5.7). Utilizing the USGS mapping of the valley as a base map, with tracing-paper overlays it was possible to block out the water, wetland, steep topography, and vegetation patterns to quickly identify the integrated corridor pattern. By observing existing roads, communities, and resource extraction patterns found on USGS maps, it was also possible to see where corridor integrity was threatened, thereby establishing priority for protection and the need for in-depth local surveys.

As rivers are defined by water drainage basins, they are contained only by natural boundaries, not human-made boundaries, but the Wabash River Valley lies partially in Illinois and partially in Indiana. The goal of the study was to help people in the valley in both states to realize the environmental and economic potential that could be achieved through resource planning. To work toward this goal, an interuniversity team was developed including the Departments of Landscape Architecture, Geography, and Urban and Regional Planning of the University of Illinois, the Departments of Agricultural Economics and Civil Engineering of Purdue University, and the Business School at Indiana University. Patrick Horsbrugh, a friend and former classmate at Harvard, was also a

Figure 5.6 Wabash River
Valley in relation to local
and national resource
values.

Figure 5.7 Wabash River
Valley related to national
and local resource value
patterns: mineral resources,
vegetation and water, soil
suitability for cultivation,
and soil suitability for
wildlife habitat.

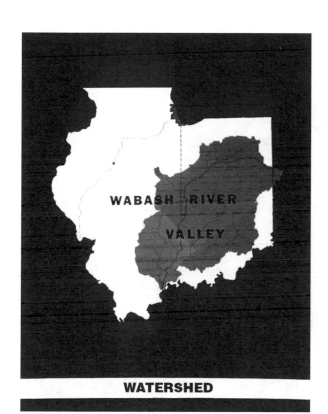

WATERSHED

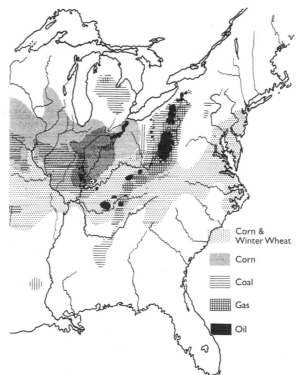

Corn &
Winter Wheat

Corn

Coal

Gas

Oil

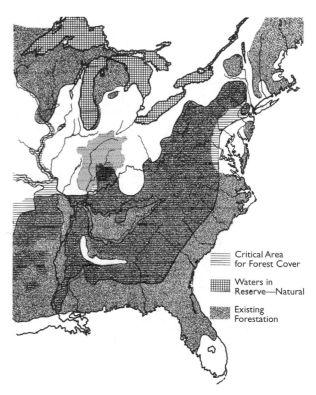

Critical Area
for Forest Cover

Waters in
Reserve—Natural

Existing
Forestation

major contributor to this project. He made no small plans and reaffirmed my conviction of the necessity to think on a broad scale, setting the context for later design detailing.

The team did very comprehensive inventories, considering the data available. However, they met with mixed success because of the priorities of the community and some of the members of the university team. Flooding was the major concern of the community and the engineers, and dams and reservoirs were the solution of choice at the time. The result was to submerge many areas with the characteristics suitable for natural and cultural diversity before they could be appraised and evaluated for possible preservation.

The reservoirs did moderate the flooding problem and later they did meet some of the growing recreational needs of the populace, but

Figure 5.7 (*continued*)

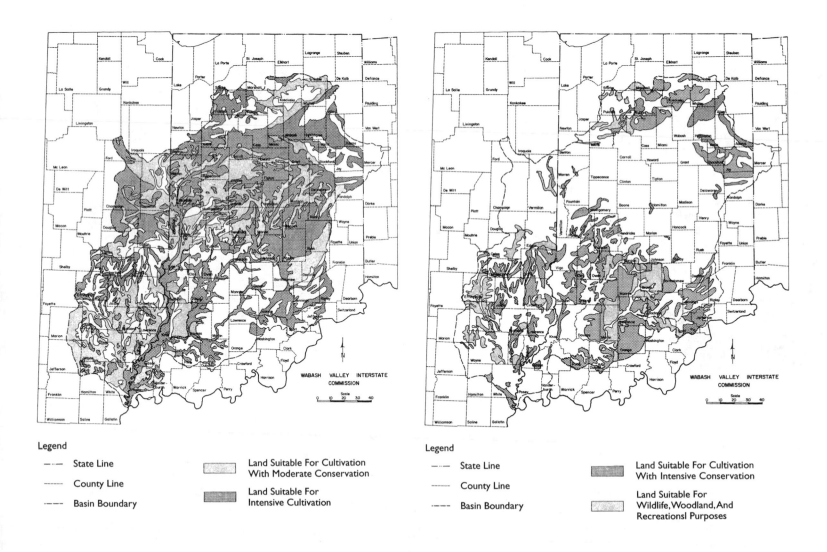

Legend

——··— State Line

———— County Line

——·——·— Basin Boundary

[shaded] Land Suitable For Cultivation
With Moderate Conservation

[shaded] Land Suitable For
Intensive Cultivation

Legend

——··— State Line

———— County Line

——·——·— Basin Boundary

[shaded] Land Suitable For Cultivation
With Intensive Conservation

[shaded] Land Suitable For
Wildlife, Woodland, And
Recreationsl Purposes

they no doubt had an unanticipated effect on the vegetation and wildlife of the area. A sheet of water replaced the plant diversity of several valleys and we will never know what was quickly traded off: rare plants and animal species, geological features, and archaeological sites.

Short-term interests and concerns won out over long-term sustainability and the interdisciplinary team was not used to its full advantage to design comprehensive options for the future. Nonetheless, the project had two surprising results. Although the project failed to inventory and protect patterns of natural and cultural diversity, it did demonstrate the power of pooling common interests across political boundaries such as state lines. It was a key lesson, even though taught partially by failure. Failure can be as instructive as success.

The Wabash River Valley study demonstrated the speed with which action can occur on a regional scale when citizen forces are effectively marshaled. A membership group called the Wabash Valley Association was formed at the beginning of the project to raise funds and implement activities. Within weeks of its founding, the association had grown into a real politi-cal force, eventually representing more than 2000 members. The political pressure they were able to bring to bear on the legislatures of two states resulted in the formation of an interstate compact, which permitted joint state funding of a staff to develop plans and public recreation programs in an amazingly short time. Despite mistakes during the project, the members of the Wabash River Association and much of the population of the Wabash watershed now recognized their river as a regional resource. As a result, the insight developed that local problems often require regional solutions and that local development invariably has a regional impact. This perspective built interest in the Wabash River watershed by emphasizing regional rather than purely local concerns.

Another key component of the evolving Regional Design Process was the recognition that public opinion and organized political action were key elements in making change happen. However, without effective communication to educate and inform the discretion of the public, results based on short-term expediency rather than long-term goals are more likely to occur.

READING THE TOTAL LANDSCAPE

Seen from the highway, landscape and townscape patterns and their relationships are not obvious. This is, however, the perspective from which most people observe the landscape, so it is understandable that their comprehension of the total landscape is limited. My applied research in the Department of Landscape Architecture, including the following Illinois study, has demonstrated how plotting resource patterns on maps drawn to the same scale and then viewing them side by side (or overlaid one on the other), can change one's perspective of the landscape.

One may be struck by the beauty of a water–wetland system, be impressed by standing on a ledge of steep topography, be shaded by a canopy of hard maples, and contemplate the history of a nineteenth-century farmhouse or a Native American burial mound, but value judgment of the total landscape is certainly enhanced when one finds all of these many features in the same landscape pattern. Overlays make overlapping of adjacent patterns obvious.

Figure 5.8 (a) Illinois water;
(b) significant topography
pattern; (c) Illinois environmental corridor pattern.

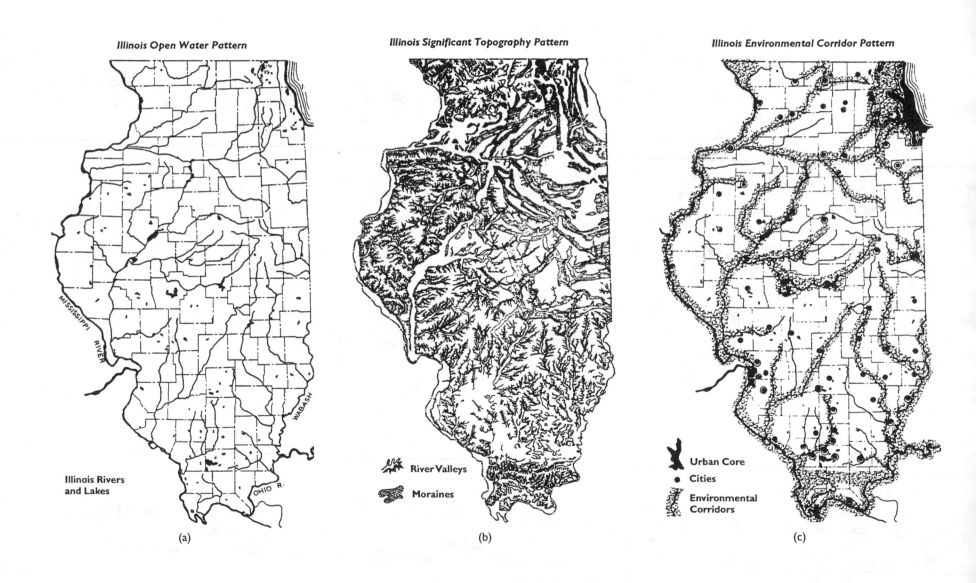

Illinois Open Water Pattern

Illinois Rivers
and Lakes

MISSISSIPPI RIVER

WABASH

OHIO R.

(a)

Illinois Significant Topography Pattern

River Valleys

Moraines

(b)

Illinois Environmental Corridor Pattern

Urban Core

Cities

Environmental
Corridors

(c)

Figure 5.9 State of Illinois.

The three maps of Fig. 5.8 show how open water and significant topographic patterns combine to form essentially linear corridors. Illinois has little steep topography outside its river valleys in glaciated areas. There are few significant wetlands, so the environmental corridor pattern is fairly simple.

STATE OF ILLINOIS RECREATION AND OPEN SPACE PLAN (1960)

The Embarras and Wabash River Valley studies prepared the way for the recreation and open space plan for the state of Illinois (Fig. 5.9). Confident that the knowledge gained by applying the Regional Design Process to the Embarras and Wabash valleys was important to growth design strategies anywhere, a proposal was made to the State Housing Board of Illinois to support such an inventory of Illinois (Figs. 5.10 and 5.11).

The funding that was granted resulted in a study that provided an opportunity to look at a region on a broader scale. In Illinois there was concern about the rapid changes in the landscape. These changes were affecting the life-

State of Illinois

support system and the diversity of the area, with the potential result of heavily influencing future tourism and recreation. It was recognized that opportunities to absorb the beauty of the diverse landscape to feed the soul might disappear if the landscape were not preserved.

The goal of the recreation and open space plan was to identify development options for Illi-

nois that minimize human impact on the land as well as preserving the life-support system, quality of life, sense of place, diversity, and options of choice. The Illinois plan confirmed the lessons of previous studies in addition to providing several additional insights to incorporate into the regional design process: the value of soil surveys in recreation planning, the need to identify and preserve landscape personalities, and how local regional design process applications fit into the larger regional context.

Following the approach developed in previous inventories, we gathered extensive information from the State Geological Survey, the Water Resource Survey, the university's archaeology department, and soil experts at the university and state soil scientists' offices and prepared maps showing the location of major soil resources. As in previous studies, the resource patterns overlapped to form linear "environmental corridors" that contain the vast majority of the state's diversity.

Timber

We looked at the timber pattern in early surveys, going back to the timber pattern of 1812. By 1969 there were about 2000 sawmills operating

Figure 5.10 Illinois timber
patterns in 1812.

Figure 5.11 Illinois sawmill
distribution in 1960.

Figure 5.12 Illinois forests
in 1960.

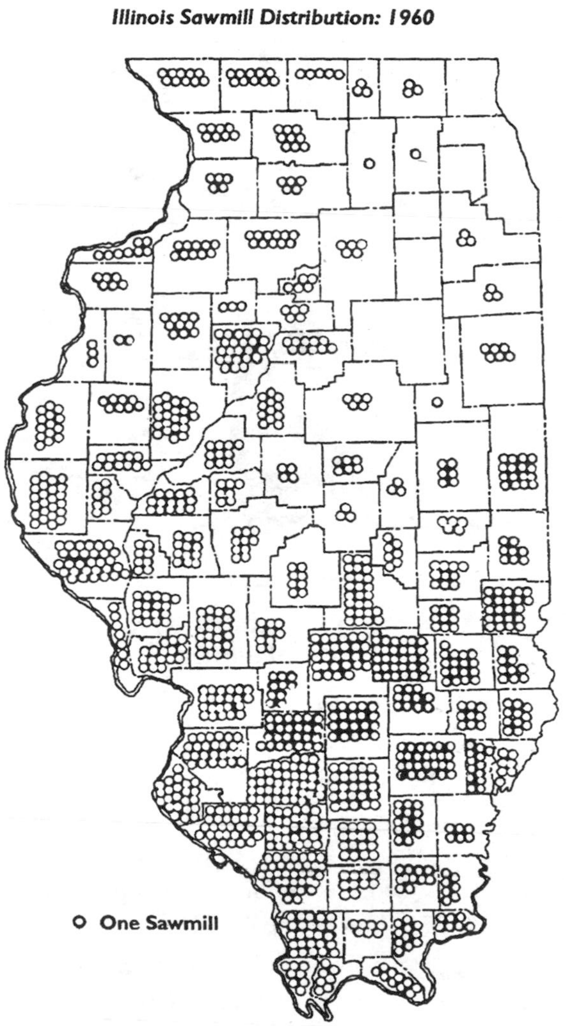

Illinois Timber Pattern: 1812

Illinois Sawmill Distribution: 1960

Illinois Forests: 1960

Forest

○ One Sawmill

Forest

Figure 5.13 Illinois archaeological sites.

Figure 5.14 Illinois historical
sites and buildings.

in this flat prairie state. The remaining timber
was on steep topography where it was too difficult to cut or where it was too wet to cut. By
1961, much of the timber outside these boundaries had been removed (Fig. 5.12).

Archaeological and Historical Sites

Working with the university archaeologists, we
identified and mapped 2000 archaeological sites
in the state, showing that practically all of these
features were on the waterways (Fig. 5.13). We
noted that their locations were determined simply because the waterway had been a transportation corridor first for Native Americans and later
for European settlers. They built most of their
early buildings on the waterways, near water for
household and agricultural use and as a refuge
from prairie fires (Fig. 5.14).

Impacts on High-Quality Resources

After identifying the high-quality resources concentrated in linear patterns, we were able to recommend to the state which areas were most in
need of protection from inappropriate development (Figs. 5.16 and 5.17). More detailed studies
revealed the resource patterns most subject to

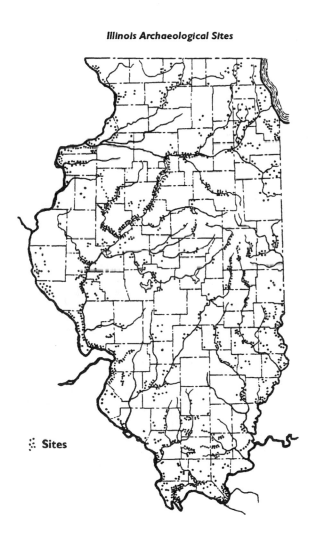

Illinois Archaeological Sites

∴ **Sites**

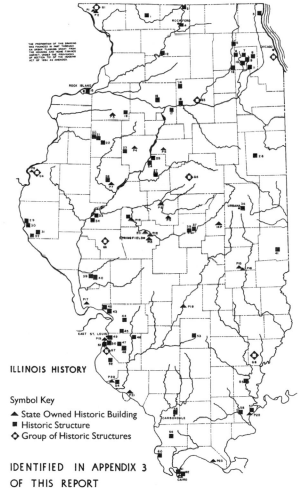

ILLINOIS HISTORY

Symbol Key
▲ State Owned Historic Building
■ Historic Structure
◇ Group of Historic Structures

IDENTIFIED IN APPENDIX 3
OF THIS REPORT

Figure 5.15 Illinois parks, conservation areas, and monuments.

Figure 5.16 Illinois's linear environmental corridors.

Figure 5.17 Major impact threats to the linear corridor system.

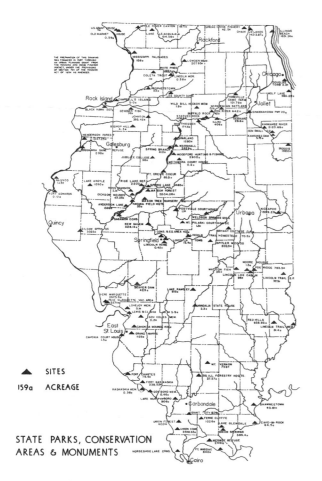

STATE PARKS, CONSERVATION
AREAS & MONUMENTS

▲ SITES

159a ACREAGE

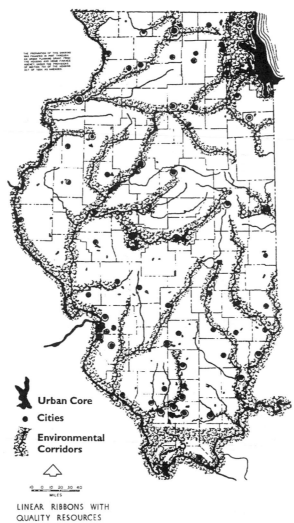

Urban Core

• **Cities**

Environmental Corridors

▼⁰ 0 10 20 30 40
MILES

LINEAR RIBBONS WITH
QUALITY RESOURCES
FOR RECREATION

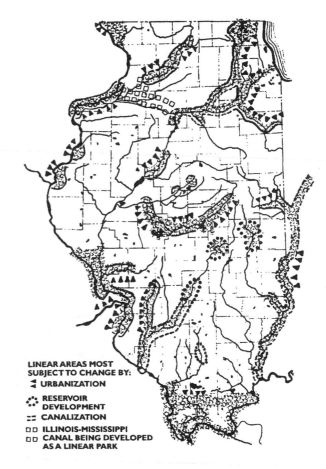

LINEAR AREAS MOST SUBJECT TO CHANGE BY:

◀ URBANIZATION

⁘ RESERVOIR DEVELOPMENT

⚌ CANALIZATION

▢▢ ILLINOIS-MISSISSIPPI
▢▢ CANAL BEING DEVELOPED
AS A LINEAR PARK

Figure 5.18 Illinois land-scape personalities.

disruption as a result of population expansion and technological change. Urbanization, industrial-ization, canalization, reservoir flooding, and new transportation systems are all aspects of such change.

Landscape Personalities

Based on the maps of the overview inventories of the state, a concept plan became clear. The state could be divided into seven distinct landscape personalities, and these personalities provide an important method of classifying the characteristic diversity in the state. Along with this identifica-tion was developed a broadscale interpretation of specific areas within the personalities, giving a more detailed picture of the resource values they contain. Each of these personalities reflects the local colors, textures, patterns, and spatial quali-ties that make each unique. As such, any plans for development should carefully preserve the varied landscape personalities.

Capturing the unique sense-of-place qualities of each landscape personality enables the designer to create palates to harmonize future development with their regional qualities. It became obvious that when the uniqueness of an

Illinois Landscape Personalities

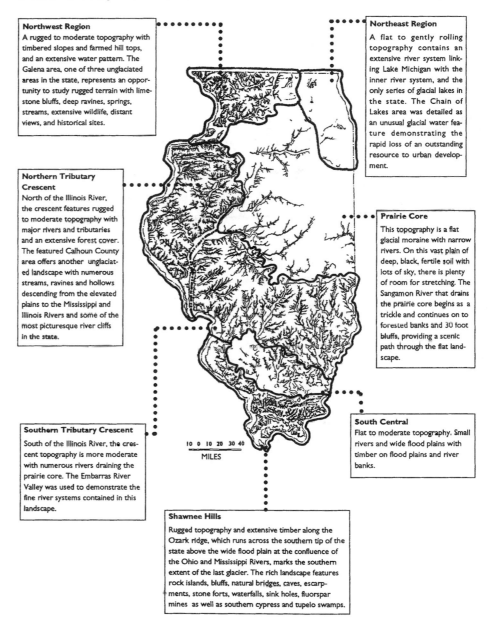

Northwest Region
A rugged to moderate topography with timbered slopes and farmed hill tops, and an extensive water pattern. The Galena area, one of three unglaciated areas in the state, represents an oppor-tunity to study rugged terrain with lime-stone bluffs, deep ravines, springs, streams, extensive wildlife, distant views, and historical sites.

Northeast Region
A flat to gently rolling topography contains an extensive river system link-ing Lake Michigan with the inner river system, and the only series of glacial lakes in the state. The Chain of Lakes area was detailed as an unusual glacial water fea-ture demonstrating the rapid loss of an outstanding resource to urban develop-ment.

Northern Tributary Crescent
North of the Illinois River, the crescent features rugged to moderate topography with major rivers and tributaries and an extensive forest cover. The featured Calhoun County area offers another unglaciat-ed landscape with numerous streams, ravines and hollows descending from the elevated plains to the Mississippi and Illinois Rivers and some of the most picturesque river cliffs in the state.

Prairie Core
This topography is a flat glacial moraine with narrow rivers. On this vast plain of deep, black, fertile soil with lots of sky, there is plenty of room for stretching. The Sangamon River that drains the prairie core begins as a trickle and continues on to forested banks and 30 foot bluffs, providing a scenic path through the flat land-scape.

Southern Tributary Crescent
South of the Illinois River, the cres-cent topography is more moderate with numerous rivers draining the prairie core. The Embarras River Valley was used to demonstrate the fine river systems contained in this landscape.

South Central
Flat to moderate topography. Small rivers and wide flood plains with timber on flood plains and river banks.

Shawnee Hills
Rugged topography and extensive timber along the Ozark ridge, which runs across the southern tip of the state above the wide flood plain at the confluence of the Ohio and Mississippi Rivers, marks the southern extent of the last glacier. The rich landscape features rock islands, bluffs, natural bridges, caves, escarp-ments, stone forts, waterfalls, sink holes, fluorspar mines as well as southern cypress and tupelo swamps.

10 0 10 20 30 40
MILES

Figure 5.19 Structure
embodying historical sense
of place.

Figure 5.20 Sangamon
Township.

area was identified and understood (Fig. 5.19), people felt a special ownership of the area and developed a desire to preserve it. Landscape personalities could be identified using readily available information that when communicated to the public could be an effective mechanism to help present the landscape as a collective work of art to be revered and protected rather than exploited and destroyed.

Diversity and the Regional Aesthetic

The varied forms and combinations of resources give each area its distinctive landscape personality. Anyone would readily recognize the differ-

ence between a desert and a tropical forest or between a mountain range and the flat expanse of a prairie. In each case the natural and cultural resources of the region have combined in unique ways to give that region a distinct, recognizable personality. Some are quite obvious, but others are much more subtle. It is these less distinct differences and gradations that make the landscape so exciting from aesthetic and spiritual perspectives and make our life-support system so complex.

In the Illinois plan, juxtaposing the water, topography, and forest patterns made certain relationships more apparent. The dendritic water pattern caused by centuries of erosive action contained much of the slope in a generally flat landscape. Most of the unexploited timber that remained was also here. Outside these corridors the patterns of agricultural production, urbanization (townscape), and transportation also had their unique characteristics. Construction materials and styles native to each region rather than generic structures must be encouraged. Each landscape heritage is worthy of expression through varied architecture in harmony with it.

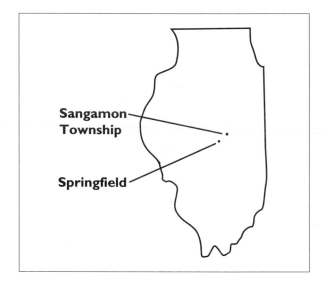

Illinois Landscape Personalities

See Fig. 5.18.

Sangamon Township

The other new concept used in the Illinois landscape study was to select a township in the state to see how developing recreational facilities should be implemented at the local level once the major regional patterns and resources had been identified. I chose Sangamon Township near Spring-

Figure 5.21 Sangamon Township soils analysis showing soils suitable for (a) embankments, (b) footpaths, (c) lakeshores, (d) golf courses, (e) campgrounds, and (f) roadways.

field, the capitol of Illinois, because it was centrally located, was the township with the most complete soil inventories, and represented a cross section through a typical linear system of diversity in the prairie core personality (Fig. 5.20).

Using readily available information to quickly define broad patterns and to buy time for more in-depth studies, soil information was considered in the inventories for the first time. This information had typically been used only for agricultural planning. The Illinois study demonstrated that this same information could also be useful in guiding decisions about recreation planning, perhaps the first use of soil information at this scale to guide human habitation and regional recreation concepts. These recommendations were guided by the appropriate uses for different soil types (Fig. 5.21). For example, class A farmland was recommended to be preserved for agriculture, and fine soils were to be left undeveloped to prevent erosion (Fig. 5.22). Most of the richer soils occurred outside the wetland/steep topography corridors, demonstrating that one can develop the environmental corridors for sustainable options and recreation without encroaching on the soils best suited for farming.

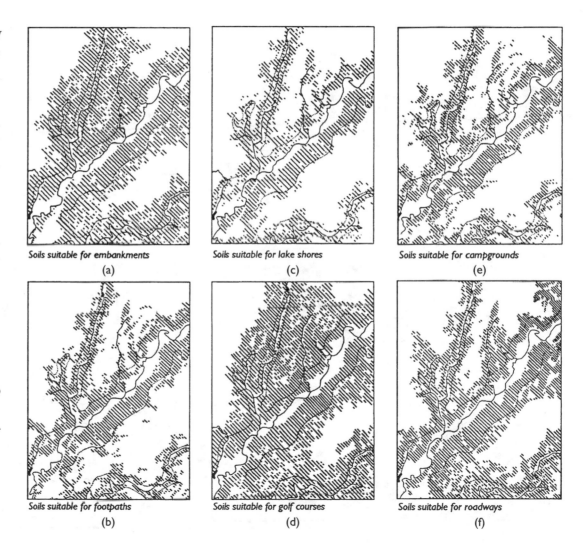

Soils suitable for embankments
(a)

Soils suitable for lake shores
(c)

Soils suitable for campgrounds
(e)

Soils suitable for footpaths
(b)

Soils suitable for golf courses
(d)

Soils suitable for roadways
(f)

Figure 5.22 Sangamon
Township agricultural soils.

Figure 5.23 Sangamon
Township perceptual study.

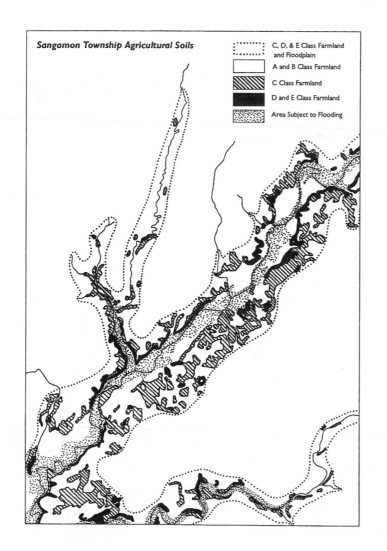

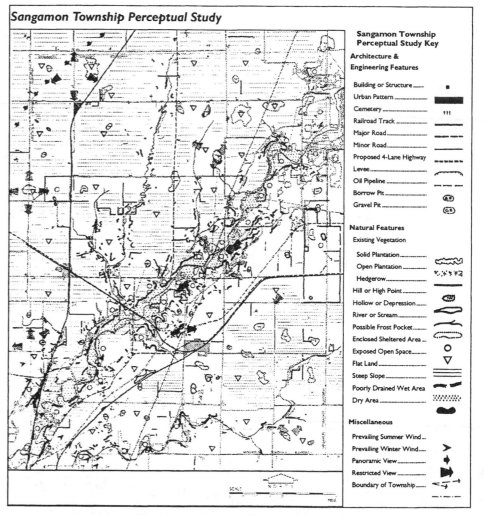

Figure 5.24 Spatial icons representing different kinds of outdoor space.

Perceptual Resources: Three-Dimensional Space

In addition to soil resources, perceptual resources such as spatial characteristics were added to the Sangamon Township inventory in recognition that three-dimensional space may be one of our most important and perhaps most neglected resources. This study showed the spatial diversity of the area and how perceptual resource inventories (Fig. 5.23) could be used to design trails linking sequences of visual delight.

There are different ways to create different kinds of three-dimensional spaces. Each space is created by walls of trees, land form, or building masses, and each space invokes different responses in people. Therefore, space is a resource that should be considered when designing spatially diverse options of the future.

I suggested that spatial *icons* representing the different kinds of space would be the most effective way to abstract this aesthetic regional resource in order to plot it and draw to it the attention that it deserved (Fig. 5.24). I charged my Australian student, Alan Correy, with identifying as many different types of space as he could and see if any symbols existed to represent these spaces. Finding none in use, he created an array

ENCLOSED PARTLY BY VEGETATION & PARTLY BY TYPOGRAPHY

ENCLOSED BY TYPOGRAPHY

VEGETATION ON ENCLOSED SIDES

ENCLOSED BY TYPOGRAPHY WITH VEGETATION

ENCLOSED PARTLY BY SOLID VEGETATION

ENCLOSED BY VEGETATION ON ONE SIDE

ENCLOSED BY TYPOGRAPHY

ENCLOSED BY VEGETATION

ENCLOSED BY VEGETATION

ENCLOSED BY VEGETATION & TYPOGRAPHY WITH HALF CANOPY

ENCLOSED BY OPEN VEGETATION WITH CANOPY ABOVE

ENCLOSED BY TYPOGRAPHY

Figure 5.25 Impacts on quality resources. Trails can be designed to maximize the experience of available three-dimensional space.

Figure 5.26 Sangamon Township landscape inventory analysis.

Figure 5.27 The Township corridor can serve as a form determinate.

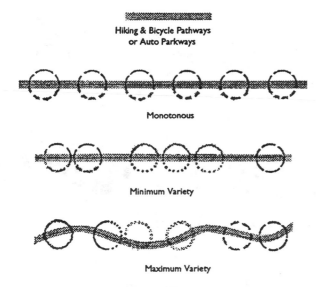

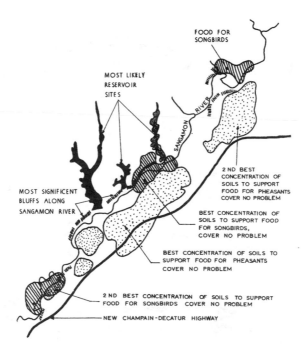

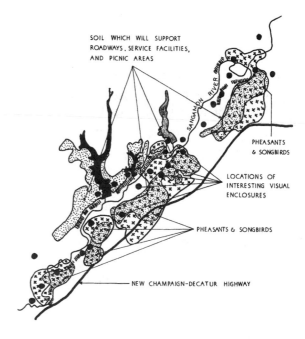

of symbols that I later used in the Wisconsin Recreation and Open Space Plan. The use of these icons to inject variety in the designing trails or parkways is shown (Fig. 5.25).

Making Recommendations

Utilizing the spatial inventories in addition to soil inventories enabled us to make recommendations about appropriate plans for recreational development, which incorporated maintenance of diverse three-dimensional spaces, soils that would

best support various recreational activities, access to existing highways and utilities, and use of areas with diverse resources all within the context of regional patterns (Fig. 5.26).

Once the inventories of the natural and cultural resources in the state were completed, it became evident what human activities had the greatest impact on the Illinois landscape. Urban-

ization, interstate highways, and reservoir development stood out. By recognizing these areas of greatest impact, meaningful priorities for more detailed studies to contain and minimize the impact were set. The Illinois study showed that carefully planned inventories could identify an integrated corridor pattern combining the water, wetland, and timber patterns with the flood-

Figure 5.28 Professor Jordahl in the capitol inner vault, Environmental Awareness Center, 1964.

plains, sandy soils adjacent to the water, and the outstanding architectural and historical resources. This corridor, in turn, became the form determinant for future development (Fig. 5.27).

STATE OF WISCONSIN RECREATION PLAN (1960)

Wisconsin is increasingly the recreational destination for the residents of surrounding states. As population, urbanization, and recreational accessibility increase, so do the pressures on the state's natural environment. In the rush to ensure outdoor recreational opportunities for as many people as possible, there has unfortunately been a great emphasis on providing human-made facilities, with little consideration for harmonizing them with the region's natural and aesthetic characteristics.

In 1960, Wisconsin Governor Gaylord Nelson recognized Wisconsin's need for comprehensive recreation planning because of the state's traditionally highly valued rich heritage of outdoor recreational resources and the potential impact on these resources created by the millions of people living in the upper midwest. He proposed to the legislature a 1-cent sales tax on the price of

cigarettes to raise $50 million to fund the purchase of key lands and preserve critical natural and cultural resources in the state that are the basis of the state's recreation and tourism industry. The tax was enacted, and because of the success of the Illinois Recreation and Open Space Plan, he appointed me to direct the resource planning division of the Wisconsin Recreation and Open Space Plan, which focused on observing, recording, and interpreting the many values in the Wisconsin landscape that make it an outstanding recreation state. The development of this state plan under the leadership of David Carley (head of the Department of Resource Development), with contributions from other outstanding environmental leaders such as Harold Jordahl (Fig. 5.28) (who dealt with land easements and planning) and Jake Beuscher (professor of law at the University of Wisconsin), whose expertise was in land-use controls and water law) had statewide grass-roots support covering a wide political spectrum. It was, and is, a landmark in environmental policy.

Recreation Impacts on Wisconsin Resources

Peace of mind seems scarce in our urbanized land. City dwellers appreciate the stimulus of crowds and lights, the abundance of stores and services, and the sophistication of city entertainment, but many feel the need for a change, for a kind of vision and perspective that cities do not provide. The great variety of recreational activities in the out-of-doors—pleasure driving, hiking, swimming, camping, and so on—provide opportunities for enjoying natural beauty. More and more people are making use of these opportunities, both as visitors and as buyers of land for recreational purposes.

Governor Nelson played a significant role in awakening the public and politicians to the need for protecting the natural and cultural resources of Wisconsin with the support of a wide range of local groups and individuals. His efforts included this statement in his resource development message to the state legislature in 1961: "I'm sure that each of us can recall a favorite picnic spot that is now a housing development, a wonderful duck marsh that has been drained for farming, a scenic highway stretch that is now cluttered with billboards and roadside stands, a once-secret trout stream that is no more, or a peaceful lake that has

been encircled and closed off by private landowners, or overrun and heavily pressured by powerboats."[1]

Communicating at the State and Regional Level

On my first day on the job with the Wisconsin outdoor recreation plan, I walked through the front door of the capitol building, entered the Department of Resource Development offices, passed the secretary and director's office, and found my way to the back room. I had one oak desk with one oak chair, and $50 million to spend.

Richard Andrews, a planner, was sitting at his desk nearby doing a microeconomics study of the state. He was quietly developing models of the state's economics on paper. A desk and a chair were all he needed, but I was oriented toward implementation and practical application, so I immediately set to work thinking about what I would need to complete the plan. I had money to spend but no staff to help me do the massive inventory required. What I needed was a

way to communicate with the legislature to show them what was to be done and to justify the staff required. What I had in mind was a place where the inventory task at hand could be explained utilizing maps, graphics, and models, a place that I was later to define as an environmental awareness center.

I asked Dr. Andrews if he knew of a space to use to establish such an awareness center. He took me back to an inner vault two stories high, filled with rusty file cabinets unopened since the early twentieth century, with a beautiful wrought-iron staircase leading up to the governor's office. I agreed that the vault would be perfect for an operations center so we obtained permission from my immediate director, David Carley, and the governor to remove the file cabinets and paint the walls white. Initially, USGS maps were pieced together presenting a map of the entire state on a scale seldom, if ever, seen. The assembled maps with three overlays, indicating the water, wetlands, and steep topography of the entire state, filled a gymnasium basketball court. Carefully, the parts of the state repre-

Figure 5.29 Rock County.

Figure 5.30 Identifying locally significant landscape features from afar.

sented by the majority of house and senate members were first displayed. The immediate effect was assurance that we were progressing rapidly with our assigned inventory task. Each day the governor and my director would button-hole another legislator and descend the spiral staircase into this awareness center. Within a month, the entire legislature was informed of what was under way and we had bipartisan support. I soon had 30 landscape architecture students employed part-time coming in at all hours of the day and the weekends to complete the inventory for the state.

As the inventory proceeded, new overlays were placed over the statewide map, and inquisitive legislators regularly dropped in to view the work in progress, especially in their home districts. The overlays were mere documentation of the intensive inventory surveys being conducted in each of the 72 counties of the state.

Natural and Cultural Resource Icons

The inventory began with a pilot study of Rock County (Fig. 5.29) to determine whether the techniques developed in the Illinois inventories could be effectively employed immediately to the north in Wisconsin. I drove every road in the

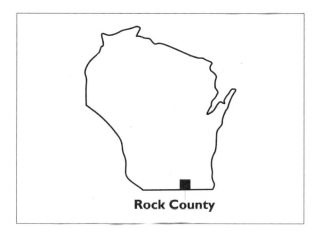

Rock County

county myself and was impressed by the degree of diversity in the state. (Fig. 5.30) I wondered if a survey of only water, wetlands, and steep topography would be meaningful in this situation. The local characteristics that local people and state agency personnel found significant needed to be plotted along with topographic patterns to see if they coincided (Fig. 5.31). Local people were interviewed to find out what resources they cherished. These interviews resulted in a list of 220 specific natural and cultural features, ranging from marshes to waterfalls, wildlife habitat to old mills, songbirds to caves. (Fig. 5.32) The next question was how to plot

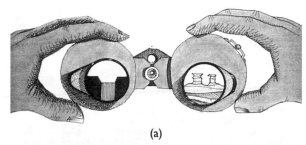

(a)

(b)

Figure 5.31 **Pilot Inventory: water wetlands, and steep topography in Rock County.** The inventory technique bears out their application to identify environmental corridors in Wisconsin.

(a)
Environmental Corridor Pattern: Rock County

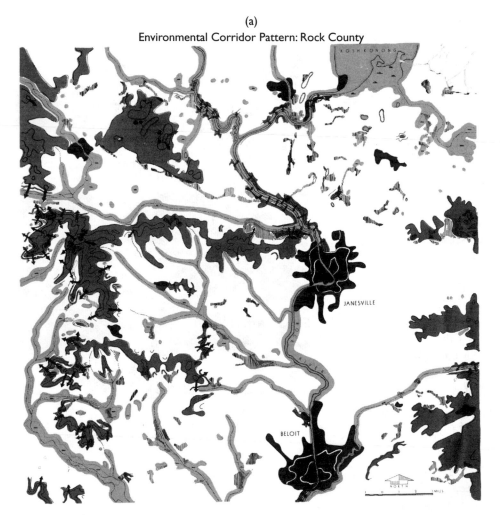

ENVIRONMENTAL CORRIDOR PATTERN
JANESVILLE-BELOIT CASE STUDY AREA

(b)
Patterns of Resource Quality: Environmental Corridors
MAJOR INTRINSIC VALUES (CONTINUOUS PATTERNS)

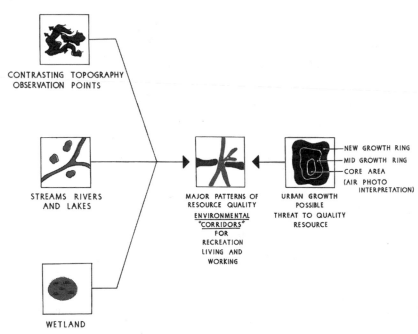

CONTRASTING TOPOGRAPHY OBSERVATION POINTS

STREAMS RIVERS AND LAKES

WETLAND

MAJOR PATTERNS OF RESOURCE QUALITY
ENVIRONMENTAL "CORRIDORS" FOR RECREATION LIVING AND WORKING

URBAN GROWTH POSSIBLE THREAT TO QUALITY RESOURCE

NEW GROWTH RING
MID GROWTH RING
CORE AREA (AIR PHOTO INTERPRETATION)

Figure 5.32 Environmental
corridor patterns and
resources, Rock County.

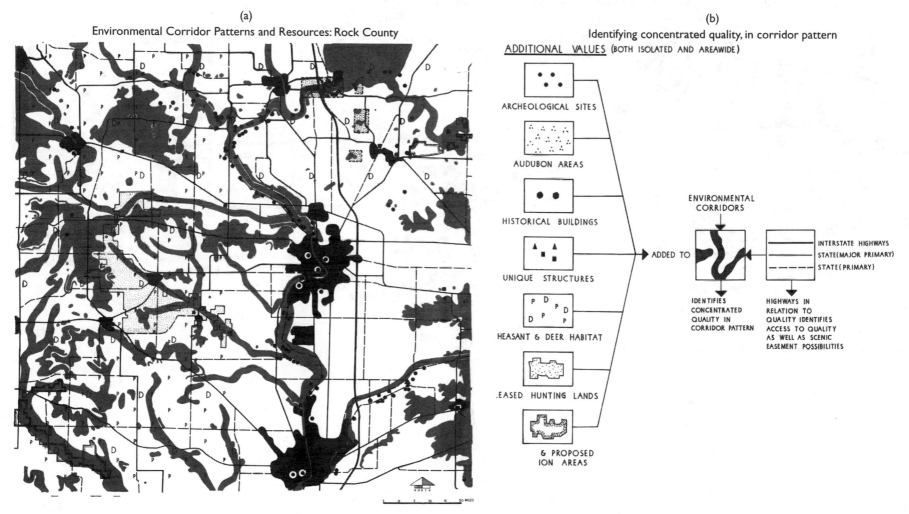

(a)
Environmental Corridor Patterns and Resources: Rock County

ISOLATED AND AREAWIDE RECREATIONAL RESOURCES AND FACILITIES
JANESVILLE-BELOIT CASE STUDY AREA

(b)
Identifying concentrated quality, in corridor pattern

ADDITIONAL VALUES (BOTH ISOLATED AND AREAWIDE)

ARCHEOLOGICAL SITES

AUDUBON AREAS

HISTORICAL BUILDINGS

UNIQUE STRUCTURES

HEASANT & DEER HABITAT

.EASED HUNTING LANDS

& PROPOSED
ION AREAS

ADDED TO

ENVIRONMENTAL
CORRIDORS

IDENTIFIES
CONCENTRATED
QUALITY IN
CORRIDOR PATTERN

INTERSTATE HIGHWAYS
STATE (MAJOR PRIMARY)
STATE (PRIMARY)

HIGHWAYS IN
RELATION TO
QUALITY IDENTIFIES
ACCESS TO QUALITY
AS WELL AS SCENIC
EASEMENT POSSIBILITIES

Figure 5.33 Symbolizing natural and cultural values: (a) viewing the landscape; (b) sketching the landscape. In addition to the corridor resources, the Wisconsin Outdoor Recreation Plan provided an opportunity to identify additional natural and cultural features in the landscape that were important to recreation and the quality of life. Unlike corridor patterns which thread through the landscape, most of these supplementary resources were found to occupy specific sites. After many consultations with local, state, and federal representatives and viewing a cross section of the Wisconsin resources in the field, we photographed and sketched the landscape as well as designed symbols to be plotted on statewide maps. Perhaps the most valuable result was that 85 to 90 percent of these resources were found to lie within the environmental corridor. When found clustered together, we identified them as nodes of diversity. The symbols we developed were not only favorably received by the general public, but they fostered an expanded awareness of diversity.

(a)

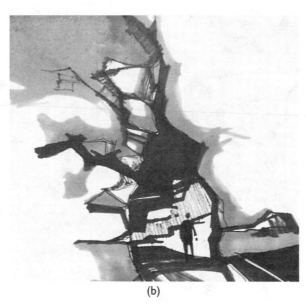

(b)

Symbolizing the Landscape

(c)

220 different resources on a single map and also keep track of each resource individually. The obvious answer was to create icons for each resource (Figs. 5.31, 5.32, 5.33) which could be placed directly on the maps. Artists were brought in to represent resources, providing a perspective that only they could provide. The result confirmed that art is another essential element of the **Regional Design Process** and that any success-

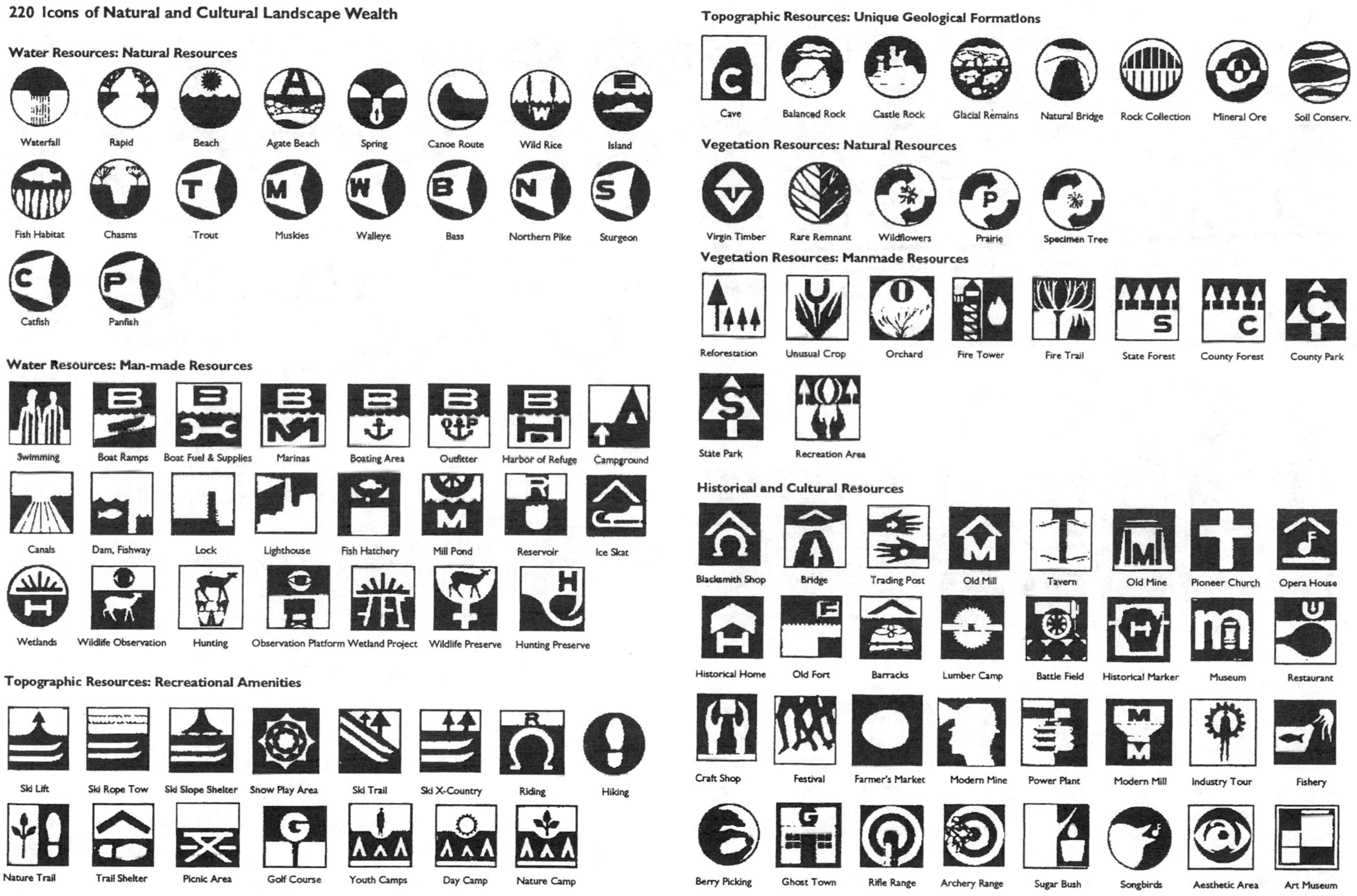
220 Icons of Natural and Cultural Landscape Wealth
Water Resources: Natural Resources
Waterfall
Rapid
Beach
Agate Beach
Spring
Canoe Route
Wild Rice
Island
Fish Habitat
Chasms
Trout
Muskies
Walleye
Bass
Northern Pike
Sturgeon
Catfish
Panfish
Water Resources: Man-made Resources
Swimming
Boat Ramps
Boat Fuel & Supplies
Marinas
Boating Area
Outfitter
Harbor of Refuge
Campground
Canals
Dam, Fishway
Lock
Lighthouse
Fish Hatchery
Mill Pond
Reservoir
Ice Skat
Wetlands
Wildlife Observation
Hunting
Observation Platform
Wetland Project
Wildlife Preserve
Hunting Preserve
Topographic Resources: Recreational Amenities
Ski Lift
Ski Rope Tow
Ski Slope Shelter
Snow Play Area
Ski Trail
Ski X-Country
Riding
Hiking
Nature Trail
Trail Shelter
Picnic Area
Golf Course
Youth Camps
Day Camp
Nature Camp
Topographic Resources: Unique Geological Formations
Cave
Balanced Rock
Castle Rock
Glacial Remains
Natural Bridge
Rock Collection
Mineral Ore
Soil Conserv.
Vegetation Resources: Natural Resources
Virgin Timber
Rare Remnant
Wildflowers
Prairie
Specimen Tree
Vegetation Resources: Manmade Resources
Reforestation
Unusual Crop
Orchard
Fire Tower
Fire Trail
State Forest
County Forest
County Park
State Park
Recreation Area
Historical and Cultural Resources
Blacksmith Shop
Bridge
Trading Post
Old Mill
Tavern
Old Mine
Pioneer Church
Opera House
Historical Home
Old Fort
Barracks
Lumber Camp
Battle Field
Historical Marker
Museum
Restaurant
Craft Shop
Festival
Farmer's Market
Modern Mine
Power Plant
Modern Mill
Industry Tour
Fishery
Berry Picking
Ghost Town
Rifle Range
Archery Range
Sugar Bush
Songbirds
Aesthetic Area
Art Museum

Figure 5.34 Symbols of natural and cultural landscape wealth.

Figure 5.34 (*continued*)

Historical and Cultural Resources

Outstanding Building	Theater	Existing Public Land	Existing Private Land	Proposed Public Land	Proposed Private Land

Archaeological Resources

Effigy Mound	Sugar Bush	Petroglyph	Quartzite	Pipestone	Steatite	Flint Quarry	Copper

Lead	Quartz	Chlorite	Campsite	Village Site	Circular Enclosure	Square Enc.	Rectangular Enc.

Wild Rice	Cornfield	Garden Bed	Trail	Ford	Fort	Battlefield	Cache Pit

<None>Workshop	Historic Village Site	Provision Cache	Shell Heap	Ceramic Artifact	Conical Mound	Mound Group	Mound-Elliptical

Historic Cemetery	Prehistoric Cemetery	Stone Grave	Burial Ground	Grave

Wildlife Resources

Bear	Bobcat	Wolf	Deer	Fox	Pheasant	Quail	Woodcock

Hungarian Partridge	Ruffed Grouse	Sharp-Tailed Grouse	Prairie Chicken	Muskrat	Beaver	Mink	Otter

Badger	Ducks	Geese	Swans	Eagles	Red-tailed Hawks	Herons	Great Horned Owls

Egrets	Ospreys	Falcons	Goshawks	Cranes	Loons	Ibis	Hawks

Tourist Facilities

Accommodations	Hospital	Telephone	Water	Pharmacies	Gas Stations	Toilet Facilities	Restaurant

Washer/Dryer

ful development study must be a true interdisciplinary endeavor.

Following the Rock County pilot study, the statewide inventory began. The USGS maps originally purchased for display in the capitol awareness center were enlarged to a scale of 2000 feet to 1 inch by the state transportation department and transferred to the transparent film, Mylar. Cheap blue-line prints were made quickly from the Mylar sheets for each county of the state.

County meetings were scheduled through the offices of University of Wisconsin Cooperative Extension and state agency personnel in the region. Meeting with representatives from these

Figure 5.35 Environmental corridors and natural corridor diversity.

organizations and selected people in each county, each with a broad understanding of local resources, we began to plot our icons on the county base maps. By selecting those who deliver oil, supplies, and mail countywide as well as the history and biology teachers of the high schools, we had ample talent for the inventory task.

Resource Inventories: Water, Wetlands, and Steep Topography

The pilot inventories confirmed that here, too, water, wetlands, and steep topography combined into linear corridor patterns, as in Illinois.

The patterns that emerged when these resource icons were plotted showed that 90 percent of all the physical resources cherished by the residents of the region fell in the water, wetlands, and steep topography corridor system (Fig. 5.35). As a result, we were able to go to the more than 100 different conservation groups in the state and tell them, "Look, instead of fighting for just your own individual resource, fight to protect this regional landscape pattern that contains most of the values we all want to protect." We suggested that by conducting inventories such as those in the Wisconsin Outdoor Recreation Plan, we could also systematically determine where to

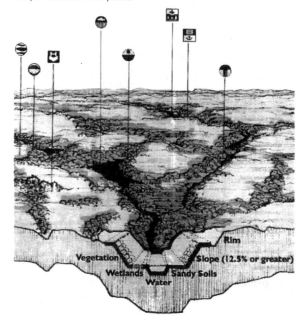

Additional Resource Values in Environmental Corridors
State-wide field checks in Wisconsin and Illinois also indicate that these additional values be for the most part within these corridor patterns.

build, where not to build, and with new design guidelines, what to build. The Wisconsin Outdoor Recreation Plan became a prototype to demonstrate the vast planning and educational possibilities that environmental corridor patterns offer. The corridor patterns are a planning guide. As such, they identified the areas that are most

critical to protect. Finally, as an educational tool, maps of environmental corridors and the resource values they contain have been used to increase awareness of the connections among a variety of natural and cultural resources worthy of protection and wise development throughout the nation.

LANDSCAPE: A COLLECTIVE WORK OF ART

I have often thought we would be less likely to destroy landscapes if more of us comprehended the beauty of these landscapes and how they sustain us. The Illinois plan revealed that landscapes each have their own personality and sense of place and if we destroy these characteristics, we are destroying the resource options among which present and future democracies depend. We cannot, in good conscience, destroy the fabric of nature on the basis of the values present in a fleeting moment of time. One of the basic rules of common sense is: "In all cases, when presented with any array that is not understood in its entirety, without a doubt, save all of the pieces." Our natural world is complex and incompletely understood, so we do not have the right to foreclose any options for our successor tenants in this place.

The question of how to promote comprehension of unique landscapes led to the conclusion that the entire state might be regarded as a collective work of art. Slashing a masterwork of fine art is not condoned, but our landscape is slashed every day. In our age of cultural, ecological, and economic instability, it is durability that we must seek. This durability is found in the discovery of uniqueness and the preservation of diversity and continuity. Most discoveries are acts of art and creation, and preservation is the result of enlightened perception, a primary product of the arts. Comprehending the state as a collective work of art requires creative education and acceptance of a unified natural and social ethic that will guide our view of the land.

ENVIRONMENTAL CORRIDORS: APPLICATION

Environmental corridors are a particularly vital pattern to protect because they are the key to regional diversity: both biological diversity, which is central for biological sustainability, and aesthetic diversity, which is vital for cultural sustainability. Since 85 to 90 percent of this diversity falls within the environmental corridor pattern, we need only inventory four resources (water, wetlands, steep topography, and timber/woodlands) (Fig. 5.36) to identify the areas of greatest diversity in the region. In addition, aquifer recharge areas are an important category to be separately identified, together with the direction of flow where information is available. These areas are the locus of examples of complex ecosystems. Other important systems are remnants of areas such as desert or prairie or forest that are also essential preservation candidates. The preservation of no single species can be accomplished apart from its surrounding habitat and the relationships of its native ecosystem.

Beyond diversity itself, there are other important reasons for identification of environmental corridors. First, without water, life is not possible. The surface waters are often flanked by wetland vegetation systems, which play a vital role in the water cycle by filtering out impurities. They provide habitat and a traverse system for many wild animals. The wetland systems are often bordered, in turn, by steep topography created by the wearing action of water and wind over centuries and millennia of time. If this steep topography is disturbed, the soils on its banks erode the slope and silt is moved into the wetland and waterway.

Collectively, the environmental corridors, class A farmlands, aquifer recharge areas, wetland, and timber vegetation (also prairie where it occurs, and desert, as well as other major vegetation types in parts of the country other than the midwest) define the areas where development is prohibited. The region outside the perimeter of this pattern, on the other hand, contains the potential for designed manipulation of the landscape guided by careful application of the Regional Design Process. Developed wisely at the scale of each level of government from town to federal, by rural and urban dwellers, these corridors can serve as countywide, statewide, and regional alternatives to advancing structures of brick, steel, glass, concrete, and asphalt. When preserved, they offer alternatives to conformity and boredom so that the landscape resource is not overtaken. (Fig. 5.37) Enjoyment and use of our natural and cultural heritage are meaningful

Figure 5.36 Components of corridors: (a) surface resources; (b) slopes; (c) rims; (d) water-oriented corridors; (e) landform-oriented corridors.

Surface Resources

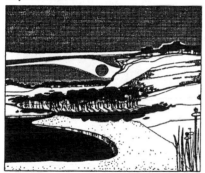

Water

All navigable waters in Wisconsin belong to the public. Kept clean, water offers vast acreages of resource quality and open space within the corridor pattern.

Wetlands

Wetlands serve as headwater marshes, wildlife habitat and sources of natural springs, and should therefore be protected as a valuable surface within the corridor pattern.

Flood Plains

The flood plains of Wisconsin offer exceptional recreational opportunities as well as natural channels for surface water drainage. Subject to flooding, these 'surface' patterns offer little opportunity for safe urban development and should be protected from such encroachments.

Sandy Soils

Sandy soils are often found adjacent to water 'surface' and offer outstanding areas for swimming if protected from second home and urban related development.

(a)

Slopes

SLOPE

Slopes

Most 'surfaces' are bracketed by slope and since slope is subject to various degrees of erosion slopes of 12.5 % or greater should be protected and stabilized to prevent silting and pollution of the 'surface' resources below.

(b)

Rims

RIM

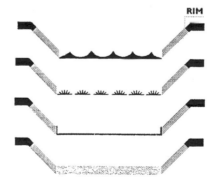

Rims

'Rims' of slope offer the very best opportunity to observe and contemplate the 'surface' resources. To assure as many Wisconsin citizens as possible have an opportunity to traverse the Wisconsin rims along bridal, hiking, bicycle trails or parkways, certain controls over rim development should be considered.

(c)

Water-oriented Corridor

Water-oriented corridors are found along rivers, flood plains, and wetlands.

(d)

Landform Oriented Corridor

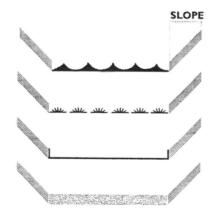

A landform oriented environmental corridor is composed of a combination of two closely related slopes which produce a ridge. It often provides vantage points for the aesthetic enjoyment of water-oriented corridors.

(e)

Figure 5.37 Washington County, Wisconsin inventory. This county in the glaciated moraine country of southwestern Wisconsin is representative of the inventory undertaken to determine what lands should be acquired. Recommendations were made to concentrate on the environmental corridors. The mapping revealed once again that the outstanding resources were in linear patterns. This more detailed county-level inventory following the state overview made information available for the establishment of more precise guidelines for future development.

Washington County

to the present generation, and through increased perception, careful planning, and sound regional design, our heritage and the extensive variety in its extensive corridor system can continue to be enjoyed by future generations.

Once broad limits to development have been identified, more detailed plans for specific land uses can be designed. The inventories required for these detailed plans are more extensive and time consuming than the conceptual inventories, so inventory efforts should be prioritized. Two areas in particular should receive first-priority attention: urbanizing areas and areas in the countryside where new large-scale residential, commercial, or industrial development is likely; and areas adjacent to existing parks, roads, reservoirs, schools, airports, and other public facilities, whose development should be carefully controlled to protect public investment.

In this phase of applying the regional design process, the resources within the environmental corridors should be inventoried in detail, identifying particularly fragile ecosystems which cannot withstand impact, so that they can be protected before they are destroyed. In addition, diverse spatial patterns and nodes of diversity,

which designate areas where a high density of kinds of resources and individually outstanding resources are found within a small area can also be identified from these ecological inventories. This information becomes useful for designing nature trails and scenic highways which incorporate the maximum diversity of the region while protecting fragile areas. These inventories help to provide a solid foundation on which to deal with the questions that residents face:

- How much natural resource protection should there be in your area? At what level of government should this protection occur?
- How do property assessment rules, tax laws, and other programs affect the local resources?
- What trade-offs are made when development is allowed in woodlands or directly adjacent to wetlands and bodies of water?
- How significant are local erosion and runoff problems? What should be done to reduce them?
- How might mineral extraction activities conflict with agricultural activities or envi-

Figure 5.38 Environmental corridors. It became apparent from my Wisconsin outdoor recreation plan that weathering and glaciation have etched linear patterns (lacelike on a regional basis) on the face of the midlands. The flat, rolling farmlands and the expansive forest to the north are beautiful, but it is the stream valleys, the bluffs, ridges, roaring and quiet waters, mellow wet-lands, and sandy soils adjacent to water that combine in elongated design patterns, tying the land together in regional and statewide environmental corridors. When combined into an environmental system, I saw that environmental corridors have the potential to provide open space for play, recreation, and enjoyment as well as spiritual and physical health and wisdom. I suggested identifying environmental corridors across the nation and using these patterns as tools for recreational, open space, and environmental planning and as tools to increase the public's awareness of the landscape. I set out to use the Wisconsin recreation plan as a prototype to demonstrate the vast planning and educational possibilities environmental corridor patterns offer.

ronmental integrity? How can these conflicts be minimized?

- Are local natural and cultural resources valued, and how can they be preserved? Do people in the town realize that many of these areas exist? How can people make land-use changes and still preserve these resources?

Designing Human Patterns in Corridor Fringe Areas

Lands adjacent to the environmental corridors can be termed corridor fringe areas. By protecting the corridors and encouraging sound development patterns within the fringe areas, the tax base of the counties can be increased and assured over a longer span of time. It is the corridor quality that attracts development in the first place (Fig. 5.38). (Loss of shoreline or ridge-top sites to single rows of cabins and other unplanned development obliterates environmental quality or creates the necessity for expensive rehabilitation by future generations.) An alternative to the obliteration of quality and expensive rehabilitation is the protection of corridor qualities through buffer zones and better design

Statewide Environmental Corridors in Wisconsin

Figure 5.39 Inappropriate development of corridor fringe. A single row of cabins along this waterfront has destroyed many of the qualities that attracted the development in the first place.

guidelines, use of present and possible forms of legislation, and voluntary participation by individuals and organizations in corridor protection programs.

BETTER GUIDELINES

Throughout the country there is a need for creative teams to design prototype land-use examples in such areas as housing, recreational facilities, and industrial parks that provide for optimum use of corridor fringe areas without destroying corridor characteristic qualities (Fig. 5.39).

By incorporation of the principles of such prototypes into enabling rules, ordinances, and codes, the quality of both the urban fabric and the rural landscape matrix can be improved upon. Thoughtful and intelligent utilization of our landscape resources utilizing the design principles of the Regional Design Process can bring about the benefits of applying good design on a broad scale, allowing for great variety in the design of smaller developed areas. Using the local natural landscape characteristics as guidelines is bound to guide development in more locally suitable and interesting ways.

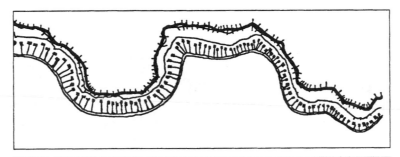

RECOGNIZING COMMON PATTERNS

The Everglades, Embarras, Wabash, Illinois, and Wisconsin studies as well as other studies of the rural landscape together suggested several key ideas that are integral components of any holistic alternative to our current approach to development. It is clear, for example, that before we can make comprehensive plans to protect our remaining natural and cultural resources, we must inventory these resources. Which resources are most important to inventory? The Embarras River study pointed to the importance of inventorying water, wetlands, and steep topography, and the Illinois Recreation and Open Space Plan showed that soils and three-dimensional space resources must be included in resource inventories.

Each study also confirmed the importance of resource patterns. Part of the challenge in identifying resource patterns was to represent them abstractly for ease of plotting on a map. As a solution, for the Illinois Recreation and Open Space Plan a series of icons was designed for this purpose, and as part of the Wisconsin Outdoor Recreation Plan, icons representing physical resources of the rural landscape were

developed. (More recently, a similar set of icons have been developed for the physical resources of the urban landscape; see See Chapter 9.) These icon mapping inventories reveal two patterns that emerge consistently and repeatedly: environmental corridors and landscape personalities (Figs. 5.40 and 5.41).

In addition, the Wisconsin Outdoor Recreation Plan showed that 90 percent of the natural and cultural values that people cherished fell within the environmental corridor pattern. By using USGS maps to identify water, wetland, and steep topography patterns that make up environmental corridors, it is possible, quickly and inexpensively, to interpret most of the features that create sense of place. On this basis sound environmental decisions can be made before more detailed and expensive studies are completed.

Further, identifying resource patterns revealed scales of thinking. Once the regional scale in which these patterns exist became apparent, it was also understood that if we are ever to achieve sustainability, we must think within a regional context, which was particularly evident in the Wabash River Valley study.

Several principles about interdisciplinary teams and communicating ideas emerged from

these rural studies as well. The Wabash River Valley study made it clear that inventorying and planning efforts must follow ecological rather than human-made boundaries. The Wisconsin Outdoor Recreation Plan demonstrated how effective an awareness center and the arts can be to inform people's discretion. In addition, each study reconfirmed the need for interdisciplinary cooperation.

The inventory of corridors and their diversity of natural, scenic, and cultural resources demonstrated that the individual valuable landscape characteristics in the broadest sense identified by various interest groups are generally included in a common corridor pattern. This corridor patterns traverses the matrix of patterns of vast areas such as prairies and plains, mountain ranges, vast bodies of water, and deserts, and a few uniquely situated resources (such as deposits of metal and other ores). Protecting corridors will protect those resources regarded as important and provide enough undisturbed territory to protect them from the onslaught of development. In Wisconsin the Open Space Plan, in which were recorded all of the available resource data and the corridors (water, wetlands, and steep topography) in which most of them fell, was used to establish

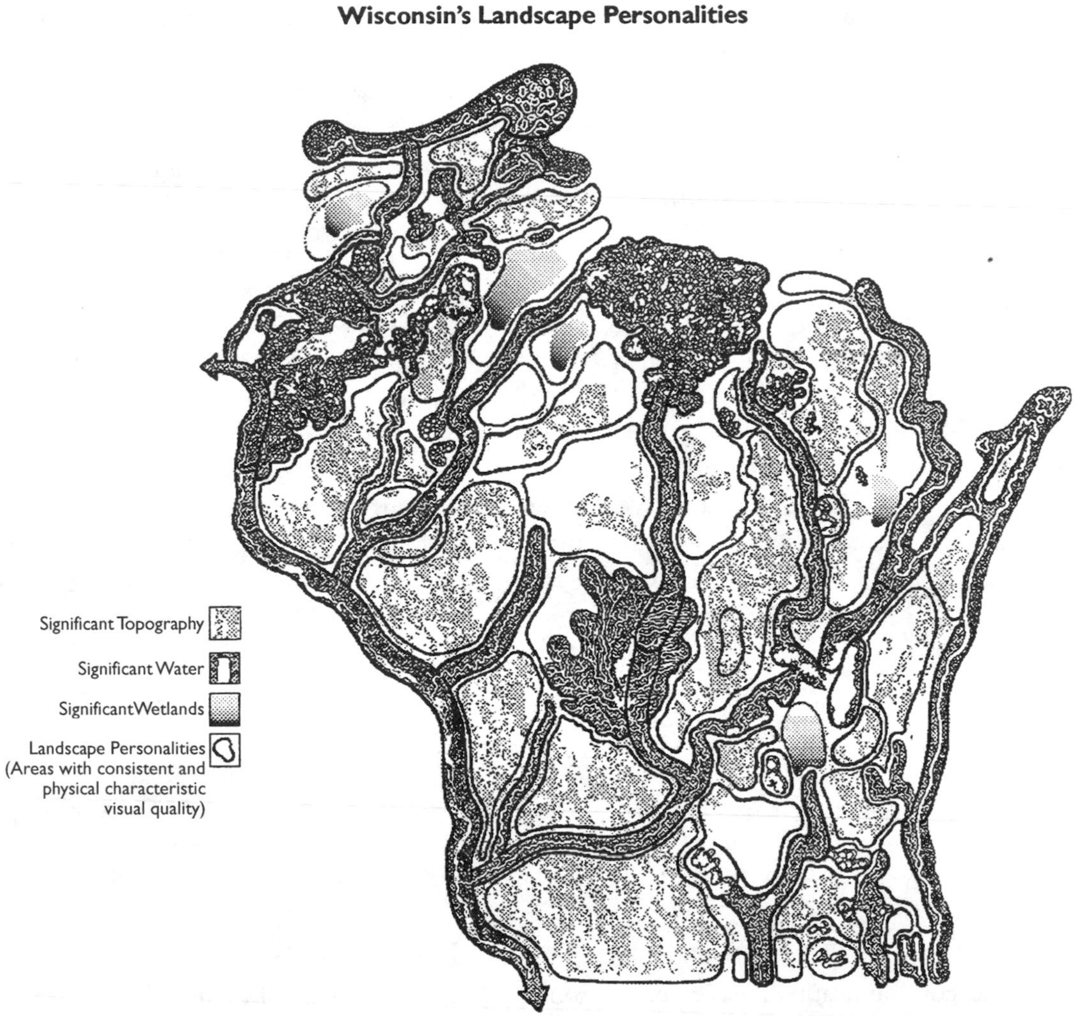

Figure 5.40 Wisconsin's landscape personalities.

Wisconsin's Landscape Personalities

Significant Topography
Significant Water
SignificantWetlands
Landscape Personalities
(Areas with consistent and physical characteristic visual quality)

which lands were of the highest priority for purchase with the $50 million for land purchase available in the 1960s.

PROTECTING ENVIRONMENTAL CORRIDORS

One of the most important legal tools for the protection of land in private ownership in the state was stated in a Wisconsin Supreme Court Decision decision [*Just* v. *Marinette County,* 56 Wis. 2d 7, 201N.W.2d 761 (1972)]. In a case in which the state's shoreland zoning model ordinance adopted by Marinette County was upheld (protecting the state's navigable waters through shoreline zoning) the Wisconsin State Supreme Court ruling includes the statement by Chief Justice Hallows that "An owner of land has no absolute and unlimited right to change the essential natural character of his land so as to use it for a purpose for which it was unsuited in its natural state and which injures the rights of others." The landowners in question wanted to fill their land. He stated further that "this depreciation in value is not based on the use of the land in its natural

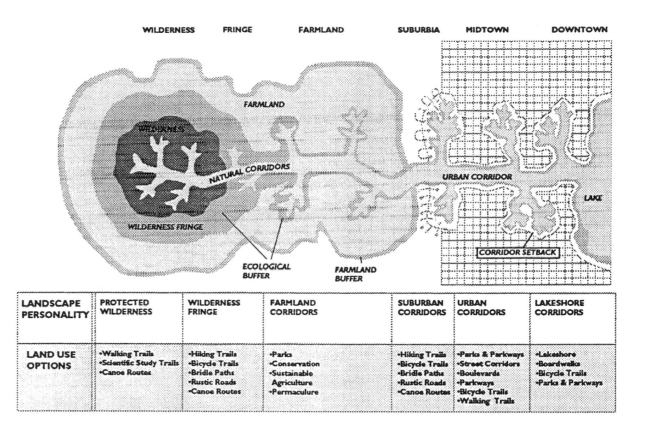

Figure 5.41 Integrating rural and urban corridor patterns.

state but on what the land would be worth if it could be filled and used for the location of a dwelling."

Currently there is much discussion and ongoing legal action as to the rights of property owners and the sort of compensation they can expect from restrictions on property rights. Our social contract is under intense scrutiny. The right of landowners to short-term profit at the expense of the public's rights to clean air and water and agricultural produce is being demanded, and the public has not articulated a recognizable response. But at least in Wisconsin, the right to water that is undiminished in quality and quantity from its natural state and condition still stands and the principle of using land so as not to injure the rights of others has been developed as a corrolary. (The rights of the public to freedom from environmental degradation at the hands of private profit taking are at issue throughout the nation, but in the Northwest Territory the public right to water was clearly articulated in its first laws.) This protection of navigable waters (including water and wetlands) and rights of the public to clean water, undamaged shorelines and wetlands, navigation, fishing, and scenic beauty derived from the

LANDSCAPE PERSONALITY	PROTECTED WILDERNESS	WILDERNESS FRINGE	FARMLAND CORRIDORS	SUBURBAN CORRIDORS	URBAN CORRIDORS	LAKESHORE CORRIDORS
LAND USE OPTIONS	•Walking Trails •Scientific Study Trails •Canoe Routes	•Hiking Trails •Bicycle Trails •Bridle Paths •Rustic Roads •Canoe Routes	•Parks •Conservation •Sustainable Agriculture •Permaculure	•Hiking Trails •Bicycle Trails •Bridle Paths •Rustic Roads •Canoe Routes	•Parks & Parkways •Street Corridors •Boulevards •Parkways •Bicycle Trails •Walking Trails	•Lakeshore •Boardwalks •Bicycle Trails •Parks & Parkways

Northwest Territory Ordinance by way of the navigable waters protection law (144.26) is still revered by the beneficiaries of the founders of the Territory.

Note

[1]*The Outdoor Recreation Plan,* Wisconsin Department of Resource Development, Madison, Wisc., 1963.

CHAPTER 6

PATTERN ANALYSIS
AND DESIGN

The earth's ecosystem and the outer universe have been a balanced system for 4.5 billion years. There have been internal shifts in the planet's dynamic system, but local changes are always balanced within the total equilibrium (energy and mass are conserved). This is not to suggest that this equilibrium is a steady state, for dramatic shifts occur. A change of enduring popular interest is the extinction of dinosaurs, but the change with perhaps the most far-reaching impact on the planet was the shift to an oxygenated atmosphere.

The current environmental crisis exists within this ecosystem, and it is inevitable that the system will remain in equilibrium. The major issue now is what changes equilibrium requires: How will we change, and what changes will be wrought on us as a species and as a civilization? We must recognize that we are an integral part of nature and therefore we must learn to guide our actions *toward* sustainability and restoration. Lest we go the way of the dinosaurs, we must learn the language of the relationships among the parts of our human ecology. My studies suggest that the one we must learn is pattern language.

Over years of observing the landscape patterns in the Everglades, the Wabash River Valley, the state of Illinois, the state of Wisconsin, the

Great Lakes Basin, and Alaska, and recognizing the importance of these patterns, I can state that the initial phases of the Regional Design Process can be considered to be pattern planning or pattern design in practice (Fig. 6.1).

The most recent and outstanding theoretical work in this area has been conducted by Christopher Alexander, who states in his book *A Pattern Language:*

> No pattern is an isolated entity. Each pattern can exist in the world, only to the extent that it is supported by other patterns: the larger patterns in which it is embedded, the patterns of the same size that surround it, and the smaller patterns which are embedded in it.
>
> This is a fundamental view of the world. It says that when you build a thing you cannot merely build that thing in isolation, but must also repair the world around it, and within it, so that the larger world at that one place becomes more coherent, and more whole; and the thing which you make takes its place in the web of nature, as you make it.[1]

Once we learn this pattern language, its use can be extended beyond analyzing the landscape in terms of topography, water, and wetland (the

Figure 6.1 Rural landscape
and urban townscape pat-
terns: (a) urban townscape
patterns: repetitive, grid-
based, rigidly geometrical;
(b) typical rural landscape
resource patterns: rich texture, curvilinear, organic.

Figure 6.2 Seeing the landscape continuum as a col-
lective work of art.

(a)

(b)

way landforms, waterways and water bodies, and
wet soils and vegetation occur on the surface of
the earth) to seeing the landscape continuum as a
collective work of art (Fig. 6.2) and a complex
design composition rather than as a set of distinc-
tively individual elements. It is a work in

progress, a mosaic of patterns of ordered elements. By means of this view, I believe that it is
possible for us to achieve sustainability.

Individual elements in the landscape continuum (such as trees, lakes, or mountains) are anal-
ogous to letters in the words of the vocabulary of
a language that can express patterns as language
expresses ideas, and just as letters isolated by
themselves have very little meaning, individual
objects within the landscape have very little
meaning out of context. The "words" (or systems, such as the *hydrologic system,* wetland system, or mountain, plain, or shoreline system) of
the landscape can form many different patterns
according to their relationships, as can our treatment of buildings, roads, or sewage treatment
plants. For this reason, at an elemental level of
analyzing the landscape, it is difficult to see relationships clearly among the endless elements of
the landscape continuum or to be able to make
decisions about priorities in guiding the growth
of human utilization of the natural world. On
the other hand, like ideas, patterns do have
meaning and are therefore a useful unit of
thought. If we base decisions on patterns rather
than on locations of individual objects, we will
be able to guide growth successfully and mini-

mize human impact on the land by aiming for harmony in and among the patterns of development and alteration of the earth's systems and their organization.

PATTERN ANALYSIS

The rural landscape is typically marked by field patterns of forests, grasslands, and crops dissected by linear environmental corridor patterns (Fig. 6.3). The water, wetlands, and steep topography in these corridors are a great source of diversity in this landscape. The spatial patterns will vary with the width of the river, the steepness and height of the bordering topography, and the vegetation and urban elements present. Nodes of diversity will dot the corridor patterns, contributing to the system's diversity. In addition, ephemeral resources that pass through the landscape system, such as wildlife, wind, rain, snow, fog, ice; glimpses of sun, moon, stars, and clouds, will affect the color and textural diversity of the landscape. Understanding these patterns, colors, and textures of the rural landscape gives a logical order to the system which makes it possible to suggest how the various elements interact.

When the urban landscape is examined in a manner parallel to the rural landscape, there is a striking similarity between the two systems. Instead of forests and grasslands, the field patterns in the urban landscape are created by residential areas, industrial areas, and park systems (Fig. 6.4). The corridors in the urban landscape follow the transportation and open-space patterns in addition to steep topography, the walls of this system are created by architectural structures. Urban spatial patterns are affected by the size and layout of streets and the height of buildings as well as by the size and nature of parks and other open spaces. Nodes of diversity add to the spice of life in the urban landscape. Just as with the rural landscape, understanding these patterns, colors, and textures of the urban landscape gives a logical order to the system which makes it possible to predict how the different elements will interact. By depicting the urban and rural landscapes together as part of a single system, it becomes apparent how intimately the two systems are interwoven and how they affect each other.

When analyzing the landscape in terms of patterns instead of objects, one can discern patterns that diminish the quality of life, sense of place, options of choice, and sustainability as well

as patterns that enhance these features. Once identified, these patterns are logical units of thought, or form determinants, to guide plans to strive toward sustainability. We must recognize that most of these patterns have not been inventoried on a state-by-state basis. Without precise inventories to locate these patterns, it is impossible to impose human patterns of development wisely and well.

Linear, Areal, and Point Patterns

Linear, areal, and point patterns comprise the basis for a pattern view of the landscape. Linear patterns are narrow strips that meander across the landscape and are commonly created by rivers and roads. Areal patterns represent areas that contain a lot of a particular resource, for example, a forest or residential area. Point patterns represent places where resources occur in an isolated place such as a cave or a single building.

Three-Dimensional Space Pattern

Perhaps one of the most basic and pervasive, and most neglected, resource patterns found in the urban and rural landscapes is three-dimensional space, a resource that does not exist without walls. These walls can be physical objects, such as

Figure 6.3 Rural landscape
patterns: linear, areal, and
point.

Figure 6.4 Urban and cultural townscape and land-
scape patterns.

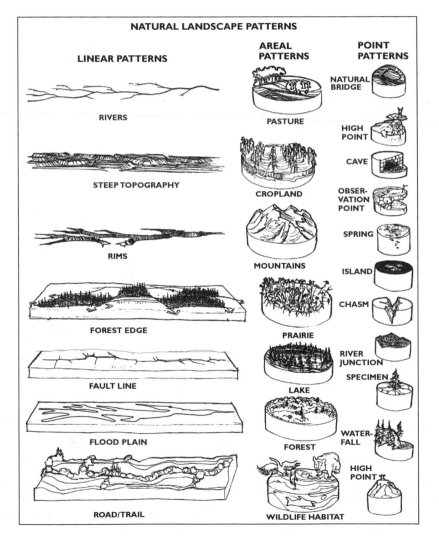

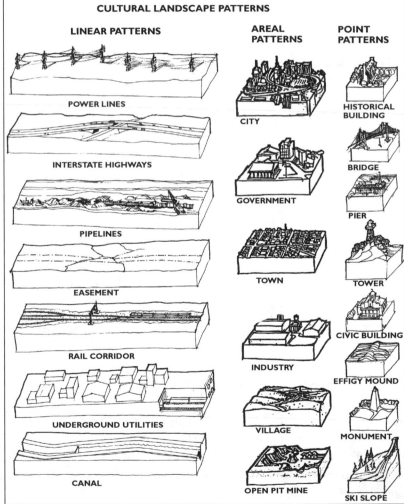

Figure 6.5 Three-dimensional landscape patterns as a cherished resource: (a) three-dimensional space does not exist without walls—walls of buildings, walls of vegetation, or walls of topography; (b) spaces exist both indoors and outdoors; (c) regional designers respect spatial resources in both urban and rural landscapes; (d) three-dimensional space flows in all directions.

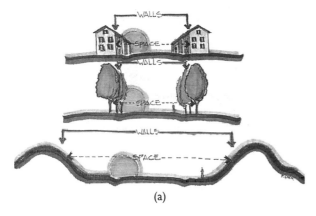

(a)

(b)

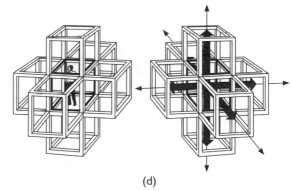

(c)

(d)

building materials, topography, or vegetation, or a natural phenomenon such as persistent mist, a geyser, or dark shadow (Fig. 6.5).

In three-dimensional space one may go in many directions: down into a subterranean cave, out on a balcony with magnificent views, or up an apple tree to pick green apples. To understand both the landscape and townscape fabric, one must understand the "space" available for manipulation.

Recognizing interesting spaces in the natural landscape defined by landform and vegetation is a simple matter when the space resource is recognized. Training in the design and art professions sharpens the ability to perceive the quality of each space based on scale, volume, textures, colors, odors, climate change, and similar factors. Using

such training consciously to develop our powers of observation and analysis combined with ecological understanding, spaces can be protected as is or enhanced by nondestructive or restorative manipulation. Perceiving how various types of spaces and sequences of space affect inhabitants and observers demands better techniques of measurement from the fields of physiology and psychology, but it is the designer that must categorize and simulate or reproduce the possible array of spaces to which humans react if the options are to be measured. An interdisciplinary endeavor needs, in addition to the designer, an ecologist, a physiologist, and a psychologist at least if we want to document what is

required to protect or create sustainable landscapes that foster the creativity and enjoyment of users.

When we focus on the built landscape, we naturally are talking about placing cubes of various sizes and functions on the landscape. Allow-

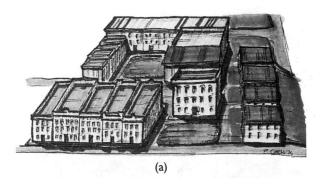

(a)

(b)

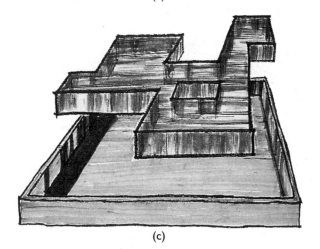

(c)

Figure 6.6 (a) Cities are comprised of three-dimensional blocks (houses, offices, industrial plants, schools, shops, etc.). (b) The city fabric can be viewed as solid block forms and voidal spaces created by building walls. (c) It is within this voidal pattern that we view the city. Its character reveals the image that we have of the particular city.

ing the life-sustaining resource patterns of the landscape, including treatment of the spatial resource, to serve as a form determinant and guide the placement of these blocks in harmony with the land and landscape and with their neighboring blocks could create more exciting community habitat. This is an expanded view of site planning on a large and integrated scale. Since these blocks (houses, offices, industrial plants, schools, shopping centers, etc.) are being produced at such a rapid rate to meet the needs of 260,000 new people a day, I believe it is useful to examine the basic box more closely to better understand the implications of the three-dimensional spaces we are creating.

First we must understand that three-dimensional space is a powerful and all-pervasive resource. Models and photographs can help further the understanding. Filling the unoccupied space in a three-dimensional model with water which is then frozen and removed so that it can be viewed as a solid-shape composition can aid in understanding its possibilities (Fig. 6.6). It is this three-dimensional space between—this voidal urban system—that can be manipulated into sequences of spatial diversity and excitement or into monotonous corridors inviting death to a livable city.

Gordon Cullen of the English *Architectural Review* long ago developed a vocabulary for describing the spatial envelope, which he called the great "out there." To help students develop this vocabulary, I encouraged them to build graphic notebooks of spatial experiences that they have personally experienced and enjoyed. This can include clipping examples of such visual values from magazines and putting them in albums, continually searching for these rare bits of quality that will add to their own personal graphic vocabulary for later application in the design process (Figs. 6.7 to 6.10).

With additional training in the design lab, including an introduction to dynamic symmetry and the golden mean (Fig. 6.11) as represented geometrically, design students become proficient in designing pleasantly proportioned and functional schemes. Integrated with regional design process talent, existing cities or new linear cities can be designed for function and beauty. In developing regional design it becomes apparent that the diversity of the rural environmental corridor can be linked to urban corridors, creating

Figure 6.7 Rare "postage stamp" of wallscape.

Figure 6.8 Macro-floorscape.

Figure 6.10 Object occupying space.

Figure 6.9 Skyscape.

Figure 6.11 The golden mean, a classic example of pleasing proportion, illustrated as a geometric construct of segments of circles in squares.

Figure 6.12 Construction of a rectangle illustrating the golden mean proportion.

integrated opportunities for maximizing the opportunities for a desirable quality of life for those who dwell in the urban areas as well as offering design form to the whole region.

The Golden Mean

One of the primary design qualities, proportion, can be introduced to students through study of a rectangle whose ratio of short to long sides is 1:1.618 (Fig. 6.12), which besides being constructible geometrically, can also be found in nature. The shell of the nautilus is the classic example of the repetition of the proportions of this classic module (Fig. 6.13).

Moving Through Spatial Systems

Design students studying architectural history, architecture, urban design, and landscape architecture and those working in design laboratories use many historic spaces created for people in the past, often building three-dimensional models to analyze composition to determine what makes a city and its spaces historically significant and beautiful (Fig. 6.14). Students in landscape architecture at the University of Illinois built models of renowned city spaces as part of their training

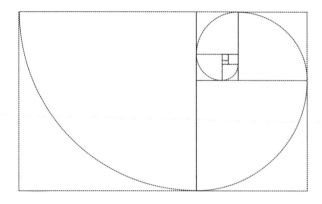

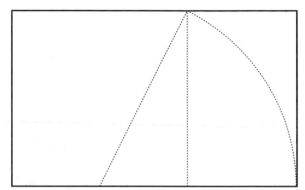

Figure 6.13 A nautilus shell illustrates the occurrence of golden mean proportions in nature.

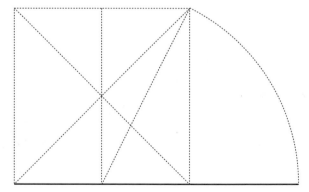

in design (Fig. 6.15). Design students also created exciting "walk-through" designs utilizing natural and human-made materials (Fig. 6.16).

Figure 6.14 Moving through
spatial systems.

Figure 6.15 Model of out-
standing urban space in
Europe.

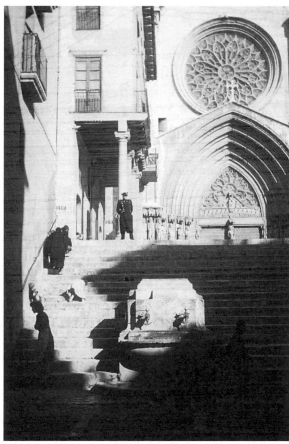

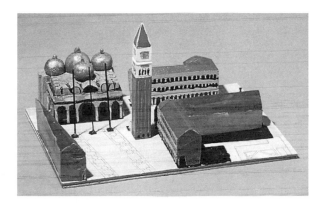

Figure 6.16 Students cre-
ated models of their own
three-dimensional space
designs in the design studio
at the University of Illinois.

Figure 6.17 (a) Cropland.

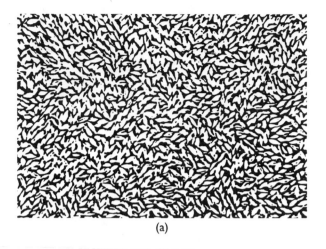

(a)

OTHER HIGH-PRIORITY RESOURCE INVENTORIES

To place creative urban design patterns in harmony with life-sustaining landscape patterns, we must understand the critical regional patterns and their characteristics.

Toxic Patterns

By a combination of predictable wind patterns and landform patterns, we can suggest where temperature-inversion layers are most probable. When a multitude of internal combustion machines or other industrial and commercial processes spew out carbon monoxide, carbon dioxide, and other poisonous gases beneath inversion layers, they can become a threat to the health of human and other components of the ecosystem.

Flood Patterns

High-water marks graphically demarcate the fringe areas of past water patterns created by early thaws and spring rains or the ravaging waters of hurricanes and tidal waves. To build within such patterns invites certain loss of property and possible loss of life.

Weather Patterns

By understanding the various patterns of weather, we may shortly and with extreme accuracy predict future paths of storms, forewarning farmers and urbanites of potential crop and property losses. We still build some of our highways within snow belts when a new alignment only a few miles farther south would save them from the hazards of slippery driving, loss of life and limb, and the cost of extensive snow removal.

Natural Area Patterns

In the analysis of various landscapes, it is apparent that areas of landscape remain as yet relatively untouched by the axe and the plow. These natural areas serve as checkpoints or baseline for recording environmental data; new drugs and new crops for medicine and agriculture may still be found within the scope of these natural patterns; and humankind can always profit by the relief afforded by these many natural textures from the brick, steel, glass, and asphalt of our cities. These area-wide patterns might vary from one-tenth of an acre to many thousands in various parts of the country.

Fire Hazard Patterns

It is relatively simple to identify textural landscape patterns that in a dry season become highly flammable and threaten all forms of life within their boundaries. Forest fires and grass-fires destroy hundreds of homes each year because of human ignorance or risk-taking in building within these scenic but dangerous areas.

Cropland Patterns

Soil scientists have identified patterns of soils that in their present state, or with the addition of fertilizers, offer the best opportunity for food and fiber production. As populations explode around the world, many areas already face famine and starvation. As responsible citizens, we should protect these most productive soils from human encroachment and see that they are maintained for even higher production (Fig. 6.17a) through new agricultural technology.

Figure 6.17 (continued)
(b) Ethnic patterns;
(c) aquifer recharge
patterns; (d) groundwater
patterns.

(b)

Ethnic Patterns

Several other kinds of patterns are important in guiding the form of the outer city. The variety of ethnic patterns are revealed by architectural, historical, and population studies; an extensive variety of local architecture, cooking, handicrafts, museums, customs, and holidays exist within cultural patterns (Fig. 6.17b). This social variety is important to human environmental quality and needs continued recognition not to be submerged in the current tendency toward conformity. Ethnic heritages serve not only as a valuable environmental quality and as a tie with the past but also as an important recreational and tourist attraction. It is a heritage not only to be used and kept active but to be protected and valued. It can continue to make life interesting and pleasant to both residents and visitors.

Aquifer Recharge Patterns

Within many of our landscapes are aquifer recharge patterns. These are porous patterns that permit surface waters to penetrate the surface of the landscape and refill natural underground storage and flowing systems (Fig. 6.17c). Protected from high-density development and assuming a

normal rainfall, underground storage systems will continue to provide water for drinking and other uses by present and future generations.

Groundwater Patterns

Geologic processes have created underground water storage systems beneath the land's surface (Fig. 6.17d). Since they contain part of the water supply for the future, it is vitally important to know the location of these patterns.

Raw Materials for Building Patterns

In many landscapes patterns of sand, gravel, limestone, and other minerals necessary for the construction and reconstruction of our expanding cities and transportation networks have been identified by geologists. Human encroachment should be prevented above these valuable deposits to ensure access to them in the vicinity of expected development. Underground excavation of minerals may also leave surface patterns unstable and subject to cave-ins and loss of property.

Volcanic Earthquake Patterns

Each year we read of loss of life and property because structures and habitations are placed in

(c)

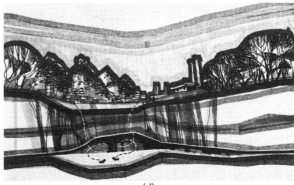

(d)

Figure 6.18 I-57 corridor
alignment study area.

the path of unstable fault lines or potential volcanic activity. Homes, highways, campgrounds, and entire cities have been known to suffer severely because of such site planning errors. What portion of the national debt could be paid from the savings gleaned by not building on geologically unstable locations? The savings in grief and misery are incalculable.

The Cost of Ignoring Natural Patterns

In the midwest it is hard to imagine a more dramatic example of the problems caused by ignoring natural patterns than the Mississippi River floods of the summer of 1993. Satellite photos taken before and during the flood illustrate the floodplain pattern clearly.

INTERSTATE HIGHWAY 57 STUDY (1969)

Using patterns to guide decision making fundamentally changes the nature of the conclusions drawn. The perspective from which decisions are made becomes an inherently larger-scale perspec-

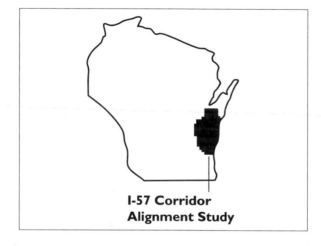

**I-57 Corridor
Alignment Study**

tive, and more comprehensive, since the patterns encompass resources as part of a larger system. A study undertaken to determine the best alignment for the I-57 highway demonstrated the benefits of using resource patterns to guide option development (Fig. 6.18).

In 1969 the Environmental Awareness Center had the opportunity to develop a corridor and alignment location system for Interstate 57 between Milwaukee and Green Bay, Wisconsin under the directorship of Ben Niemann. The study area was a rectangle approximately 120 miles

long and 60 miles wide. The intent of the corridor selection study was to develop a system by which social, economic, aesthetic, and ecological patterns could simultaneously be used to determine an interstate location. Historically, highway location decisions have been based on the evaluation of a limited factor bank. From an analysis of highway determinant factors, the Center originated a list of 130 factors that would influence, should influence, or would be influenced by the location of a major highway system such as an interstate. An evaluation of current methodology showed that there were limited means suitable to handle this number of factors. Since typical planning–design methods are restricted when a multiplicity of variables are to be evaluated simultaneously, it was evident that systems methods utilizing computerized geographic information were the relevant and necessary technology.

Suggesting using computers to analyze data may seem obvious today, but in 1969 it was almost unheard of. Most analysis was restricted to what could be incorporated on a physical map, so the extent and flexibility of analysis were greatly restricted. Simultaneous satisfaction of such a variety of needs as required by a comprehensive analysis could be accomplished only by using a computer program.

We established a database that included inventory information for the area from previous studies. We divided these variables into three categories: (1) use characteristics, the physical use of the area; (2) environmental characteristics, the significant characteristics of the landscape; and (3) constraints, those variables that would possibly impose limitations on the corridor location. We extracted this information from many different sources, including USGS maps and aerial photographs.

Initially, the variables were grouped into nine "corridor determinants," which reflect the basic economic, social, and environmental determinants used in highway location. Each variable was assigned a weighting by establishing the interrelationship between the selected variable and the others in its resource category. The interpretation then became a reduction of the total variable list into nine groups of variables: corridor determinants that provided for manipulation of variables to select a single highway corridor.

The second phase of analysis involved relating one corridor to another and by various weightings.

The speed of data manipulation by a computer allowed comparison of a multitude of different relationships among variables. Comparing variables in this way made it possible to find the path of least resistance among the various impact costs and benefits between Milwaukee and Green Bay.

Corridor Variables

When we laid out an alignment for Interstate 57 between Milwaukee and Green Bay, the goal was to determine the path that would be not only the most cost-effective but also be scenic and preserve the natural and cultural resources that are the life support system and the basis for the tourism industry (see Table 6.1). Especially since Wisconsin's varied landscape personalities have contributed to making tourism one of Wisconsin's largest industries, it would be foolhardy to destroy that resource. In order that the alignment recommendations be as comprehensive as possible, we compiled a list of variables important to different perspectives. Computer analysis allowed us to weigh the importance of the different variables and combine them to compare the advantages and disadvantages of different alignment options (Fig. 6.19).

WISCONSIN ELECTRIC POWER COMPANY TRANSMISSION ALIGNMENT STUDY (1972)

In the summer of 1970, the Wisconsin Electric Power Company entered into a contract with the Environmental Awareness Center to conduct a study critiquing the transmission alignment methodology they typically employed. The study team, directed by Bruce Murray, was charged with analyzing the current methodology, as expressed in two proposed alignments, one system south and one system west of Milwaukee, Wisconsin (Fig. 6.20). Unlike the I-57 study, which employed computer GIS (Geographic Information System) technology, this study demonstrated using the overlay process to determine alignments that made the least impact on critical resources.

Increased population and affluence had resulted in increased power consumption, more power lines, and a greater visual impact on the landscape. As a corollary to the visual impact of electric power transmission, the physical effects of these components on biological and cultural systems had to be investigated and undesirable practices corrected. The public and private sup-

TABLE 6.1   Highway Location Variables

Least Acquisition Cost

Residential	Commercial
Rural	Industrial
Vacation	Recreation
Suburban	Institutional
Urban	Proposed commercial
Proposed residential	Proposed recreational
Proposed industrial	Town road
Proposed institutional	Unpaved
Limited-access highway	Paved
Interchange	County road
Railroad	State highway
Soils	Federal highway
Surface	Landowners
Subsurface	
Substratum	

Least Damage to Potential Conservation and Recreation Lands

River or lake zoning	Barren land
Intermittent stream	Forest
Streams	Upland
Rivers	Lowland
Minor	Open swamp
Major	Slope
Pond	0–2%
Lake	3–6%

Lake Michigan	7–12%
Scenic highway	13–20%
Degree of orientation	21%+
Drumlins	Sand dunes
End moraine	Eskers
Intrinsic resources	Escarpment
Elevation change	

Areas Most Scenic from a Highway

Barren land	Agriculture
Forest	All water
Upland	Rural towns
Lowland	Slopes
Open Swamp	One
Slope	Two
0–2%	Three
3–6%	Four
7–12%	Elevation change
13–20%	Sand dunes
21%+	Eskers
Drumlins	Escarpment
End moraine	Extrinsic resources
Intrinsic resources	

Least Destruction to Productive Agriculture Lands[a]

Slope	Surface
0–2%	GF
3–6%	SC
7–12%	SF
Subsurface and substratum	ML
GC	CL
GF	OL
SC	CH
SF	PT
ML	
CL	
CH	
Bedrock	
OL	
PT	

Least Damage by Highways to Ecological Systems

Intermittent stream	Pond
Stream	Lake
River	Lake Michigan
Minor	Barren land
Major	Upland forest

[a] GC, gravels without fines; GF, gravels with <50% fines; SC, sands without fines; SF, sands with <50% fines; ML, inorganic silts, etc.; CL, inorganic clay with <50% fines, low plasticity; CH, inorganic clay, with <50% fines, high plasticity; OL, organic silts, organic clays of low plasticity, <50% fines; PT, peat.

Figure 6.19 (a) Path least destructive to agricultural variables; (b) path least destructive to cultural patterns; (c) path least destructive to ecological systems. (Darkest cells)

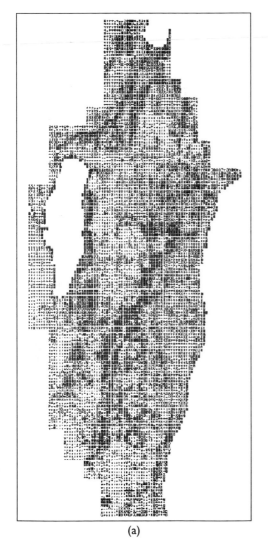

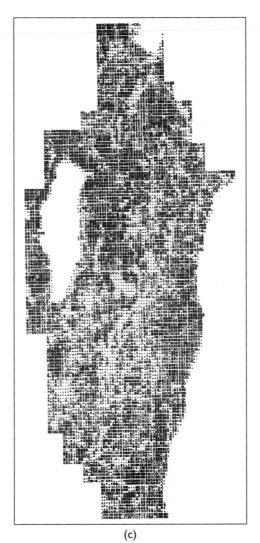

(a)   (b)   (c)

Figure 6.20 Transmission
alignment study area.

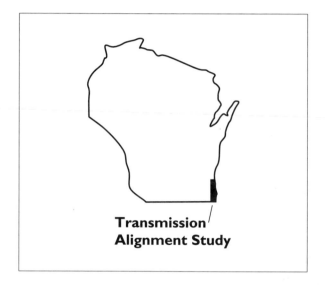

**Transmission
Alignment Study**

pliers of electric energy in this country were coming under scrutiny by individuals, private-interest groups, government, and professionals associated with energy production. This increasing concern with the natural and cultural implications of energy production and transmission by the industry was the result of many influences. The suppliers of electric power faced the possibility of more stringent standards of operation relative to practices that affect the equilibrium of the environment.

More than this, however, management and practical professionals in the power industry were to face the significance of current and potential future environmental effects of more generating plants transmission lines on the landscape and were moving to modify and improve their applied practices.

The ultimate intent of the Environmental Awareness Center's plan alignment critique was to:

• Generate data relevant to ecological, social, and economic aspects of transmission alignment.
• Map relevant variables at a uniform scale.
• Plot each of the two proposed alignments in the context of the relevant variables.
• Assess the positive and negative aspects of implementing each proposed alignment in the context of maintaining the stability of the natural and cultural environment.

The I-57 alignment project provided extensive graphic information for corporate training and awareness. An exhibit of beautiful colored maps of critical resource patterns was displayed at the power company's headquarters, which gave notice that initial consideration for new power

alignments should take careful notice of these form-determinant patterns (Fig. 6.21). A timely event occurred that focused attention on these patterns when to the north a row of transmission towers fell in a wind storm because they had been built on unstable soil patterns. Had the soil patterns been considered as a determining factor in tower location, this expensive disaster might have been averted. Engineering specifications for high-stress situations may not take all factors into consideration, and basic considerations should prevail over reaching to the limits of physical specifications.

Both of these early computer studies were utilized in the agency offices, in classrooms across the country, and were well documented in the *Journal of the American Society of Landscape Architects.* Besides having a beneficial impact on the final alignment of these two corridors, they also assisted in stimulating the interest and almost common use today of computer technology in such alignment studies.

Reducing data to patterns at many scales and for many purposes is a means of preparing data for design and planning in a manageable and uniform way so that relationships and guidelines can be discerned. For clear and carefully considered

Figure 6.21 Wisconsin Electric power-line study: (a) existing land use; (b) landform and elevation analysis; (c) topography, 30-foot contour intervals; (d) soil type map; (e) soils suitability for construction.

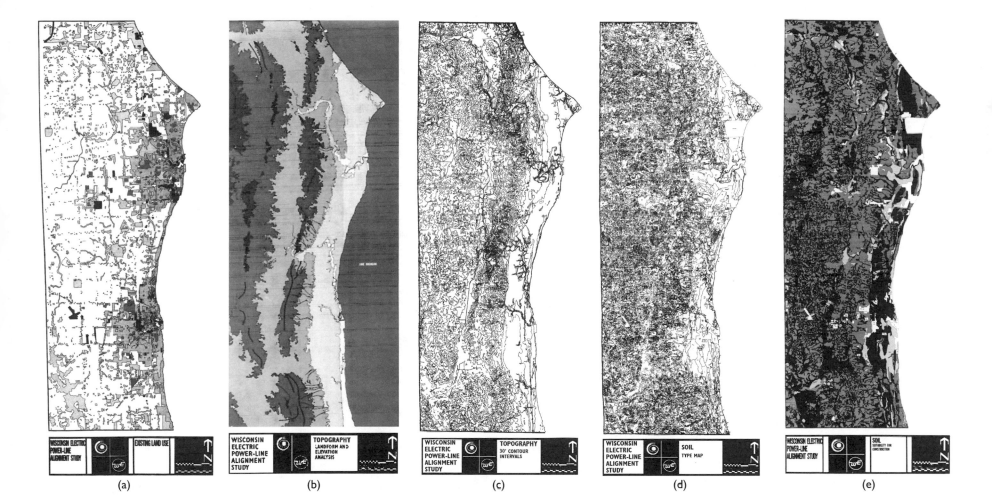

design and land-use decisions it is absolutely essential that we take advantage of both urban and rural patterns and use them at the scale appropriate to the situation. We are immensely aided in this endeavor by contemporary technology, beginning with the lowly copying machine and ranging through all of the computer-aided ways of dealing with massive data. Decision makers today responsible for major land-use proposals can identify the most important patterns to be considered, based on well-defined criteria. Graphically presented data augmented by explanation is the form in which information is most easily understood when presented to the public for their consideration. We can also present projections, to some extent, of the effect of our decisions by using our knowledge and simulation techniques to present past and present trends in aiding in the decision process.

Identification of urban patterns in their rural matrix led to the utilization of the idea of urban constellations. The recognition of 23 constellations in the United States as described in Chapter 2 set the urban context for a regional study of the constellation within our most studied landscape in the midwest, discussed in Chapter 7. In fact, it was here in Circle City that it occurred, growing out of the detailed regional studies of the Embarras River Valley, Wabash River, state of Illinois, state of Wisconsin, the Mississippi River Valley, and the Great Lakes Basin.

Note
[1]Christopher Alexander, *A Pattern Language,* Oxford University Press, New York, 1977.

Figure 7.1 (a) National and
(b) upper midwest contexts
of Circle City.

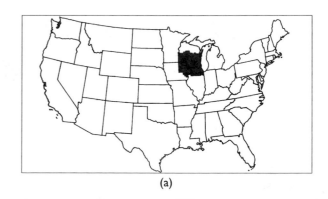

(a)

CHAPTER 7

RESOURCE

PATTERNS AND

CONSTELLATIONS:

TERRESTRIAL

URBAN STAR

TRACKS

REGIONAL CONSTELLATION DESIGN CASE STUDY: CIRCLE CITY

The constellation concept discussed in Chapter 3 arose from the image of a satellite photograph of the United States at night, an image containing in one picture a consolidation of all the airplane views of the nation and a compilation of the information about the United States contained in geographic atlases. The concentrations of lights in the photographs are the glow of terrestrial concentrations of urbanization. These bright spots can easily be joined in the same way stars are joined into constellations into 23 terrestrial constellations. Various regions of the country can be studied in detail using these outlines as a guide to where existing urbanization and adjacent less-populated areas are. The characteristics of each region are different, but the striking patterns of adjacent cities, towns, and urbanized areas occur nationwide.

A more detailed study of the midwest regional constellation begun about 1981 was attractive because it provides an organizational framework for the detailed resource inventories that are described in Chapter 5 (Fig. 7.1). To uti-

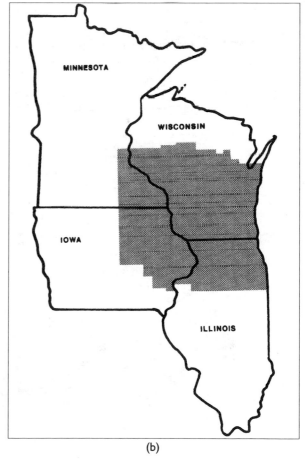

(b)

Figure 7.2 (a) Primary cities in Circle City region, showing population densities by township and the overall connecting pattern (Circle City, population 17 million); (b) connecting high population densities in the Circle City constellation.

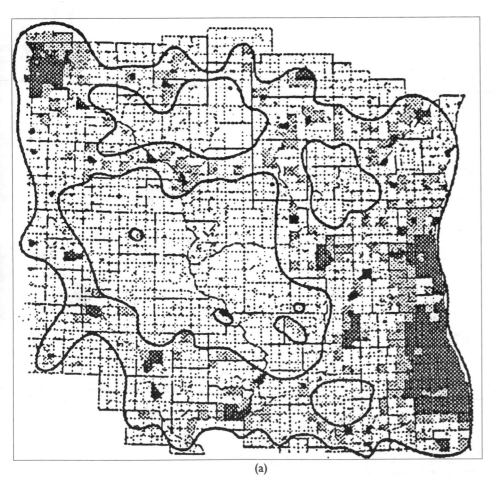

(a)

(b)

Figure 7.2 (*continued*) (c)
Population densities in Circle City region.

lize these identified natural and cultural patterns
as form determinants to guide midwestern
growth it remained to identify urban population
density patterns by township so that they could
be linked in a regional configuration that would
cause the least disturbance to the identified critical patterns (Fig. 7.2a).

Circle City is an urban constellation within
the upper midwestern region. It is the fourth
largest of 23 such patterns nationwide, which, by
definition, are determined by the existing distribution of population. It is not the uniformly
dense urban megalopolis described by Jean
Gottman in 1961, but an irregular ring of cities
with fewer urbanized and rural areas between
and around them (Fig. 7.2b).

The urbanizing ring of Circle City extends
from Chicago to Milwaukee, up the Fox River
Valley, across Wisconsin to Minnesota's Twin
Cities, down the Cedar River into northeastern
Iowa, and across northern Illinois back to
Chicago (Fig. 7.2c). The shape of this pattern of
cities draws attention to the "hole in the
doughnut," which corresponds very closely to
the *driftless area,* most of which is in southwestern Wisconsin (Fig. 7.2d). In the Great Plains
this weathered and geologically worn landscape

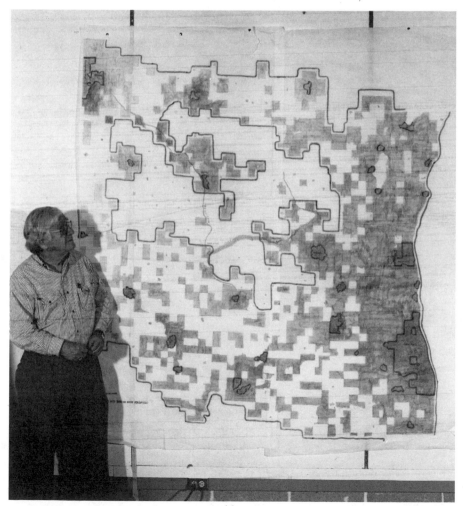

(c)

Figure 7.2 *(continued)*
(d) Cross section of the
driftless area. (e) View of
Wyoming Valley, Iowa
County, showing a valley
typical of the driftless
region.

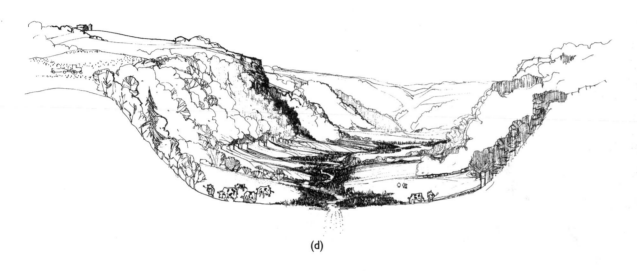

(d)

(e)

of unglaciated hill country, timber, rivers, small farms, and historic sites is an outstanding open space pattern in scale with Circle City, functioning similarly to the way that Central Park serves Manhattan Island. The driftless core (Fig. 7.2e) separated from concentrated urbanization, can absorb much of the future recre-

ational needs of Circle City. Protected and wisely developed, the constellation's environmental corridor patterns are an adequate foil to the evolving Circle City. This could be done with better statewide land-use standards and recognition of the unique driftless region as a biosphere reserve.

The objective of the Circle City study was to show how regional resource patterns can serve as form determinants to guide existing regional urbanization and its expansion into a meaningful midwest form (Figs. 7.3 and 7.4). The method of analysis involved asking necessary questions about the resources available to a region or constellation

Figure 7.3 Circle City and
the Driftless Area as a
potential biosphere reserve.

Figure 7.4 USGS relief map
of Wisconsin showing the
driftless hill country in
southwest Wisconsin.

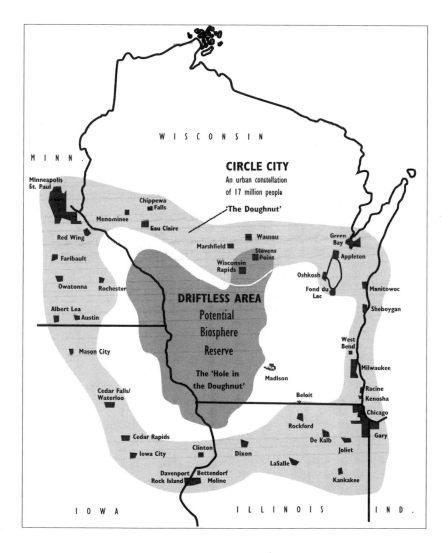

Figure 7.5 Evolution of Circle City (a) during the latest, or Wisconsin period of glaciation of North America, a sheet of ice with a thickness generally of about 2000 feet, whose various lobes advanced over North America. (b) The farthest extent of this glaciation was the Ozark Ridge region of southern Illinois. (c) The lobes advancing from the Keewatin, Labrador, and Patrician centers bypassed the Driftless Area. (d) This area of southwestern Wisconsin, southeastern Minnesota, northeastern

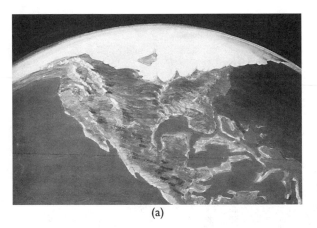

(a)

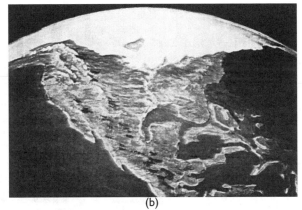

(b)

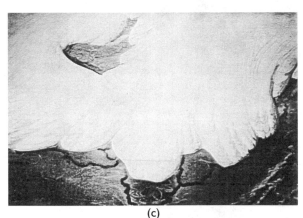

(c)

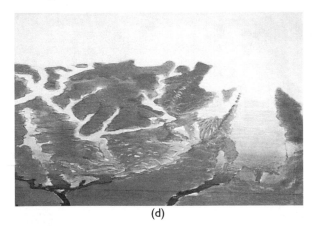

(d)

both from within its boundaries and from outside the area. Consideration of priorities for appropriate consumption, conservation, and reallocation of resources as well as possible substitutions for nonrenewable resources; and strategies utilizing the placement of the arteries of growth (transportation, integrated utilities, and communication facilities) are essential to establishing guidelines for regional growth. Developing regional consensus on growth issues is the starting point for local action to achieve local goals.

Quality of life is highly regarded among the residents of Circle City. Deeply embedded in the midwestern consciousness, it is personified by the writings of John Muir, Aldo Leopold, and Jens Jensen, among others. We cherish the availability of woods, lakes, streams, and rivers; prairies and fields, hills and valleys: the out-of-doors. It is an important consideration in determining where development occurs. The natural amenities with which the area is endowed arose over the prehistoric period when the land was shaped and formed. The recent period of human habitation of the area gave rise to the pattern of settlement: farming, urbanization, transportation routes, and all the adornments and appurtenances

Iowa, and northwestern Illinois remained hilly, with a mantle of older soils, a dendritic drainage pattern, cliffs, caves and sinkholes, and towering "castle" rocks; all due to a longer period of weathering. (e) During a period of warming, the glacier retreated, leaving in its track eskers, drumlins, and moraines. (f) Recently, a period of human glaciation began with the return of native Americans, followed by European immigrants' farms, roads, railroads, and buildings.

of contemporary civilization (Fig. 7.5). The availability of parks, open space, museums, sports facilities, boating, beaches, and recreations areas in urbanized areas plus access to the countryside to hike, bike, hunt, fish, swim, or otherwise enjoy our surroundings within minutes of home provides many amenities as well as fostering good air and water quality. These features embody much of the quality of life we value.

A large portion of the new jobs in our national economy are in the service-producing sector. Most firms offering these new jobs choose their locations with quality-of-life criteria as either first or second in importance.

Using the form of the Circle City constellations as a guide, together with resource analysis and the constraints developed from that analysis, an existing transportation and communication corridor (Fig. 7.6) can be utilized and developed to ensure the continued existence of recreational and scenic resources, productive lands, and economic resources for an expanding population by making better use of existing knowledge about our resources and their wise use.

Lying in the nation's upper midwest, Circle City encompasses much land that is generally

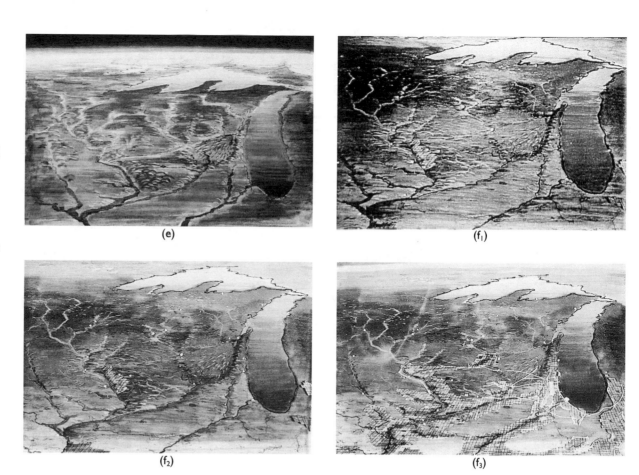

(e)

(f₁)

(f₂)

(f₃)

Figure 7.5 (*continued*)
(g) These settlers were
joined by their offspring, rel-
atives, and other immigrants
who formed the pattern on
the land of Circle City. (h)
Today, this is the form of the
impact of 17 million inhabitants and their urban constellation surrounding the
Driftless Area, which was
touched but lightly in comparison.

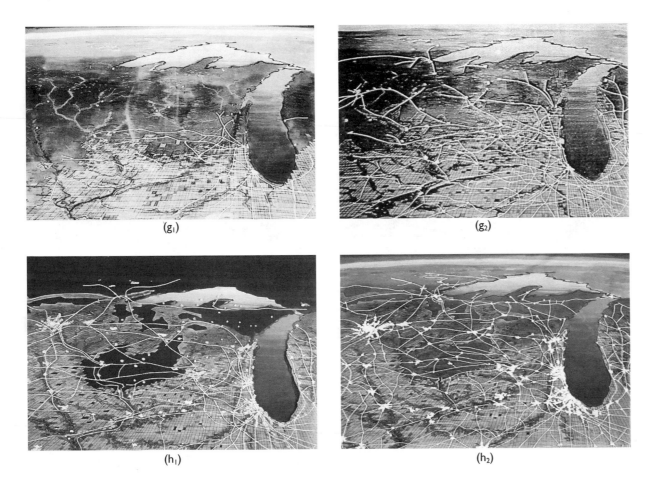

(g₁)

(g₂)

(h₁)

(h₂)

considered rural. However, Circle City contains 17 million people and should be considered as a single urban pattern. A constellation is a system of cities rather than a series of individual unre- lated cities. It can be a system of cities in har- mony with the sustaining regional resources within its core and on its flanks.

Population densities with this sort of distribu- tion can support regional transportation and inte- grated utilities and communication lines. As arteries of growth, these corridors linking cities can serve new development, building new livable densities and an increased tax base. They can retard sprawl by utilizing a framework to guide regional growth. Transportation and utility/com- munication corridors can retard sprawl by utiliz- ing that framework to guide regional growth, provided that development occurs only at suit- able nodes along those corridors. Sufficient pop- ulation densities to support use of the corridors must be linked by those corridors to make their services available. The corridors serve as linear magnets for growth.

The region includes low-urban-impact rural areas in the pattern of development of a high- impact urban constellation. Nationwide, between 1970 and 1980, population in metropolitan areas

Figure 7.6 Rail lines with
Circle City access.

increased 9.8 percent, and in nonmetropolitan areas it increased by 16.9 percent.[1] In the 1980s this movement resulted in lower overall urban densities, and much more widely spread areas of urbanization; also the rate of migration to rural areas diminished greatly. As the trend of suburbanization continues, this process has put great pressure on smaller units of government: villages, towns, and smaller cities. County governments are dealing with much greater social and land-use responsibilities than they were designed to handle and are subject to great pressures for both development (in the form of zoning petitions, particularly) and containment of development (unwise development can cause inflation of property taxes because of the expense of supplying services and transportation to far-flung and widely scattered development). Counties lack the statutory power in Wisconsin to deal with matters not specifically assigned to county government. Other units of government are permitted to deal with matters not specifically assigned elsewhere by state law, and local units of government are responding in a competitive way to foster development. Counties undertake functions of other units of government only with their agreement and cooperation. Experimental measures to deal with growth, land

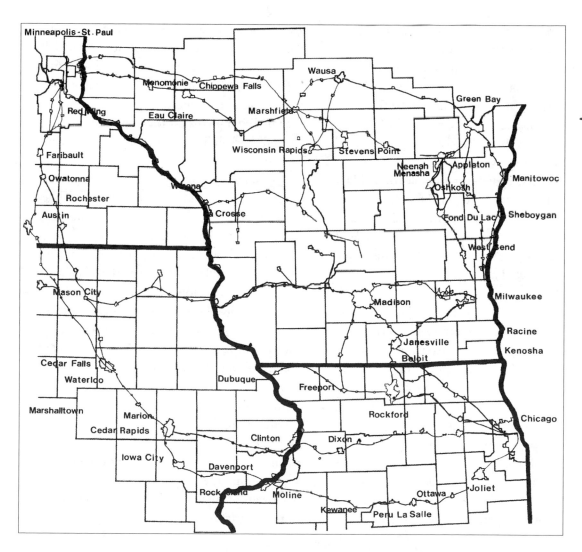

use, and development can be used on a trial basis and as continuing policy by local units of government to respond to pressures (the town of Dunn in Dane County has had a long-standing policy against any more platting of land for development until all lots designated for building are used). State enabling legislation setting standards for local plans as well as enforcing their integration into acceptable, workable, desirable, and internally consistent regional plans would do much to reduce the tension at the local level and encourage the pursuit of goals in a time frame of more than a year or two. Ad hoc decisions often result in unexpected and undesirable consequences for public policy.

Transportation policy is set largely at the state level, so counties and local units of government are at a disadvantage as far as determining the kind and extent of local transportation networks. This illustrates the need for state policy to include land-use goal setting and participation in the process at the county and local level.

The tools of county governments are limited, but they can do regional planning as required by federal legislation (to receive federal open space or highway funds, for instance) either alone or in conjunction with adjoining counties. This

involves some level of awareness of the design element: some visualization of how plans will look must be involved. Standards and reinforcing regulation at the state level could enable agreements among contiguous units of government. A primary emphasis on the appearance, esthetics, and workability of regional design is sorely lacking.

Consideration of Circle City as a regional structural unit provides a basis for the development of such a Circle City design including transportation, schools, parks and open space, and urban services planning in a coordinated way. Further, the implementation tools for such a design can be developed among the governmental units involved (including the state) so that agreement on various goals can be achieved and priorities assigned among those goals, some of which are bound to be mutually exclusive. Circle City urban areas are accessible to small rural farming communities, and their interactions are multitudinous.

After seeing their relationship to a large urbanizing system, questions about the place of rural communities in the region are being asked by citizens of small towns and cities which are currently growing formlessly.

- How does this regional urban form relate to a smaller community within its boundaries?
- How does the region relate to its large cities?
- How is this circular urban region supplied with food now, and what future changes are possible or desirable?
- How can a clean water supply be assured to its many inhabitants?
- How can we maintain or improve the quality of air of the Circle City region?
- How will accessible parks and open spaces for natural and cultural diversity be provided?
- How can wastes within the circular system be collected and recycled for maximum use and value to the residents of the region?
- How can the reduced residue be returned as harmlessly as possible to ground, water, or air?
- How might available renewable wood resources be utilized to build and rehabilitate this growing urban form?
- How can Circle City best be linked with all its needed resources?
- How can we design and produce new affordable urban forms that encourage habitable densities and avoid sprawl?

Figure 7.7 (a) Midwestern breadbasket; (b) the driftless area in the center of Circle City contains rich farmland for food production to support the surrounding urban ring.

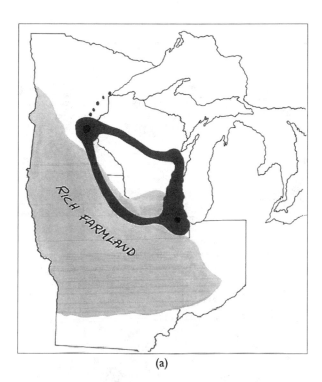

(a)

CIRCLE CITY REGIONAL RESOURCES

Food Supply

In using Circle City as a model framework that could be applied elsewhere, a general review of both the physical and social resources of the region is required. These sustaining resources for Circle City are the food supply, water supply, and other natural resources (e.g., timber) as well as energy sources, transportation system, utilities, and communication corridors.

Circle City includes productive prairie soils of the Great Plains in the part of its range that extends from northern Illinois into southern Wisconsin (Fig. 7.7). Because it is a nationally significant area in food and fiber production, for domestic use as well as surpluses for international trade, it is essential that these land patterns be protected for this and future generations.

A conflict exists between patterns of ongoing suburban sprawl (Fig. 7.8) and the continued farming of the finest agricultural soils in the midwest. The constellation concept provides guidelines that can divert new growth from priceless soil boundaries and assure many opportunities to feed Circle City as well as the rest of the world.

There are ample areas in which to build without destroying key agricultural soils or natural diversity *if* proper planning and regional design process teams are made available to our residents. The sooner that priorities are recognized and implemented, the less likely the land uses they concern will be preempted for lesser needs. Wisconsin and other states are experimenting with farmland preservation programs to diminish the economic pressures for development of farmland, such as the Farmland Preservation Act, and county agricultural zoning and land-use plan changes.

State and county legislation currently provide the means to implement open space, water, and wetland protection by outright purchase and other measures. We still lack state policy to require all parts of the state to form land-use plans. Local and regional plans are needed that are consistent with priorities arrived at by democratic procedures, that are consistent with overall generally accepted state criteria and each other, taking into consideration the needs and desires of neighboring units of government. We lack the tools to apply site-specific direction for the location of development.

(b)

(a)

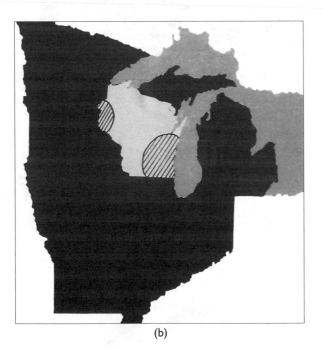

(b)

Figure 7.8 (a) Major urban sprawl threatens the sustainability of the breadbasket; (b) intensive urban growth invades Wisconsin from the Chicago area and the Minneapolis–St. Paul area.

Given regional recognition, the 17 million people of Circle City have the population, resources, and economic base to develop broad sustainable design and management options as well as the ability to communicate regional values and models of organization and operation to regional constellation inhabitants. Regional facilities, located conveniently within the constellation, would be the means by which the Regional Design Process, as described in Chapter 10, would be initiated. Education and political discussion are necessary to develop popular awareness of the needs of the region and the methods of supplying solutions.

In Circle City, comprising portions of Wisconsin, Minnesota, Iowa, and Illinois, this multistate pattern, like other constellations, would depend on integrated support from existing regional inventories, governmental agencies, corporations, regional foundations, and citizen organizations. Presently, support for the Circle City concept comes from all of these sources.

Water Resources

Circle City has convenient access to the largest and finest freshwater network in the world at such a great distance from the sea (Figs. 7.9 and

7.10). Again, through understanding and acceptance of the Regional Design Process, major efforts to protect and enhance this Circle City treasure by the region are called for. Pressures and demands for the use of this water will increase steadily as the population of Circle City expands and other regions of the country short of water demand use of this abundant midwest source. Wisconsin is fortunate to have one of the tightest set of water standards in the nation, but there is a continuing need to maintain and improve these standards.

Natural Resources

In Circle City, a critical natural resource is timber (Figs. 7.11 and 7.12). Ample supplies of timber lie within easy reach of Circle City. Their future availability will depend upon farsighted understanding of these key landscape patterns in which they occur by those responsible for their management. Developing guidelines for their most conservative use and preservation of their structure and diversity is appropriate now before the demand for their use increases any further. Transport networks to and within Circle City are an essential part of ensuring availability of timber and wood products. Many of the forests of

Figure 7.9 (a) Greatest freshwater body in the world so far from the sea; (b) Lake Superior shoreline.

Figure 7.10 Water resources of the Circle City region.

(a)

(b)

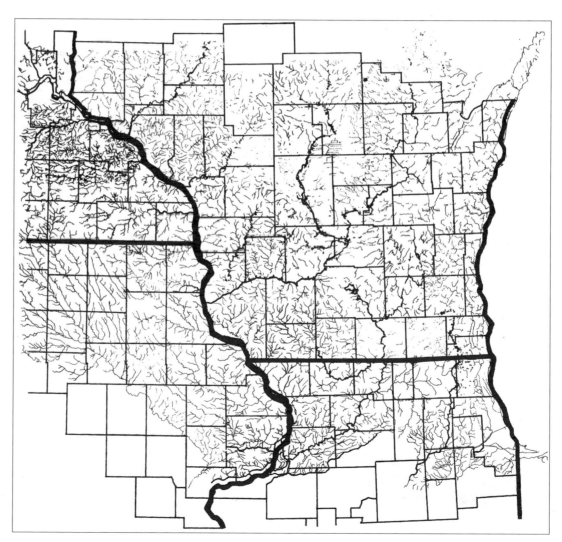

Figure 7.11 Timber supply:
(a) the north woods; (b) the
beauty of the forest.

Figure 7.12 Circle City vegetation cover.

(a)

(b)

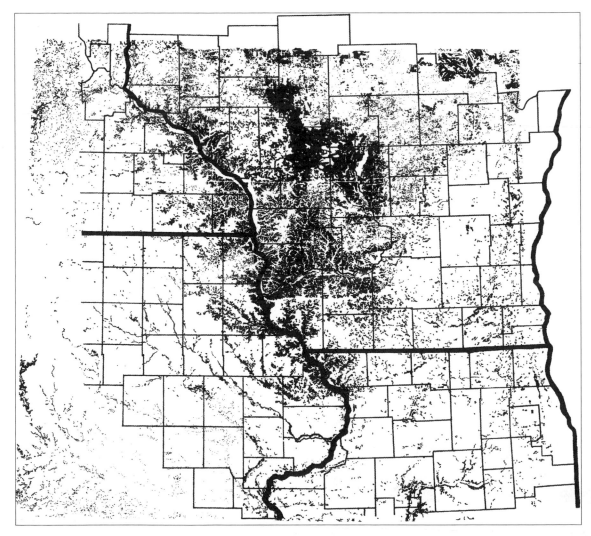

northern Wisconsin have wisely been placed in public ownership and offer Circle City an outstanding recreational resource.

Open Space

The driftless area, the environmental corridors, the farmlands and wooded areas within the core of Circle City, the area surrounding Circle City, and the nonurbanized areas within the circle of cities, and the parks and open space pattern within cities, towns, and villages, constitute the open space resources. With increasing populations, more of this system will require protection from development, and further easements and purchase for public access and use. Different kinds of recreational, water-quality protection, and conservation strategies developed by a Regional Design Process team used and required by the citizens of Circle City and its region can maximize the use and preservation of this resource (Fig. 7.13).

Wisconsin demonstrated leadership in the 1-cent sales tax on cigarettes to finance the $50 million acquisition program of the 1960s. More recent financing of a $250 million state stewardship plan continues to allow open space acquisi-

tion and protection. Additional programs include scenic easements, land trust programs, and local park and open space funding that has protected thousands of acres of critical open space resources. Open space and vegetation not only provide outstanding recreation and tourism opportunities but also contribute to the improvement of air and water quality.

Energy Resources

With virtually no petroleum-based energy resources, limited present use of solar energy, and no massive hydroelectric capability, Circle City is dependent on outside sources for most of its energy supply. Conservation, cogeneration, and district heating are capable of producing savings in the future. This is another incentive for encouraging population increases at suitable points on mass-transit routes by planning utilities and urban services there and providing financial incentives for housing within walking distance of transit routes. Limited local energy resources also imply economic and environmental benefits from making more use of mass transit as well as rail- and water-based freight movement.

MULTIMODAL TRANSPORTATION NETWORK

If 17 million people[2] now live in Circle City, surely the regional city can support a mass-transit system. At present, Amtrak service for Circle City is minimal. By utilizing the Soo Line (20 miles greater in length than the current route from Chicago to Minneapolis–St. Paul), seven times the population could be served (Fig. 7.14). In addition, using this route would encourage growth within the Circle City urban framework instead of in the driftless area core.

As existing rail corridors presently connect the major cities of Circle City, all forms of passenger and freight transit within this circle of concentration of population need to be considered. The existing corridors provide the opportunity to construct new utility and communication lines in an integrated corridor. They can serve as the locus of linear growth of urban densities between constellation corridor cities. Careful planning requires such growth within the corridors to be placed where it interferes least with existing natural and cultural treasures. Major rail corridors connecting constellation cities in all parts of the country should be

Figure 7.13 (a) Landscape features that separate ridges and rims from their valley floors are known as slopes. Building or farming on slopes of 12½ percent or greater creates serious erosion problems. (b) The land may be too steep to plow, but for people it is a place to scale either in body or in mind. (c) Steep topography in the core of Circle City.

(a)

(b)

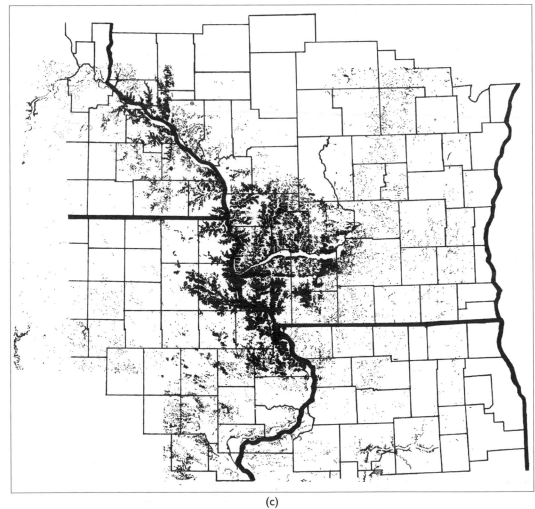

(c)

Figure 7.14 Circle City and
Amtrak alignment.

preserved by the individual states, as their replacement would be almost impossible because of the basic land cost, and the other uses to which land has been put. They provide the major opportunity for a new and desirable urban form. Rail transit within existing cities plagued with noise, vibration, and air pollution in their corridors can be replaced with new elevated systems such as the PRT 2000 owned by the Raytheon Corporation, which is currently being readied for demonstration as a working system. Such *personal rapid transit* and other elevated systems can serve new and attractive "infill" development by integrating practically noiseless transit with enclosing wraparound architecture. Such redevelopment and higher livable population densities can rehabilitate and increase the tax base of central-city areas, and make the alternative of sprawl economically and aesthetically less attractive. (There is further discussion of this in Chapter 11.)

In addition to moving people within Circle City and heavy freight between industrial centers, regional self-preservation priorities demand public policy and financing to assure rail-centered multimodal transit, including many interconnections: for instance, ship/truck/train/barge transfer and movement of containerized freight, move-

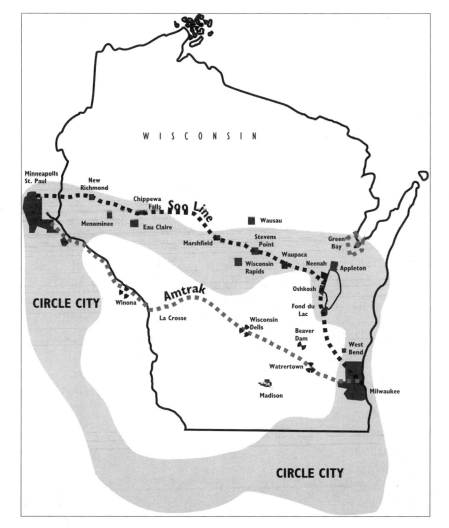

ment of tourists and their cars together, and transfer centers where different modes of transportation interact: park and ride parking lots, provision for storage and moving of bicycles, containerized freight transfer, bus–rail transfers points, and so on. Such access between Circle City and our identified resource patterns is essential for convenience and economy.

Fortunately, we do know where our outstanding natural and cultural diversity is located, and as mentioned, the Wisconsin Outdoor Recreation Plan established that most high-quality resources are concentrated near major river and lake networks in patterns called environmental corridors. These corridors contain much of our rail network which was built in these minimum-grade networks. It is possible to provide access to the major population concentrations and to these high-quality recreational resources and experiences by protecting and enhancing key rail systems.

The key rail links joining our natural and cultural quality patterns within Circle City might be considered as a state or national rail park network. We have national parkways, national wild rivers, national walking trails—why not national rail and water parks that join and penetrate our natural and cultural heritage?

One of the greatest difficulties the new National Park Urban Park Program has faced is getting people to the parks and home again without massive traffic snarls. Our key rail networks could handle this problem with ease and at one-tenth the energy cost.

Wisconsin state-level efforts to redirect and expand Amtrak services in the state and within the region of Circle City as well as to acquire and rebuild many miles of neglected trackage may be cut off by current national policy changes. A policy of allowing new private short-haul operators to manage rail systems is in place here, currently serving primarily to move freight.

Circle City has an opportunity to direct growth in an area of increasing population using transportation links and resource patterns both to preserve the amenities and desirable characteristics of the area and provide additional development.

Notes

[1] U.S. Department of Commerce, "General Population Characteristics of Wisconsin," in the *1990 Census of Population,* U.S. Government Printing Office, Washington, D.C., June 1992.

[2] Ibid.

Figure 8.1 Upper midwest core landscape inventories, 1950–1991:

(a) Embarras River Valley,
(b) Wabash River Valley,
(c) state of Illinois,

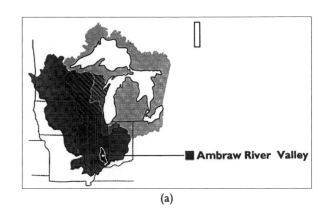

■ Ambraw River Valley

(a)

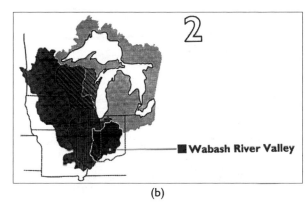

■ Wabash River Valley

(b)

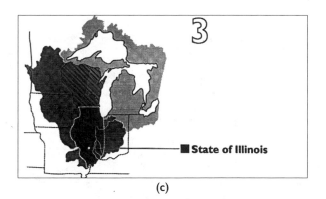

■ State of Illinois

(c)

CHAPTER 8

COMMUNICATING REGIONAL VALUES AND VISIONS

INDIANA TERRITORY (1800) TRAIL

At the regional scale, application of the Regional Design Process involves recognizing and utilizing regional resources and characteristics. These are clearly identified with tourism, travel, and education—the general public familiarizing themselves with regional features of interest and enjoying themselves in the process of partaking in the regional experience. To travel and enjoy, there must be accessibility to the traveler. Features linked geographically, visually, and aesthetically are those that are visited the most. Facilities for overnight accommodations, restaurants, and activities for all age groups need to be available, together with the dissemination of information.

In my series of studies of the upper midwest (Figs. 8.1, and 8.2) it is evident that the core of the landscape I have been studying all these years was the Indiana Territory of 1800 (Fig. 8.3). Water surrounds the territory: Lake Superior, Lake Michigan, and the Tippecanoe, Wabash, Ohio, Mississippi, and St. Croix rivers (Fig. 8.4). The shorelines of these major water systems (as well as those of all other environmental corridors

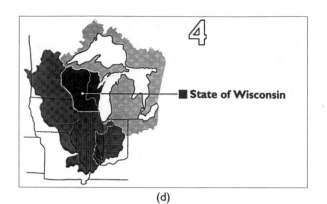

(d)

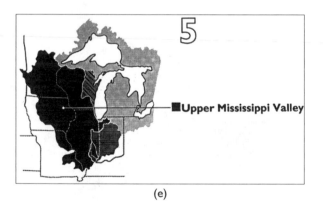

(e)

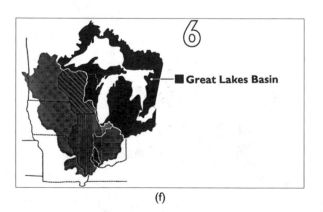

(f)

Figure 8.1 (continued)
(d) state of Wisconsin
(e) Upper Mississippi Valley
(f) Great Lakes Basin

Figure 8.2 Composite map of upper midwest landscape inventories, 1950–1991,

showing location in the United States

Figure 8.3 The western segment of the Indiana Trail parallels the mighty Mississippi River and all of its natural and cultural features.

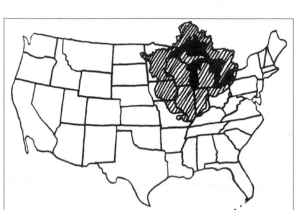

(a)

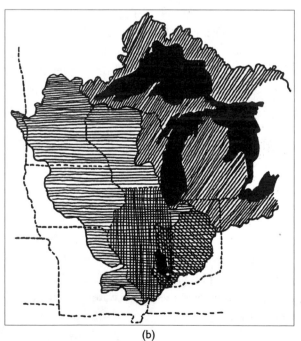

(b)

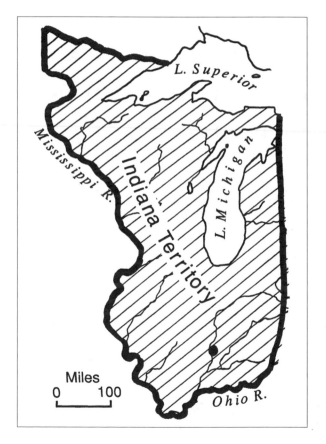

Figure 8.4 Indiana Territory
in the upper midwest study
area.

within Circle City) have been shown to contain most of the natural and cultural diversity that characterizes them as outstanding settings for all forms of trail networks. Most rail systems, because of a requirement for low gradients, have followed river corridors in which we have found most of our national natural and cultural diversity. The same opportunities are found at the regional and local levels.

A design opportunity similar to the proposed national rail spine exists here in the form of a regional rail corridor running north–south through this midwest island and a shoreline corridor around the island. Traversing all its major landscape personalities by rail would provide an exceptional tourism/education (Fig. 8.5) experience. Broadening the north–south route to include the exceptional water corridors would link the historical (transportation, recreation, and tourism) resources that developed along these transportation routes of the past. (Fig. 8.6)

Such a regional rail/water trail (the Indiana Territory Trail) would offer outstanding tourism opportunities, and in addition there is the educational possibility of classrooms on boats and rail-cars easily accessible to 1.4 million two- and four-year college students and 90,000 university

and college staff members in the region who hardly ever speak to one another as things are now. (Fig. 8.7) One can imagine how a "public works for college credit" program for students from area academic institutions could be coordinated and focused on an interdisciplinary process team effort to protect and enhance these local resources for future generations.

Of the many resource jewels on the Indiana Territory Trail necklace to be linked, none have greater potential than that of adding to the present number of undeveloped Mississippi floodplain acres. The history-making flood of the Mississippi River of 1993 should certainly demonstrate the folly of building in the wide floodplain. If we slowly return this area to the state of a natural ecological buffer, we could prevent billions of tax dollars being lost, prevent additional hardship for thousands of people,[1] and offer a new ecological and aesthetic resource in the center of the nation parallel to a proposed national prairie a bit farther west.

Schools of landscape architecture, planning, and architecture, as well as many youth programs, are abundant in every constellation of the country. Many of these students are seeking meaningful work related to their fields of study.

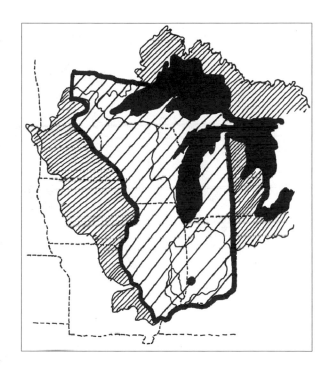

Figure 8.5 Landscape personalities

Figure 8.6 Indiana Territory Trail

THE 'IT' TRAIL

INDIANA TERRITORY
RAIL & WATER E-WAY

● COLLEGES & UNIVERSITIES (26)
'BIG TEN' UNIVERSITIES (6)

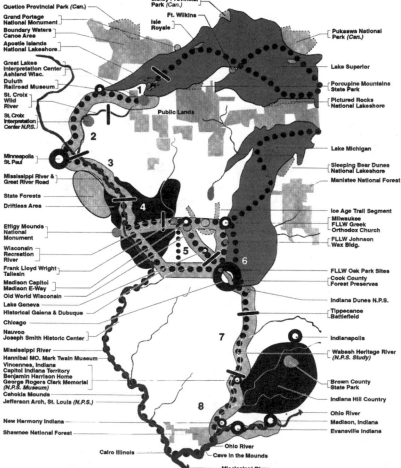

800 MILE HERITAGE E-WAY CONCEPT

Figure 8.7 Two- and four-
year colleges in the Indiana
Territory Trail area

Inventorying the remaining resources adjacent to
these E-Ways and trails in every constellation
region fits into the curriculums of many areas of
study (science, history, etc.), and the goals of
many employment and training programs, such as
work-study, conservation corps, community service organization projects, and scouting. Future
leaders will benefit from an intimate knowledge
of the resource values gained from inventories
and learn respect and appreciation of their native
landscapes by participating in their protection
and restoration. In Wisconsin in the 1960s the
state planning program provided the modest
funding for training and employing 30 University
of Wisconsin landscape architecture students to
do the inventories necessary for the resource survey of the state. Later a contract with the
National Park Service permitted my professional
office and some of these same well-trained students to inventory the Upper Mississippi Valley
and the Great Lakes Basin. It is well within the
reach of existing programs to integrate a common resource inventory goal that would contribute to the health of the nation and the goals
of education. Such an endeavor could certainly
benefit from the historical experience of establishing CCC programs (the present Youth Con-

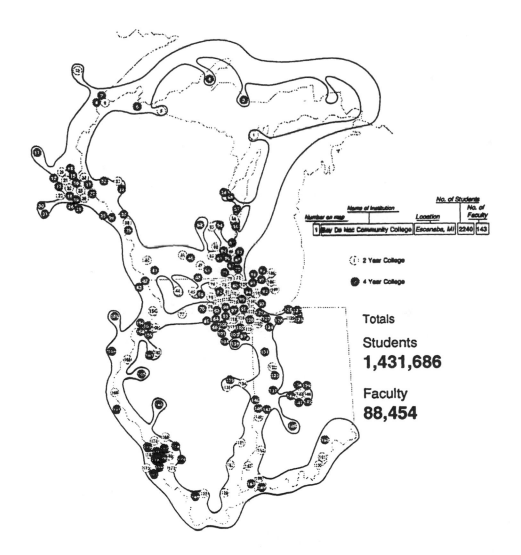

No. of Students

Number on map	Name of Institution	Location	No. of Students	No. of Faculty
1	Bay De Noc Community College	Escanaba, MI	2240	143

⊙ : 2 Year College

● : 4 Year College

Totals

Students
1,431,686

Faculty
88,454

Figure 8.8 Scenic rail
tourism/education route
(Heritage Necklace)

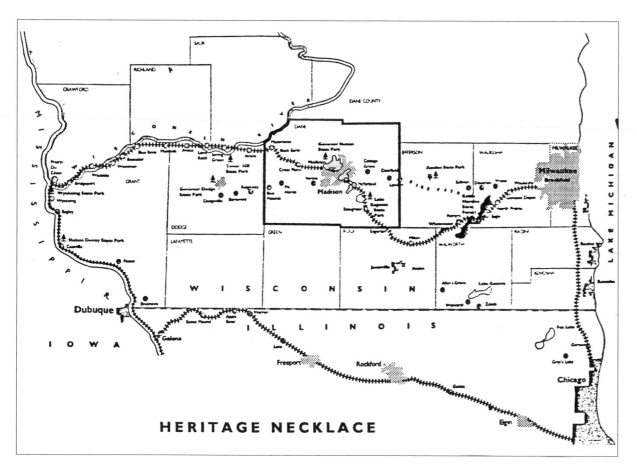

HERITAGE NECKLACE

servation Corps) Peace Corps activities, and the
"public works for college credit" program.

INTERSTATE HERITAGE NECKLACE

As noted earlier, it is one thing to have inventoried the key resource patterns of a region, and quite another to persuade the voters and politicians that it is to the advantage of all to see that the resources are protected and enhanced. While developing the concept of promoting integrated tourism and education opportunities within the Indiana Trail, it occurred to me that an inner loop designed to connect such resources within the highest population density areas of Wisconsin and Illinois would be important, as they would serve as a demonstration area for the more extensive Indiana Territory Trail (Figs. 8.8 and 8.9). This design proposal, the interstate heritage necklace, was designed as an educational tourism loop which provides easy access to the region's big cities, small towns, and rural areas. Within the core of the Indiana Territory Trail area, the heritage necklace was designed as an opportunity

Figure 8.9 Circle City heritage necklace

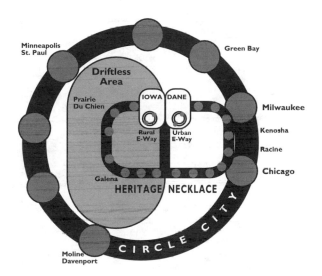

17 Million People

Impact‹–›Market

to experience the natural and cultural diversity of the region, thereby providing an outstanding opportunity to inform people about critical rural and urban landscape resource patterns and options for the future.

The heritage necklace design is intended not only to educate people about the nature and history of the region but also about transportation alternatives and human impact on the landscape. Taking these issues into account, this tourism loop can also transport tourists by a combination of boat and rail methods. These transportation modes reduce automobile traffic and control human impact by limiting where passengers alight at locations predetermined to be capable of supporting the impact. Linking the Indiana Territory Trail and the interstate heritage necklace to the transcontinental rail spine would offer exciting tourism/education options for the future. (Fig. 8.10)

At this time, the national rail spine, the Indiana Territory Trail, and the interstate heritage necklace are proposals based on the many studies documented in this book, the opportunities provided by the existing rail and water corridors, and the need for more economical, available, safe, environmentally sound, and convenient trans-

portation. Making the opportunities and the design possibilities known is the way to make implementation possible. We have the national resources, the necessary organizational structure, and lack only knowledge of the possibilities and the will to carry them out.

THE WISCONSIN IDEA

In the Progressive era, Robert LaFolette, Charles McCarthy, and the University of Wisconsin "brain trust" promoted the idea that academia and state government should pool their efforts to improve the physical and social character of the state. Lincoln Steffens, the political journalist and muckraker celebrated the notion—particularly in the area of railroad legislation and reform of the election laws—as the Wisconsin Idea. In later years the Wisconsin Idea also came to be identified with University Extension, whose mission has been to extend the boundaries of the university to the boundaries of the state. Since 1967 the Environmental Awareness Center, with participation by undergraduate and graduate students and staff from many university departments, has

extended regional design concepts and options for sustainable use of the land to fill state needs.

One such long-range concept central to Environmental Awareness Center work on applying analysis and design to the resources of the state was to develop a series of local land-use demonstrations along a common rail corridor.

Figure 8.10 Linking the
upper midwest heritage
necklace with the transcontinental heritage rail spine

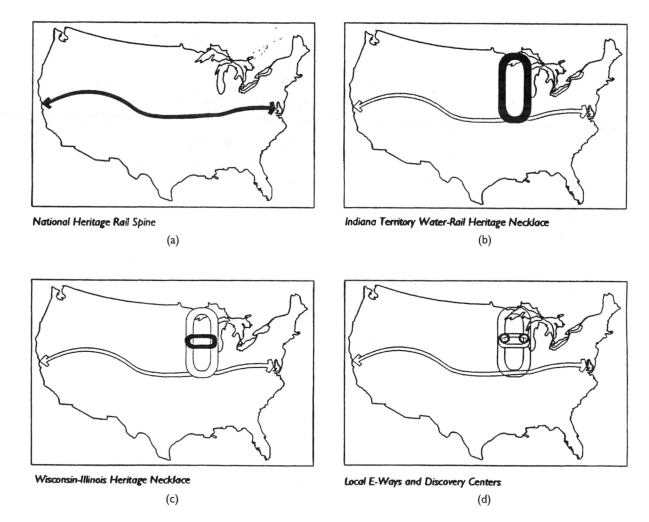

National Heritage Rail Spine

(a)

Indiana Territory Water-Rail Heritage Necklace

(b)

Wisconsin-Illinois Heritage Necklace

(c)

Local E-Ways and Discovery Centers

(d)

We call this corridor the Wisconsin Idea Guideway. It constitutes the northern segment of the
Interstate Heritage Necklace.

Wisconsin Idea Guideway (Fig. 8.11)

The Wisconsin Idea Guideway is a subsidiary
part of the Indiana Trail within the interstate
heritage necklace. This rail guideway route transects southern Wisconsin and its rapidly growing
population, running from Milwaukee to Prairie
du Chien via the capitol city of Madison. It connects the Great Lakes and the Mississippi River.
It traverses nearly every type of landscape and
townscape within Circle City.

It has, through the years, served well as a
landscape laboratory for staff and students of the
Environmental Awareness Center, and since the
right-of-way has been acquired throughout most
of its length by the state department of transportation, it offers an outstanding opportunity to
serve as a tourism/education system.

The guideway encompasses many opportunities to prepare prototype demonstrations of land-
use options to serve as models for *local* action
with respect to land use, transportation, and local
relationships to the encircling 17 million population of Circle City, as well as the interstate her-

Figure 8.11 Wisconsin Idea
Guideway

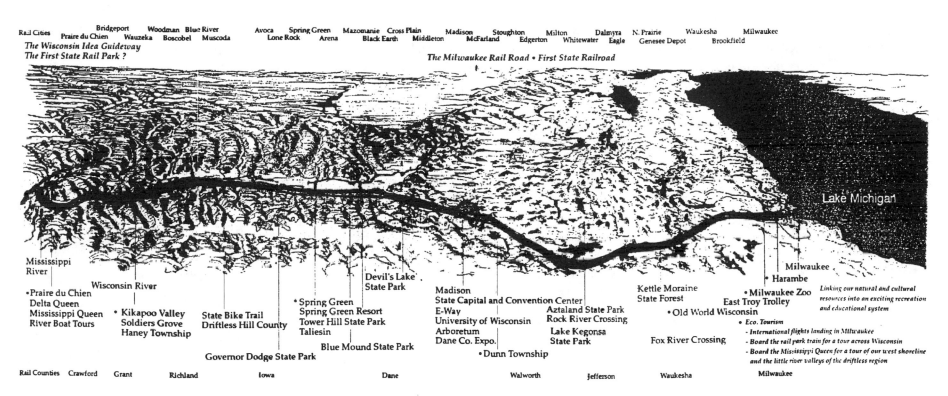

Rail Cities · Praire du Chien · Bridgeport · Wauzeka · Woodman · Boscobel · Muscoda · Blue River · Avoca · Lone Rock · Spring Green · Arena · Mazomanie · Black Earth · Cross Plain · Middleton · Madison · McFarland · Stoughton · Edgerton · Milton · Whitewater · Dalmyra · Eagle · N. Prairie · Genesee Depot · Waukesha · Brookfield · Milwaukee

The Wisconsin Idea Guideway
The First State Rail Park ?

The Milwaukee Rail Road • First State Railroad

Lake Michigan

Mississippi
River

• Praire du Chien
Delta Queen
Mississippi Queen
River Boat Tours

Wisconsin River

• Kikapoo Valley
Soldiers Grove
Haney Township

State Bike Trail
Driftless Hill County

Governor Dodge State Park

Devil's Lake
State Park

• Spring Green
Spring Green Resort
Tower Hill State Park
Taliesin

Blue Mound State Park

Madison
State Capital and Convention Center
E-Way
University of Wisconsin
Arboretum
Dane Co. Expo.

• Dunn Township

Aztaland State Park
Rock River Crossing

Lake Kegonsa
State Park

Kettle Moraine
State Forest

• Old World Wisconsin

Fox River Crossing

Milwaukee

• Harambe

• Milwaukee Zoo
East Troy Trolley

*Linking our natural and cultural
resources into an exciting recreation
and educational system*

• *Eco. Tourism*
  - *International flights landing in Milwaukee*
  - *Board the rail park train for a tour across Wisconsin*
  - *Board the Mississippi Queen for a tour of our west shoreline
    and the little river valleys of the driftless region*

Rail Counties · Crawford · Grant · Richland · Iowa · Dane · Walworth · Jefferson · Waukesha · Milwaukee

itage necklace, the Indiana Territory Trail, and the national rail spine. A select few of the local studies along this rail trail by Environmental Awareness Center staff and students are discussed in more detail in Chapter 9.

By way of many land-use demonstrations it has been possible to inform the public of

national, regional, and local values and visions for the future. The Wisconsin Idea Guideway is a rail transportation route with the capacity to make accessible in many ways the regional resources of Circle City by way of transportation of goods and people as well as providing travel and education programs and amenities.

Following the present practice of the National Park Service to locate parks near major cities (e.g., the new seashore parks near New York and San Francisco and the Indiana Dunes near Gary and Chicago), the guideway rail route transects the center of Circle City. It connects the Great Lakes and the Mississippi River, passing through towns, villages, rural townships, river valleys, and villages.

Along the guideway an awareness of the importance of Circle City, whose 17 million people are a nationally important group, is developing. The smaller communities as well as large cities are taking notice that there are consequences to their geographic, economic, and transportation relationships, and there is uncertainty as to the nature of these effects. It is already apparent (by the appearance of second homes and recreational and tourism facilities) that residents of Circle City are turning for recreation and relaxation to the lovely hills of the driftless area, sand country, glacially created lakes, hills and ridges, rivers, and small towns in Circle City's central core. People are already coming; proper accommodation for them is needed.

What are the present and future total effects of increased auto traffic, new second homes, absentee ownership (nonvoting taxpayers often exert considerable economic influence), and all the other effects of such growth? The consideration of the concept of Circle City and the guideway route has provided a focus for local attention to the consequences of this growing trend.

Many absentee farm owners in this area, unaware of local resource values and local customs, have made blunders in the effort to extract as many dollars as possible from agriculture without applying conservation practices to the land designed for continued farming. Others have built second homes, without the sensitivity in building and site treatment necessary to coexist with fragile local resources. Traffic on local highways and byways is increasing by their comings and goings in addition to locally generated traffic. In the guideway stretching from Milwaukee on Lake Michigan to Madison and on to Prairie du Chien on the Mississippi River, there are ample opportunities to prepare prototype demonstrations of land-use options to serve as models for local action with respect to land use, transportation, and development issues.

A basic principle guiding these demonstrations is that projects be a joint venture between the citizens of the community and the newcomers, recognizing that public involvement in the decision-making process is an essential task of land-use design efforts and that local citizens will be better informed to educate and direct local and absentee owners toward development processes that will involve them in the effort toward sustainable use of existing resources.

The Wisconsin Idea Guideway is designed to make available to the people along its route a unique recreational network that will provide a diverse travel and education experience. Rehabilitation and reuse of a continuous right-of-way formerly owned by the Milwaukee Road Railway is the goal. This rail route, the first in the state, provides the setting for an outstanding rail parkway connecting over 150 unique cultural attractions amid the scenery along its right-of-way.

Trial Excursions

Following state acquisition of the rail corridor, recent joint private and public actions formed a transit authority to acquire and lease the rail corridor to a short-haul operating rail company. Recently, a lessee of the trackage began testing the system for passenger use through quickly arranged excursions, utilizing the equipment they were restoring in Janesville, Wisconsin. These first excursions met with success. One destination, Spring Green, was surprised when one weekend the train rolled into town, disgorging hundreds of passengers eager to see the local scenery and shops. By the second or third visit the local leadership had prepared maps of the downtown stores and the excursion company had

Figure 8.12 Model of the
Wisconsin Idea Guideway

arranged for 10 school buses from Dodgeville to meet the visitors and take them on short excursions to nearby Governor Dodge State Park, the House on the Rock, and the Spring Green Restaurant.

Later, plans were made to visit Frank Lloyd Wright's Taliesin, just across the river from Spring Green. Since rail acquisition by the state, rehabilitation work has been completed and future excursions are planned to move people from Madison–Middleton to Prairie du Chien. The trip along the Wisconsin River ends at the historic Villa Louis, on an island in the Mississippi River.

Increased commercial rail freight carriage will be necessary for a rail company to survive and thrive. Trials indicate that adding recreational excursions to freight operations offers an additional incentive for the overall success of the total effort.

To encourage implementation of the Wisconsin Idea Guideway concept, the Environmental Awareness Center has constructed a 52-foot three-dimensional model of the area between Milwaukee and Prairie du Chien. The model, and the thousands of acres of public lands and local attractions identified along the rail corridor,

illustrate the Guideway's communication value to both urban and rural dwellers and the present and potential tourism value to the state and region. (Fig. 8.12)

Note

[1]Bruce Hannon, "A Ten-Million Acre Wetland River Park," *St. Louis Post Dispatch,* February 2, 1994 (paper obtainable from author, 220 Davenport Hall, University of Illinois, Urbana, IL 61901).

PART III

LOCAL OVERVIEW

In Part III we apply the evolving Regional Design Process at the local scale to the landscape within Circle City. Now that a survey of the national and midwestern regional resources has been established, a review of local resource values and visions is appropriate.

It is easily demonstrable that local sprawl occurs where establishment of transportation lines, integrated utilities, and communication lines is allowed and found possible and desirable. Where these "arteries of growth" occur automatically predicts the patterns of growth. Where such arteries are lacking, growth is prevented or inhibited. Adopting a growth strategy of controlling the location of arteries of growth suggests that after identifying national and regional resource patterns of great value and deciding to protect them from further impact, the placement of such arteries should occur only outside the boundaries of patterns exempted from development. By

placing integrated utilities and communication lines (wire cables and fiber optic lines) in present and identified future transit corridors (for heavy or light rail or personal rapid transit lines), these corridors can serve as strong organizing frameworks for future growth within identified constellations and provide the opportunity to connect corridors.

First the Regional Design Process as applied to local prototype studies is discussed. The study projects are located along the Wisconsin Idea Guideway, which was described briefly in Chapter 8. From these studies the value and uses of interdisciplinarity can be seen as essential to the process and instrumental in achieving effective design solutions and plans of action.

Next, interdisciplinary teams are discussed and what is important in their composition, as well as facilities that could house and foster such interdisciplinary analysis and design activities. Appropriate

regional facilities and the sort of budgets they require are discussed. Also suggested in Chapter 10 are possibilities for utilizing interdisciplinary expertise, and creative designs for properties as Regional Design Process teaching and demonstration prototypes for other constellations of populations and cities.

Assuming the strategy of utilizing arteries of growth to define development, the 1994 graduate regional design class developed a local design proposal for a segment of the rail corridor within the Wisconsin Idea Guideway which is presented in Chapter 11. The goal of these studies was to establish higher livable densities along a transportation spine (a rail corridor) as an alternative to sprawl in all directions that becomes supplied with roads, services, and utilities without regard for either their complete cost or total effects. By organizing development along existing transportation rights-of-way, more economical, higher volume transportation can be supplied and more efficient and aesthetically pleasing use made of the land and its amenities. In addition, energy and environmental savings can be realized—in general, a higher quality of life can be achieved in view of the available physical, social, and economic resources. Simple, straightforward guidelines can be provided by utilizing the Regional Design Process. The most complex problems are capable of solution by utilizing a broad view of regional considerations. It is hoped that others will benefit from considering these ideas and that understanding will bring about further development and support for regional design and popular participation as well as appreciation of how we can achieve the goal of maintaining and benefiting from the world in which we live.

CHAPTER 9

EAC COMMUNITY PROJECTS ALONG THE WISCONSIN IDEA GUIDEWAY

The many land-use demonstrations on the Wisconsin Idea Guideway are like jewels on a necklace. Taken together, they demonstrate the variety of projects that have contributed to the evolution of the Regional Design Process over the years. Through large- and small-scale projects, the Environmental Awareness Center (EAC) has studied a variety of aspects of this guideway corridor. These diverse projects have focused on small towns, city neighborhoods, natural and recreational areas, and open space. Recommendations for the conservation of historic architecture, wetlands, and unique natural areas have been made as EAC designers[1] and students worked together with local officials and residents. Each project has been unique and has generated a variety of responses from communities. Other products have included published reports and guides, such as the *Land-Users' Handbook,* which was developed to help landowners and prospective land buyers make informed decisions about the use of land within the ridge and valley lands of the driftless region.

Overall, the studies have contributed to an understanding of the interrelationship between Wisconsin land and the uses to which it is put. Application of the Regional Design Process developed at the Environmental Awareness Center incorporates necessary human and natural variables and is based on an interdisciplinary team approach. The nature of the team components have varied according to the demands of the individual project and the funds available for each one.

Projects undertaken by the EAC to date were funded by grants from federal and state agencies, private foundations, and local communities. In addition to giving planners, private entrepreneurs, public agencies, and community groups new ways to perceive and work with the environment, hundreds of undergraduate and graduate students have gained valuable experience. Members of the landscape architecture department faculty have also had the opportunity to test and refine a broad range of innovative methodologies, design concepts, and technological tools.

In the following section we illustrate the variety of projects developed to study the rural and urban components along the route of the Wisconsin Idea Guideway. This cross section starts in Milwaukee and terminates at the Mississippi River with the Master Plan Study of Prairie du Chien. Studies of Milwaukee's inner city, the town of Dunn, Madison's E-Way, upper Iowa

Figure 9.1 The Milwaukee
central business area and
the Harambe neighborhood

County, Spring Green, Boscobel, the Kickapoo
Valley, and Prairie du Chien were specifically
chosen to illustrate a few examples of landscape
planning and design along the rail guideway. The
range of projects completed demonstrates the
potential for applying the evolving Regional
Design Process and preservation principles in a
community participation framework. Perceived
as many individual projects composing an integrated regional system, the Wisconsin Idea
Guideway offers outstanding potential as an
exciting educational/tourism system and a model
for applying the regional design process to
resource corridors and resolving local issues
across the nation.

HARAMBE NEIGHBORHOOD, MILWAUKEE, WISCONSIN (1978) (FIG. 9.1)

The Harambe neighborhood in the inner city of
Milwaukee offered an opportunity to study allevi-
ating the plight of a depressed city core. The
study was initiated because the residents in the
Harambe neighborhood felt a lack of sufficient
access to open space and recreational opportunities together with many other serious problems.

Figure 9.2 Measuring the townscape (a) Where are the homes located? How far are they from the street curbs? (b) We measure the alleys. Where are the garages? How wide are the alleys?

To understand how the residents could remedy this deficiency, it was necessary to discover the physical structure of the neighborhood and determine if available open space could be reconfigured to better meet residents' needs. The first step in the study was to conduct an inventory of the neighborhood's resources. Milwaukee's inner city is typical of large urban centers. Although it occupies only about 10 percent of the city's land area, more than 20 percent of the city's population lives here, a high percentage being minorities. At the time of the Harambe study, the inner city contained only 2 percent of all the publicly owned parkland in the city, an unfair application of public policy. The dearth of recreational opportunities for youth is in part due to the lack of open space and recreational facilities conveniently located within neighborhoods. Concerns about crime and the lack of park and recreational facilities were the top two items in a list of six problems perceived by inner-city residents and representatives of human service agencies. Although nearly 45 percent of families in the inner city did not own a car, about one-third of all land area in the inner city was paved streets and alleys. In addition, hundreds of lots were vacant as the result of arson and accidental fires which, together with tax delinquency, led to the transfer of these properties to city and county ownership. This lack of respect for landscape and people is not conducive to combatting the existence of crime and the fear of crime (which is a form of rebellion against society).

In the Harambe neighborhood (Fig. 9.2) (where the majority of occupants did not own automobiles), the wide roadways and vacant and derelict lands typified the ineffective use of this available space, which resulted in the residents' dissatisfaction with the neighborhood opportunities for recreation and open space. Analysis of studies of the neighborhood resulted in the proposal to reclaim half of the streets to be developed as open green spaces for pedestrian corridors. If these corridors were linked with the city and county lands, including the vacant lots, the park and open-space areas available to this high-density community could be tripled. (Fig. 9.3)

To communicate our process and possible changes for Harambe to the residents of the neighborhood, every streetscape was photographed and a series of sketches prepared incorporating the proposed park system. Finally, two busloads of residents were brought to the Awareness Center in Madison, where a 360-degree theater with nine screens and nine projectors was arranged to show the neighborhood as it

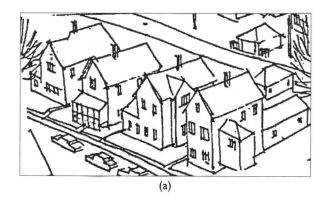

(a)

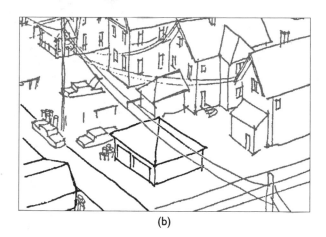

(b)

Figure 9.2 (continued) (c) We want to know where the sidewalks are located. We want to know where the driveways are located. We want to know where the grass and dirt surfaces are located. We want to know where the streets and curbs are located, and the width of the streets. (d) and (e) We want to know where the trees, shrubs, vines, and flowers are located. We want to know where all the utilities are located. We can see telephone poles but sometimes more research is needed to know where the sewer, water, gas, and underground electric lines are located. (f) We want to know where public facilities are located on the block. How many square feet of open space exist adjacent to the buildings?

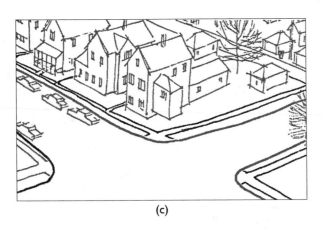

(c)

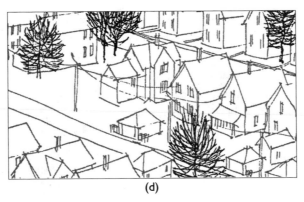

(d)

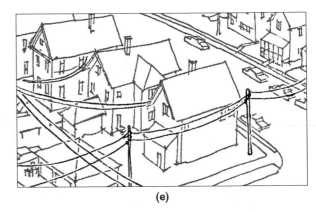

(e)

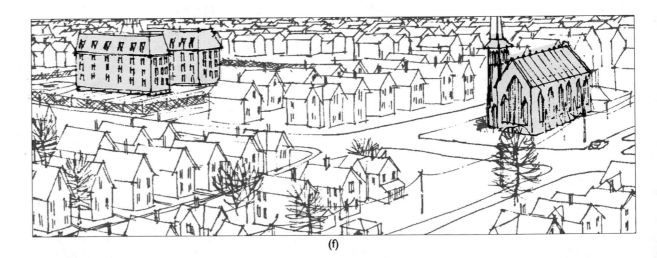

(f)

Figure 9.3 Reclaiming half
of the existing street scene
for the neighborhood

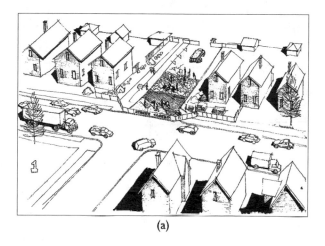

(a)

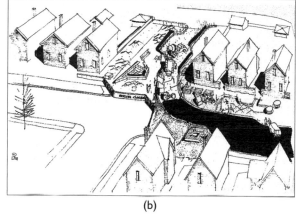

(b)

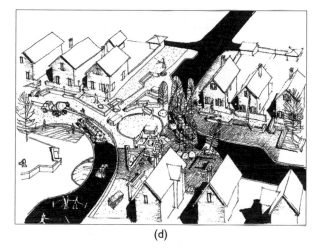

(d)

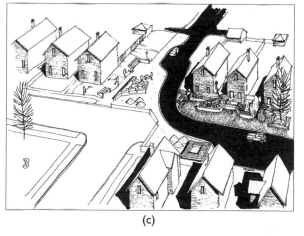

(c)

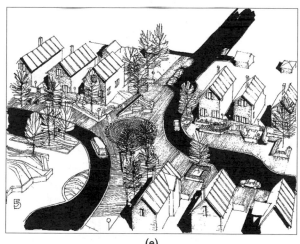

(e)

presently appeared (Fig. 9.4) and what it could look like if plans were carried out. For instance, streets narrowed at intervals can leave parking bays for a commercial area with pleasant stopping places for pedestrians and a system of walking paths (Fig. 9.5). Possible locally accessible vacant lands and street amenities (Fig. 9.6) were shown connected to existing public parks and open spaces (Fig. 9.7). The use of presently vacant lots for urban gardening and vacant houses for auxiliary indoor uses such as greenhouses or indoor plant-starting and storage facilities was explored. Both monetary savings and high-quality food could result, as well as a visual amenity (Fig. 9.8).

Figure 9.4 The EAC 360°
theater utilized to show
neighborhood options.

Figure 9.5 (a) Extrapolating
development possibilities
into the future; the redevelopment of an existing commercial area is shown.

(b) Plan of parking bays and
street amenities.

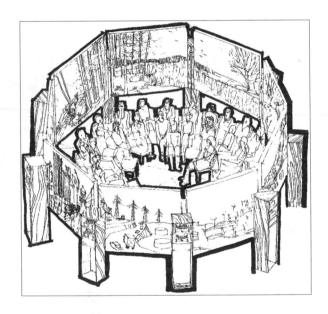

providing fuel for heating. At the time, meeting
basic needs took precedence over developing the
proposed park, and the proposal remains unim-
plemented today. Should a national service or
environmental CCC program be initiated in the
future, combined with a training program for
youth, the youth of the inner city could yet play
a major role not only in rehabilitating their home
corridors but also gain experience and new trade
skills to assist in other similar projects. The concept is valid but awaits the recognition of new
endeavors and the availability of funds to solve
inner-city problems.

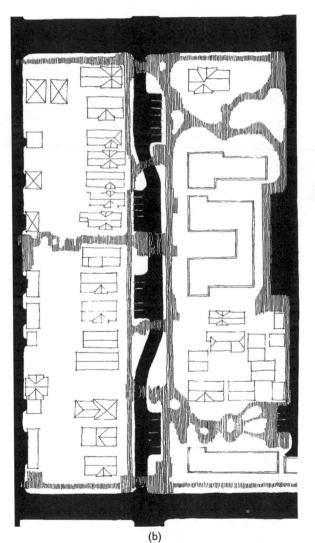

The residents were shown the Harambe neighborhood in different versions to provide a forum
for their response to our ideas.

The Harambe residents expressed interest in
developing the suggestions and would have liked
the proposed park and open space system to be
developed. Declaring these public corridors a
state park might have been a way to secure part
of the funds. In addition, block grant programs
were available at the time, but instead these funds
were required for weather-proofing homes and

(a)

(b)

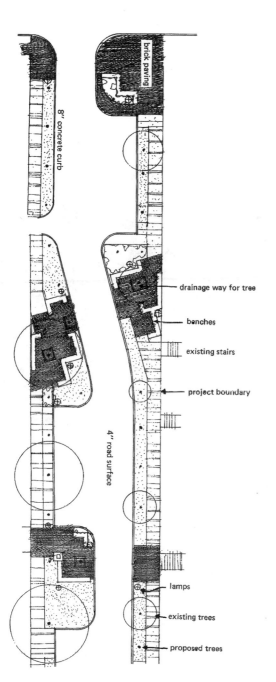

(c)

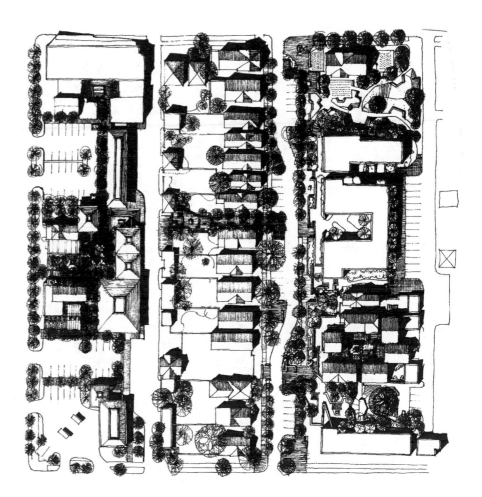

Figure 9.5 (continued)
(c) Walking paths and motor
vehicle accommodations.

Figure 9.6 The redesigned
neighborhood area.

Figure 9.7 Near-north-side
Milwaukee parks and open
space showing proposed
connected system

Figure 9.8 Urban gardening:
mapping of empty lots
shows ample area for growing food, and possibly a market area for produce.

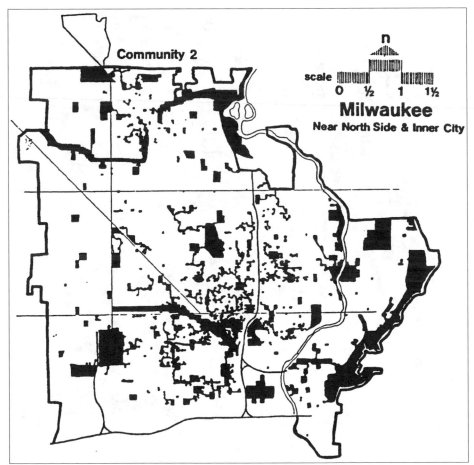

RURAL TOWNSHIP PLANNING (1979)

The unincorporated areas of Wisconsin (where population density is the least) remain the source of many of the state's natural resource problems and conflicts, primarily because they contain the largest percentage of land area. Dane County, for example, is one of the most urbanized counties in the state, yet 73 percent of its 786,676 acres were in agricultural use in 1990. The annual rate of new home construction is 1000 new homes, many of which encroach on rural farmland, resulting in significant land-use conflicts.

In Wisconsin, incorporated areas are governed by counties and county subunits called towns, which have jurisdiction over townships of 36 square miles each. Wisconsin's 1270 towns represent 69 percent of the 1841 municipal units in the state.

Although most towns do not have community institutions such as their own schools, churches, and newspapers, a legal entity and sense of community do exist which provide an important element in the development of natural resource identification, planning, and implementation programs. There was a significant need to develop the skills of town officials and citizens to ensure that these programs were devised within local planning concepts to determine where to avoid building and where building would be acceptable.

TOWN OF DUNN LAND-USE PLAN

For instance, in the town of Dunn (Fig. 9.9) in southern Dane County the EAC inventory and design process was applied to provide town officials and citizens with information and design concepts to deal with local planning issues. An inventory of all land platted for future development showed no need for further increasing the number of buildable lots, so the town board adopted a plan which directed that no more platting be permitted until all approved plats had been developed. This proved to be one of the most successful efforts to control sprawling development in Dane County. The town of Dunn received a national award, the *Renew America National Environmental Award,* presented in Washington, D.C. in January 1995, for a land-use plan preserving a wide variety of natural resources and maintaining farming. The plan, put in place in 1979, has accommodated a growth of 13 percent in population over the past 10 years in areas designated as suitable for development with strict controls on subdivision and lot sizes. The numerous colorful Environmental Awareness Center resource value maps used in formation of the plan have been displayed on the walls of the Dunn Town Hall (Fig. 9.10), easily accessible to the public and town board for reference in regard to planning questions.

THE OPEN SPACE PRESERVATION HANDBOOK (1979)

The award to the town of Dunn was the result of a study by the town which began with research on the land and water configurations that make up the natural heritage of the area. Open space resources and their preservation techniques were analyzed to serve the needs of the town. The geological regions within the township—the glacial moraine area in the southern part and the Yahara River Valley basin in the northern two-thirds—were evaluated. Woodlands, lakes, streams, wetlands, and underground water pat-

Figure 9.9 Dunn Township
in the County of Dane

terns were discussed as well as wildlife, fisheries, and historical resources in the area (Fig. 9.11). The resulting information was published in *The Open Space Preservation Handbook,* which provides a practical experience for other communities interested in preserving their open space resources. Composed by W. Thomas Lamm of the EAC, the 36-page *Handbook* was designed "for people who intend to play a part in preserving those things they value about their town, ranging from good quality farmland to scenic views and vistas." It concentrated on the important first step in preserving those resources, how to prepare a town plan to guide change in the community, and it focuses on helping towns develop programs to preserve their unique local resources. It takes a step-by-step approach to the town planning process, describing initial organization and enumerating the steps in a resource analysis and long-range plan drafting.

MADISON, WISCONSIN'S CAPITOL

Madison, the second largest city (Fig. 9.12) in the state, is also located in Dane County and on the

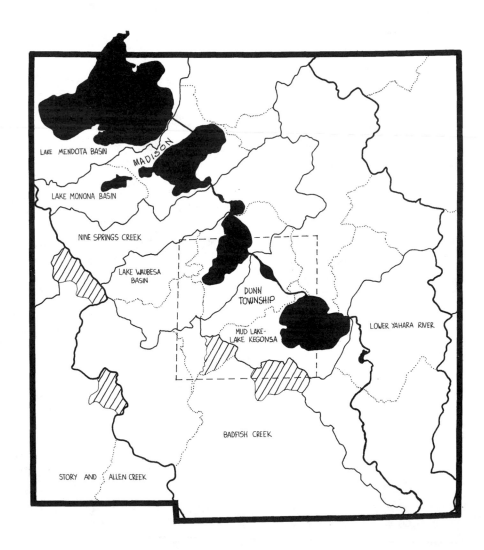

Figure 9.10 Dunn Township resource inventory plates displayed in Dunn town hall as a basis for growth strategy planning

STUDY AREA ANALYSIS

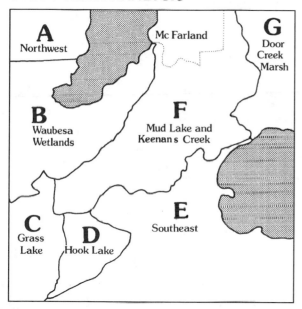

A — Northwest

G — Door Creek Marsh

McFarland

B — Waubesa Wetlands

F — Mud Lake and Keenan's Creek

C — Grass Lake

D — Hook Lake

E — Southeast

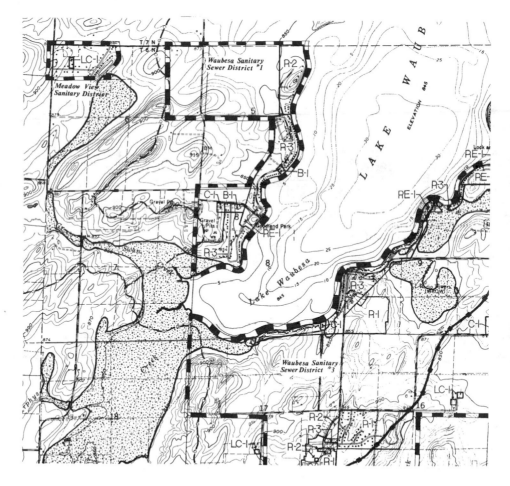

Zoning, Flood Plains, & Sanitary Sewer Districts

R-3 — ZONING Boundaries

100 YEAR FLOOD PLAINS

SANITARY SEWER DISTRICT Boundaries

Figure 9.10 *(continued)*
Dunn Township

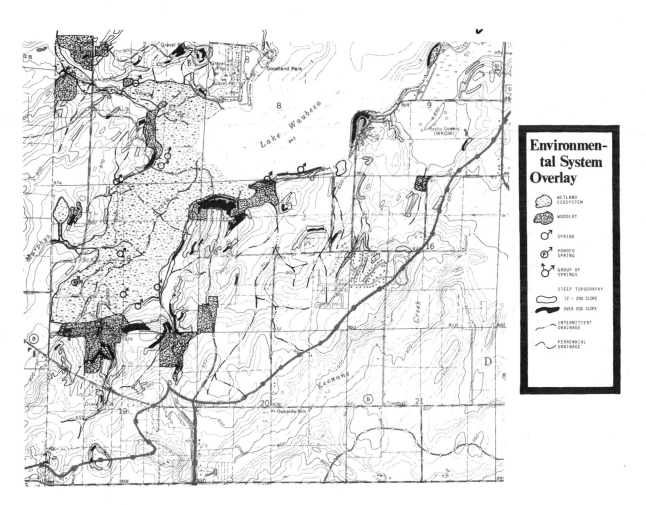

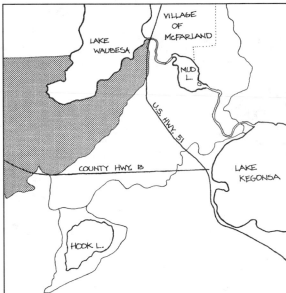

B. WAUBESA WETLANDS

Figure 9.10 *(continued)*
Dunn Township

Figure 9.11 Even when protected from direct alter-
ation, wetland quality can be
destroyed by unwise land
use in upland areas

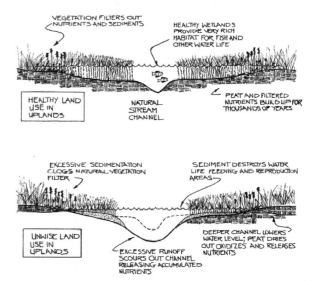

Even when protected from direct alteration wetland quality can be destroyed by unwise landuse in upland areas

Wisconsin Idea Guideway. Since 1960, Madison has increased in population from 126,058 to 170,616 in 1990, an increase of 26 percent. Dane County has increased in population from 222,095 to 367,085, or 65.28 percent, during that time. During this time a national trend toward suburbanization and subsequent thinning of the urban density and solidification of suburbs into urbanized areas has occurred, with the consequence that traffic, parking, development pressures, property taxes, and environmental degradation are all current issues here. Dane County and Madison have always been considered good places to live, but the present trend of growth has eroded that sense of self-contained well-being (Fig. 9.13). The area's lakes now require remediation of *point-source* and *non-point-source pollution*. Air quality has deteriorated. Many historic and beautiful structures remain despite losses to parking lots and aesthetically less distinguished structures. Adoption by the city and county of parks and open space plans commensurate with population growth has occurred, and acquisition and development are being funded. All of the necessary democratic institutions are alive and well and the opportunity is here and now to do battle against the incursions of traffic congestion, architectural uglification,

environmental pollution, social problems, neglect of education, and the rest of the panoply of modern urban dragons.

The key to protecting and enhancing urban patterns that enhance the quality of life and minimize environmental degradation is to recognize desirable and undesirable features so as to integrate the natural and cultural resources in the urban fabric to provide for outstanding quality of life, sense of place, diversity, and a range of options from which to choose one's own personal preferences.

Shortly after I joined the University of Wisconsin–Madison's faculty in environmental design, I taught a course in environmental aesthetics in the Urban and Regional Planning Department. I used Madison as a prototype to explore with my students those aesthetic features that made Madison a particularly attractive place and those which were objectionable.

First, I asked the class to identify worthy physical features in the urban fabric. This inventory included attractive blocks with street trees, historical buildings, topographic overlooks, monuments, and statues: the urban landscape features that create sense of place and therefore contribute to quality of life. I then challenged them

to link the features they identified into a walking tour (Fig. 9.14) to demonstrate the best that the city had to offer. This exercise was followed with a parallel assignment to identify the undesirable features and link these into a similar walking tour demonstrating the features in the city that diminished the quality of life, sense of place, diversity, and a wide range of options from which to choose in all aspects of life.

We were excited to find that the resulting walking tour routes provided a set of criteria to use in comparing desirable and undesirable features in the urban fabric. The walking tours developed our discriminatory powers and gave us a basis on which to make informed decisions about options for the city's future: a street lined with telephone poles, wirescapes, and billboards or a street enclosed with green, shade-giving, carbon monoxide–absorbing trees. Streets can reflect the unique character of the land uses through which they pass such as residential, commercial, institutional, or streets that reflect a hodge-podge of uses with no definite orientation. Streets can present enclosing walls that embody and reflect the colors, textures, and patterns of the local region or present a maze of metal, glass, and imitations of various styles in

Figure 9.12 Madison, capitol
city of Wisconsin

Figure 9.13 During 30 years
of watching Madison's urban
fabric change, there has
been a gradual loss of features in the city that make it
a unique and pleasant place
to live. A concerted effort
is required to preserve and
enhance its sense of place.

materials of no particular distinguishing character. A street can be wide, monotonous, and lacking in vistas, or it can present a sequence of
spatial and visual delight. In the process of evaluation one must become aware of the percentage
of townscape and cityscape that is devoted to
streets, highways, expressways, alleys, and parking
lots. Accept the realization that better ways of
moving people have been and will be devised,
and the benefits of streets without undue noise

Figure 9.14 Linking urban resources: Walking tours that link valuable natural and cultural resources in the urban fabric are a powerful tool that use the urban landscape as a teaching laboratory to promote preservation. This tour links buildings in the historic district of Madison.

Figure 9.15 This series of linked open spaces, parks, wetlands, urban corridors, institutions, and other natural and cultural resources constitutes the Nine Springs E-Way, a real-world laboratory for studying the regional design process.

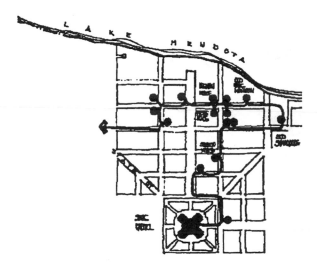

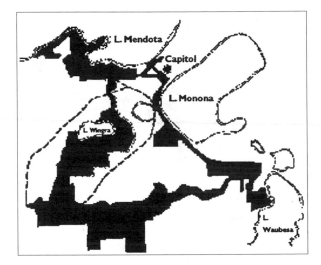

and exhaust can be imagined. We discovered how powerful a tool walking route corridors can be for displaying options among architectural styles, urban amenities and styles, and the multitude of activities in cities: the freedom of choice that is the basic freedom of a healthy democracy.

NINE-SPRINGS E-WAY (FIG. 9.15)

Expansion of the identification of urban corridors such as the ones that these students had desig-nated to a larger scale, to link the urban core to the neighborhood, to suburban sprawl, to farmlands, and to recreational and semiwilderness areas (Fig. 9.16), led to proposing a 21-mile E-Way for the capitol city of Madison and Dane County. It was the result of an Environmental Awareness Center design project funded by the National Endowment for the Arts in 1969. The E-Way was designed to show how a community's existing natural and cultural resources could be identified and accentuated to elevate environmental, ecological, and aesthetic planning decisions to a higher priority within the community development decision-making process and to provide a permanent aesthetic and recreationally enjoyable corridor system for the use of residents. The E-Way was therefore proposed as a community-wide system that would link many of Madison's natural and cultural features, providing the city with an environmental awareness way for the city, county, and state. The term *E-Way* was chosen as a symbol for an educational, ecological, esthetic, exercise, and environmental system.

The E-Way brings many environmental aspects of the community clearly into focus by unifying the city's prominent educational, ecological, and environmental characteristics. The basic framework for the system consists of existing public roads, streets, walkways, and open space systems. The E-Way connects these corridors with open space in a loop system through urban and urbanizing areas including diverse land uses. It includes many of Madison's most prominent and aesthetically pleasing environmental landmarks, including the state capitol building, the University of Wisconsin, the State Historical Society Museum, the Elvehjem Art Center, the Dane County Zoo, and the University of Wisconsin Arboretum. Additional existing features include many historical monuments,

Figure 9.16 (a) The Dane County Nine-Springs E-Way interpretation nodes: (b) Linking these diverse attractions both contrasts and harmonizes naturally and culturally defined three-dimensional space. More exposure to natural surroundings can inspire solutions for human habitation that have minimal impact on our life-support systems.

beautiful old homes, and three of the city's five lakes (Fig. 9.17), as well as stretches of wetlands and areas of rural beauty. The landscape in this area has been used and enjoyed by people for thousands of years and includes relicts of Native American society and culture. Much of our remaining native landscape lies in the E-Way corridor.

The 22 interpretation nodes in the E-Way link the downtown facilities with important open spaces by way of bicycle and pedestrian trails to the southern fringe of the city. The particular open spaces were chosen because they formed a linear system for public enjoyment. They, too, are capable of being enhanced in value to users through demonstration of their history, environmental function, and relationships to each other or through addition of related public educational facilities.

One of the major tasks in implementing the E-Way loop was to secure privately owned properties that would complete the chain of existing open space. Most of the Nine-Springs corridor properties have since been purchased using federal, state of Wisconsin, and local public and private funds. It has been brought about by continued effort on the part of all levels of gov-

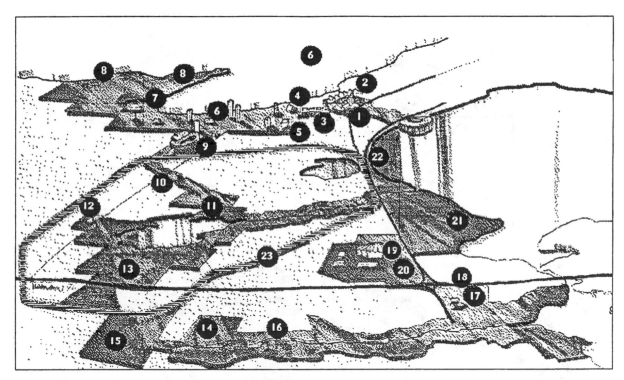

1. State Capitol and Historical Society Museum
2. Historical Homes
3. State Street and Civic Center
4. State Historical Society Library
5. Elvehjem Art Center
6. University of Wisconsin & Lake Mendota
7. UW Marsh
8. Picnic Point Indian Mound
9. Camp Randall Stadium
10. Oakland-Campbell Sts.
11. Henry Vilas Zoo
12. Day Care Center
13. Arboretum
14. Fish Hatchery
15. Nine Springs Creek
16. McCoy Farm
17. Sewage Treatment Plant
18. Marsh Protection
19. Dane County Fairground
20. Regional Discovery Center
21. Turville Point
22. Monona Causeway
23. Mini-Mass Transit Right of Way Proposed

Figure 9.17 E-Way interpretative nodes: (a) The University Arboretum, (b)Elvehjem Art Museum, (c) Dane County Exposition Center, (d) shoreline design concept for access to views of the lake and distant state capitol.

Arboretum

(a)

Elvehjem Art Museum

(b)

Dane Country Exposition Center

(c)

Campus Shoreline Design

(d)

ernment with the help of many private individuals and organizations.

The E-Way has proven to be an effective tool to promote local awareness of and knowledge about Madison's and Dane County's natural and cultural resources. Its trail provides a mechanism for people to see and enjoy the vegetation, birds and animals, topography, and natural attributes of our landscape in all seasons of the year. It thus informs the public consciousness concerning how and where development should take place in the future in the county, the region, and municipalities and how our total landscape can look and function best.

The student study of Madison demonstrated ways in which human-scale spaces in Madison's urban fabric could be revitalized. The city right-of-way of State Street, which connects the state capitol and the university, a busy shopping street, was the ideal site for a pedestrian way, as an adjunct to the E-Way (Fig. 9.18). Major efforts on the part of the Madison planning department and its urban designer, John Urich, ensured creation of the pedestrian mall that is in place today. It is thriving commercially and is a distinct asset to the city, the university, and the region. Trees, flowers, banners, pedestrian-scale lighting,

Figure 9.18 The State
Street Mall

benches, summertime outdoor eating, a small park, and the Civic Center are among its pleasures. It is demonstrably successful and is part of the summer farmers' market scene, the annual art fair, and musical and entertainment events. By enhancing the downtown/campus area it contributes to higher livable downtown residential and commercial density.

FRANK LLOYD WRIGHT CONVENTION CENTER (FIG. 9.19)

Where central downtown Madison used to be full of life, there are now a number of empty storefronts around the state capitol square and on the nearby streets. People in outlying areas now frequent the malls to shop at the edge of town, where the highways take them to vast parking lots east or west of downtown Madison and the smaller ones north and south of town, together with many on the major streets threading the fringe areas. The way to reverse this trend is to increase utilization of available lots for development or redevelopment by urban infill techniques. Together with more compactly placed buildings, easy access to the downtown sector

must be provided and there must be major downtown facilities such as a long-debated downtown convention center. It is proposed as a community focus to revitalize central Madison and serve as a regional gathering place. A version of the center designed and redesigned over 50

years ago by Frank Lloyd Wright (Fig. 9.20) has been approved in a citywide referendum. It is to include a rooftop garden overlooking Lake Monona, restaurant facilities, a meeting hall for weddings and parties, and a discovery center displaying the values and visions of the region. It is

Figure 9.19 Monona Terrace is meant to provide a dramatic link between the capitol square and Lake Monona.

Figure 9.20 This view from Lake Monona shows the Frank Lloyd Wright Convention Center as a fitting enhancement to its monumental neighbor, the state capitol

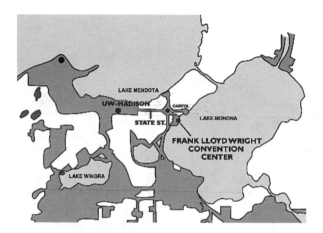

intended to be a host to local, state, and national meetings and conventions as well as local events. Since the center is designed to be built over the rail and roadway corridor along the lake utilizing their air rights, the center can be combined with an effective transportation system so that people will frequent downtown in far greater numbers than at present. A vital active downtown area will slow the dilution of area population and slow the rate at which it scatters over the surrounding landscape by providing a focus and hitherto unavailable urban amenities. The bridging over of the transportation corridor will link the capitol to Lake Monona, creating a satisfying downtown sense of place and at the same time

Illustration by Jim Anderson

illustrate how higher livable densities can be developed utilizing the air rights over any rail corridor.

URBAN CORRIDORS

A key to designing cities that enhance the quality of life requires evaluation of their elements to determine those that make them attractive places and those that detract from their desirability. The urban icons recently designed indicate the range of elements present. (Fig. 9.21) About 90 percent of all rural values (represented by the rural icons) occur within or near water, wetland, or steep topography (i.e., in environmental corridors). When mapped (Fig. 9.22), most of the urban icons appear on the street corridors of cities. By determining which streets have the highest concentration of urban icons, protection and enhancement programs for urban corridors can be chosen for protection, care, and rehabilitation efforts. These corridors offer linkages with key rural corridors in a regionwide network of open space and of ecological and cultural diversity. The Nine-Springs E-Way has demonstrated the value of such a design process that is being applied

elsewhere. In successful projects outside the Wisconsin Idea Guideway, E-Way concepts were applied in Beloit, Wisconsin (1991) and Schenectady, New York (1992). Although Beloit and Schenectady are widely separated geographically, they have similar populations and both cities suffer from recent significant losses to their industrial base. As a result, both cities' economic stability has been badly damaged. The cities have slowly deteriorated and the quality of life has decreased to the point where a need for rehabilitation has been recognized. Beloit and Schenectady both needed rehabilitation policies that would enhance the cities' appearances to attract skilled employees and their families to the area. Both cities needed to identify and utilize funding sources for the work. The concept plan for both cities centered on their respective rivers: the Rock for Beloit and the Mohawk for Schenectady. The rivers provide an urban connection to the rural landscape, so the concept was to design a corridor that would link this element of the rural landscape with significant features in the urban landscape.

After developing the concept plan, more extensive inventories of the features (such as river shorelines, historical homes, civic centers, muse-

ums, churches, outdoor market squares, transportation stations, parks, parkways, college campuses, local schools, and recreational facilities) in the urban landscape mapped as icons were completed and the local people were consulted to determine which features were perceived as being particularly important to the city. Plotting these features on an aerial view map suggested patterns of key elements in the urban fabric and provided a firm basis on which to design specific plans for bold urban corridors.

The detailed plans for both cities linked most of the exciting features of each that could be traversed in a relatively short walk. In Beloit, both shorelines of the Rock River corridor were designed to connect the downtown, the Beloit Corporation, Beloit College, historical buildings, two bridges, rehabilitated structures, and the high school. Beloit (Fig. 9.23), a typical "rust-belt" city, had lost a great deal of its charm along with its tax base as its manufacturing base declined. Despite this decline, it possessed all the necessary elements, including an underappreciated and underutilized riverfront, for a successful revival. Focusing attention on this neglected resource was the key concept in a plan to link natural and urban corridors. Civic leaders were brought together to learn about

Figure 9.21 Urban icons

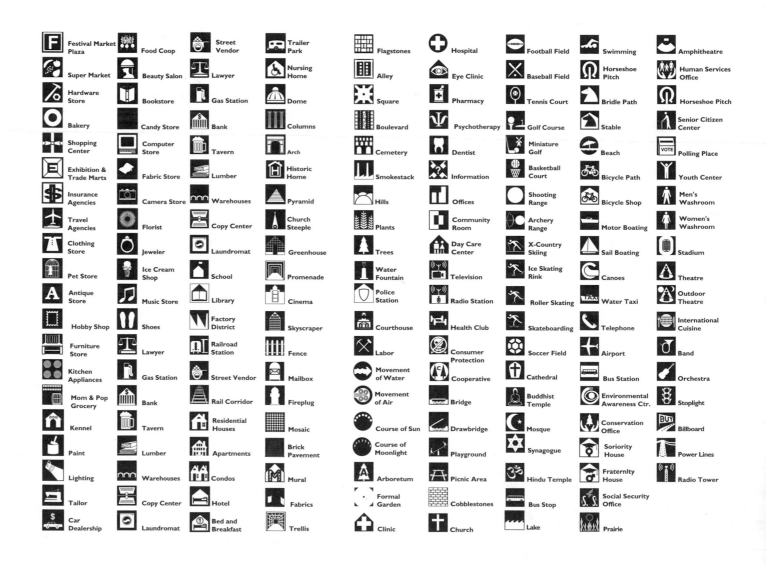

Figure 9.22 Symbols of diversity in the urban landscape. Linking key resources in the rural and urban landscapes first requires identifying the diversity of objects that enhances both landscapes. As in earlier rural corridor studies, symbols representing the milieu of interesting urban features were identified and mapped.

From such inventories the streets with the greatest diversity and interest were thus identified as streets to be preserved and enhanced.

Figure 9.23 (a) Beloit, Wisconsin. (b) The basic plan for Beloit was derived from the Regional Design Process to identify major natural and cultural corridors, then used more detailed information to design urban links to the Rock River natural corridor to be attractive to both residents and tourists.

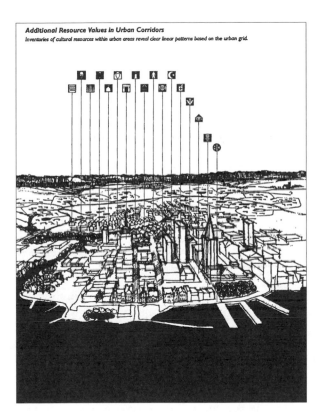

on the river, the transportation junction of the bus system and Amtrak, a proposed civic center connected to the business district by a narrow pedestrian mall, a unique cathedral, Union College, a regional museum displaying values and visions of the region, and a proposed electric museum celebrating Schenectady as the home of Thomas Edison and George Westinghouse (Fig. 9.25).

Linking the main features of the urban fabric serves several important functions. First, these corridors integrate the natural and human-made environments into a single continuum, allowing people to enjoy its diversity without destroying the Regional Design Process and to see how a holistic plan is developed and endorsed by the various sectors of the community before proceeding.

In Schenectady (Fig. 9.24), the proposed urban corridor connected the historical district

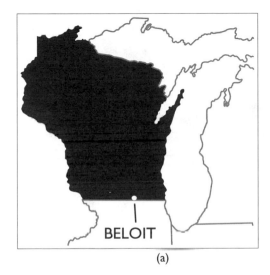

(a)

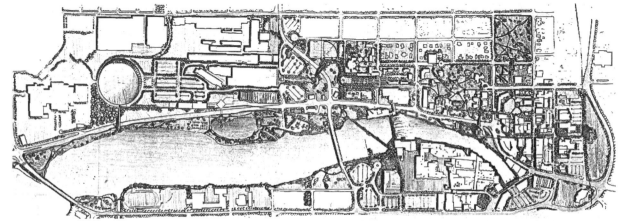

(b)

Figure 9.24 Schenectady,
New York

Figure 9.25 (a) Schenectady,
New York, once a major
port on the route from
New York to Lake Erie and
the original home of General Electric and Westinghouse.

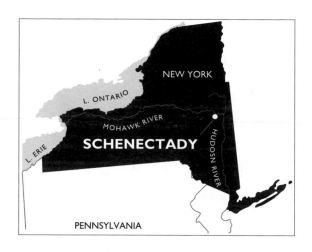

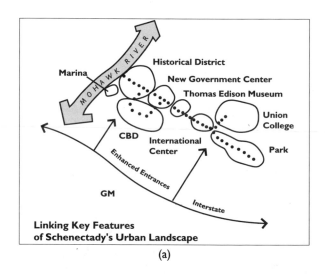

Linking Key Features
of Schenectady's Urban Landscape

(a)

it when the whole is properly designed to make the best use of the desirable features, facilitate transportation, and make things work harmoniously and effectively as a whole. An urban corridor can be used as a form determinant to modify spaces and buildings by means of color, texture, and pattern themes to characterize and distinguish different parts of the city. These urban corridors permit viewing the urban fabric as an integrated and internally consistent urban system rather than an accidental conglomeration of isolated features.

In Schenectady part of the design was a proposal for nighttime awareness of the integrated system by means of a flow of light and color, using the expertise of General Electric (headquartered there) to design a street lighting system that could be used in different ways anywhere in the country. Through distinctive lighting at night and imaginative street tree plantings the corridors by which we see our cities could be identified and enhanced.

Developing urban corridors like the ones in Beloit and Schenectady can be a strong catalyst for stimulating additional rehabilitation investment. In Beloit the urban river corridor has in the last two years[2] stimulated $40 million in investment. The corridors serve as visible working prototypes, and once the possibilities are made apparent, investors are encouraged to expand these available, exciting, and diverse corridors.

THE LAND-USERS' HANDBOOK (1979) (FIG. 9.26)

The *Land-Users' Handbook,* a publication for rural landowners resulted from an Environmental Awareness Center study of the driftless area of Wisconsin through which the Wisconsin Idea Guideway passes. The objective as stated by Environmental Awareness Center staffers

W. Thomas Lamm, Kent Anderson, and consulting planner Brian Vandewalle was to "provide a better fit between what . . . people want from the land and what the land can offer." Behind this objective lies the assumption that along with the rights of property owners to use their land comes the responsibility to use it in a way that shows respect for neighbors, the community, the environment, and future landowners. It urged minimal changing of the landscape to preserve the resources that attracted owners in the first place, planning for energy conservation when building, respecting local values, and being a

Figure 9.25 (*continued*)
(b) Relocation of manufacturing left this once-thriving
city in serious financial trou-
ble. Resource inventory and
design of a creative renewal
plan to enhance the quality
of life includes the waterfront, extensive park and
landmark industrial buildings, and a graceful college
campus together with natural features.

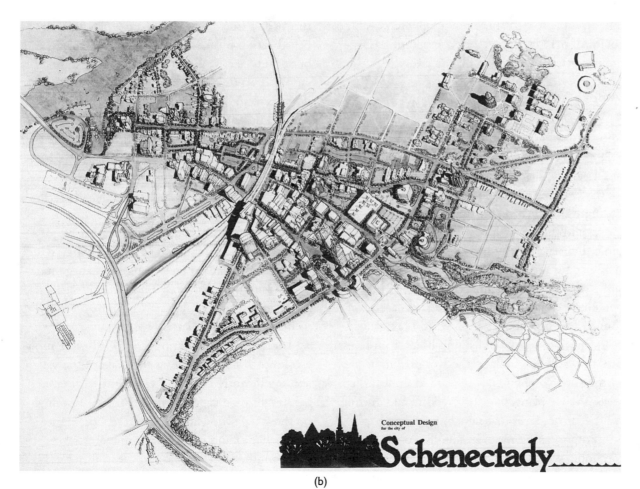

Conceptual Design
for the city of
Schenectady

(b)

member of the community economy by working and spending there.

The *Handbook,*[3] designed to be used by anyone living in the driftless region, raised conflict-
of-interest issues related to agricultural lands,
including loss of topsoil, road and utility expan-
sions, changes in energy use and farming methods, interference with aerial spraying and
irrigation practices by high-tension wires, the
extent of soil conservation practices, changes in
the pattern of ownership and its concomitant uses
of land, the effect of creating small parcels and
access to them, the effect of absentee owners on
farming operations, and the effect of speculative
land purchases on farmland prices and taxes.
Absentee farmland owners often live hundreds of
miles away, lack an understanding of local values,
and have purchased the land to produce the highest return from crops without respect for what
happens to the land and landscape. Recreational
landowners not in permanent residence do not
take part in agriculture and resent agricultural
intrusions such as noise, odors, straying animals,
and incursions by hunters. Often, outside land
buyers pay high prices for farmland, driving up
assessed values and causing increased taxes because
of demands for increased services such as roads,

Figure 9.26 The *Land-Users'*
Handbook

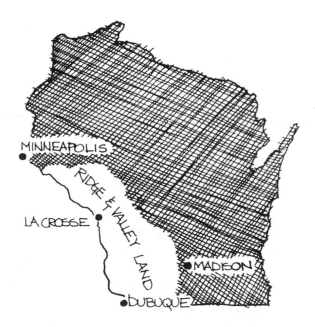

drainage and sewerage, solid waste disposal, and
law enforcement.

Also addressed are maintenance and husband-
ing of class A farmland (Fig. 9.27), assisted by the
use of Soil Conservation advice and plans; and
cost-sharing programs for such measures as ter-
races, grass waterways, and runoff management
for profitable use of farmland, including pasture
renovation and managed livestock grazing rather
than the raising of cash grain crops on thin, steep,

and erodible soils. Where row crops are possible,
rotation, strip cropping, and conservation tillage
are urged as soil, cash, and labor savers.

Where to Build in Rural Areas

The *Handbook* offered guidelines for finding and
using buildable sites in the driftless region (Fig.
9.28). Walking across a typical valley in the driftless area, one descends from the rim and its grand
views. Down the slope of an enclosing valley a
distinguishing feature of the ridges, rock out-
crops, and the steep slopes is stands of white
pine, their evergreen canopy contrasting with
white snow and bare oak trunks in winter and
shiny green leaves in summer. On slopes of 12.5
percent or greater, the pines and rocks are surrounded by mixed deciduous trees. Oak grubs
with multiple trunks and stump holes from forest
fires may still be visible in the woods, and in the
spring showy ephemerals abound in undisturbed
areas. Prairie plants that survived fire and grazing
still occur in places that remain open, perhaps
around protecting rocks and bluffs. At the foot of
the slope, where the descent becomes more
gradual, the valley was once or still is pastured.
Here prairie remnants occur. Where fire and
grazing have been removed as controlling factors,

shrubs and trees are growing up—patches of
blackberries, birch, pine, and oak are typical, and
butternuts occur. Wider valleys with pasture or
cropland on the deeper soils appear lawnlike,
with surrounding walls of wooded slopes and
bluffs. The entire landscape, well worn by water
and wind, is dissected by a dendritic pattern of
spring- and surface-fed streams, creeks, and tributaries of the Wisconsin and Mississippi Rivers.
A few perched wetlands occur on the slopes, and
there are wetlands in flat areas where there is wet
soil near waterways. There is a great variety of
vegetation and habitat and constant change with
the seasons, weather, and changing management
and agricultural practices. There are fish, game,
birds, and all the animals native to the area, as
well as some exotics such as pheasants.

Building on the rim (Fig. 9.29) of these modest slopes visually threatens the scale of the valley
and significantly alters the views and vistas that
are sought by escapees from urbanism. Building
on the steep wooded slopes requires the removal
of vegetation and incurs erosion that removes the
soil from the slopes and dumps it in the waterways below. Waste disposal for a dwelling of any
modern style or permanency involves either a
mound-type septic system or removal of wastes

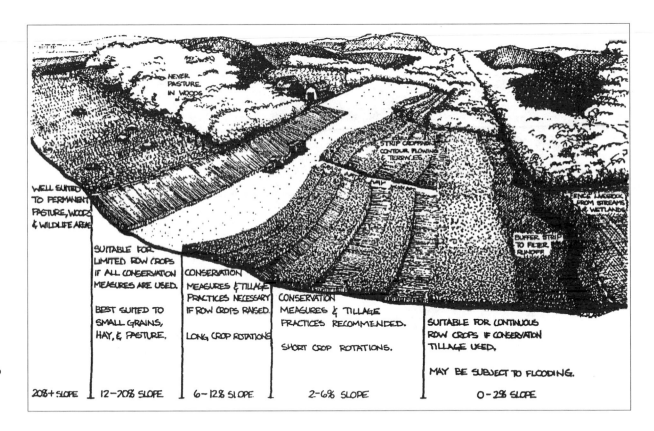

Figure 9.27 In addition to soil type, topography also appropriately influences agricultural practices

by sewers or trucks. It is the gentle slopes of the valley that offer the greatest opportunity for building where there are secondary soils suitable for septic fields, and the necessary area to cluster housing in village-like groups where coloring and style can make them appear appropriate to their surroundings.

In and near towns and villages, development can occur in urban service areas. The best soils can still be reserved for agricultural use, and buffers maintained between the farms and the water/wetland corridor. Pasture and forage for dairying as well as habitat for deer, turkeys, and other wildlife remain with such a scheme.

Steps to Knowing Your Land

The first step in the *Handbook* is for the owner to decide whether the land is to be used in a developed state or to be kept as a natural area. If it is to be developed, are new or existing buildings to be used? Is income to be derived from the land, and if so, how much and by what means? These decisions lead to choice of a suitable site. (Fig. 9.30)

Step 2 is to determine the topographic character of the land, what crops could be grown, how access drives can be aligned, where buildings could be placed, and so on. Indicate on a

copy of the base map (from the U.S. Geologic Survey topographic map) the direction and steepness of slope and drainage ways, which look like small valleys, particularly evident during or after a heavy rain (Fig. 9.31).

Step 3 is locating information about soils from Soil Conservation Service soil surveys. The site is first located on the appropriate map and soil types listed. Suitabilities for these can be found in the soil ratings with the aid of an SCS conservation-

Figure 9.28 Steps to knowing your land: a sample
study site

Figure 9.29 Building on the
rim

Ten Steps to Knowing Your Land [2]

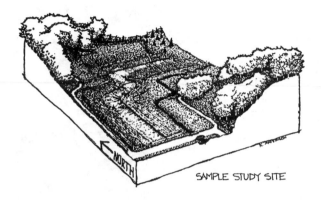

SAMPLE STUDY SITE

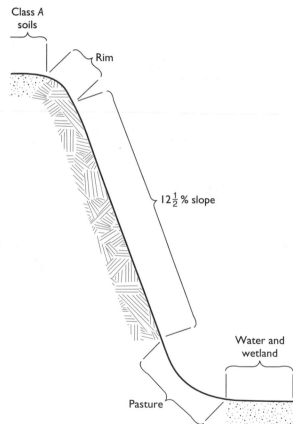

Class A
soils

Rim

12$\frac{1}{2}$ % slope

Water and
wetland

Pasture

ist. For septic system suitability a licensed soil
tester's services are required (Fig. 9.32).

Step 4 is to determine site features such as
existing wells, springs, paths, and roads, and to
note the health of existing fields and wooded
areas. All such features, plus conservation practices
already in place on the land. Field guides, local
university resources, county agents, foresters,
neighbors, and local conservation organizations
can help in the identification of vegetation and
communities as well as wildlife. (Fig. 9.33).

Step 5 concerns energy considerations. Slope
affects energy use as airflow, wind, and exposure
to the sun affect rates of heat exchange. Existing
vegetation and new plantings can be taken
advantage of to block winter winds and channel
summer breezes. Climate varies on a local scale
from hilltops and ridges to valleys. While noting
these effects in different seasons, a compass will
aid in measuring their source and direction
(Fig. 9.34).

Step 6 involves planning for service and utility connections, such as electric power and telephone lines. Planning can avoid interfering with
farming activities and natural views as well as the
neighbors' established way of life. Soils suitable
for septic systems can be located and if a well is

Figure 9.30 Step 1: site map

Figure 9.31 Step 2: topography and drainage

Figure 9.32 Step 3: soils (a) soils map (b) soil ratings chart

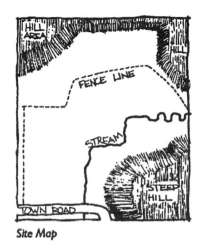

Site Map

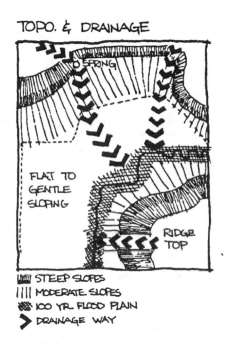

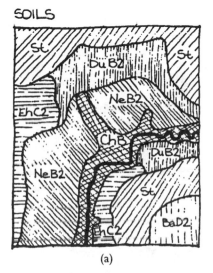

(a)

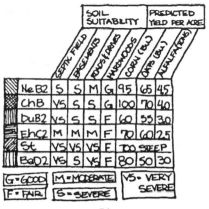

(b)

required, a well driller consulted as to the depth of neighboring wells. Driveways need to be designed for all-weather access: not too steep, too narrow, or with too tight a turning radius. Trash collection and road plowing are the owner's responsibility, as a rule, in rural areas (Fig. 9.35).

Step 7 is to consider how use of the site will affect the neighbors' view, farming activities, and so on (Fig. 9.36).

Step 8 is to assess problems and opportunities via the map: outlying slopes too steep for farming or building, productive soils, water and wetlands, and the best building conditions on the remaining area if building is planned (Fig. 9.37).

The final step is to compare the results of the foregoing analysis steps with the expectations for the site and to assess its suitability; perhaps another site is better suited, or expectations for the site in question may have to be revised (Fig. 9.38).

In addition to guidelines for building, the *Handbook* offers methods for dealing with development on the pastureland above the rich soils and views of the valleys. In general, for local land-

Figure 9.33 Step 4: vegetation and site features

Figure 9.34 Step 5: energy considerations

Figure 9.35 Step 6: services and utilities

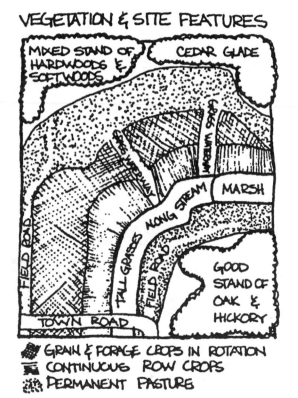

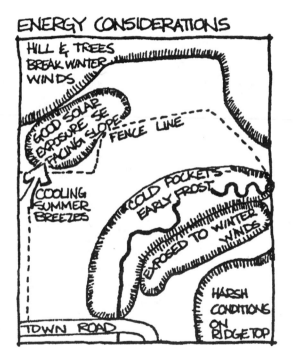

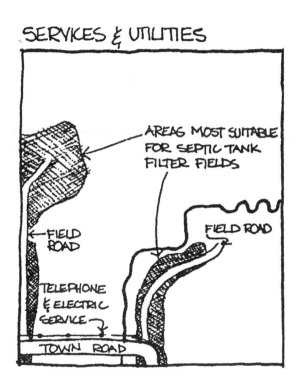

use decisions, complete and detailed inventories of land uses, soils, zoning, floodplain boundaries, transportation, schools, and the natural and cultural resources of the area are the beginning of the process. Whether population is growing or declin-

ing, what impact rural homes and nonfarm uses have on schools, taxes, roads, municipal services, and the rest of the local infrastructure, whether unsewered development is occurring in poorly suited soils, whether inspection of septic systems occurs, whether land with slight limitation for septic systems is also good farmland, whether zon-

ing and land-use regulations are having the desired effect, how local planning relates to surrounding communities, and whether current services are adequate for an expanding population are issues connected with development.

Identification of landfills, truck yards, and other sources of pollution and their relationships

Figure 9.36 Step 7: relationship of site to surrounding
area

Figure 9.37 Step 8: prob-
lems and opportunities map

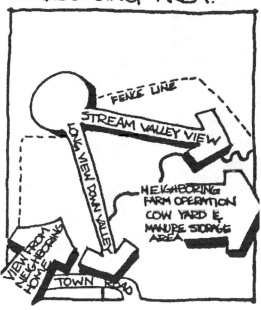

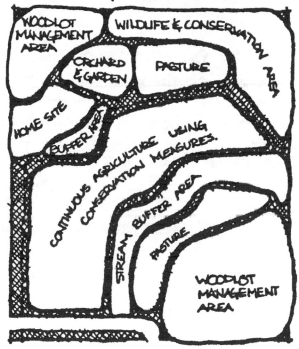

to subsurface aquifers that can be contaminated
by seepage through soils or fractured bedrock can
avoid disastrous results. The same applies to
floodplains, wetlands, streambeds, and seasonal
streams. Floodplains serve as reservoirs, storing
floodwaters at high water rather than sending it
downstream, where it will cause more damage.

Valleys often contain the soils that are most valuable for agriculture. Constructing buildings only
where there is more than 6 feet to the highest
possible groundwater level prevents basement
flooding and drainage problems. New buildings
that harmonize with the scale, color, materials,

and architecture of nearby structures avoid conflicts with the existing character of the environs
and is respectful of neighbors and their community. Hunting can be a source of conflict in rural
areas: Hazards to people and property can be
avoided by posting and requiring permission to
hunt. Hunting can serve to keep animal populations in balance, avoid crop damage, and provide
food and enjoyment for hunters (Fig. 9.39).

Local conditions are also affected by nearby
metropolitan areas: their electrical transmission
lines, roads, airports, railroads, and air- and
waterborne dissolved and particulate matter. The
Handbook summarized the steps and considerations for deciding where to build in rural areas
such as the driftless area.

In an era when individual rights are in many
instances deemed to be all-important, the *Handbook* made clear that property owners have
responsibilities to use land with respect for neighbors, their community, the environment, and the
next generation of owners as well as rights to the
use and enjoyment of their property. Landowners
are acquainted with many ways to meet these
goals. An ethical approach to wise development
requires substantial research, teaching, and university extension activity to bring about sustain-

Figure 9.38 Step 9: comparing expectations to new information

able development and sustainable regional design and plans for land use.

VILLAGE OF SPRING GREEN MASTER PLAN (1980)

The village of Spring Green, located in southern Sauk County, is in the heart of the driftless region. Rich valley soils surround the village, producing abundant feed grain and vegetable crops. The village is framed by the scenic bluffs of the Wisconsin River Valley (Fig. 9.40). The area is also rich in cultural resources. Frank Lloyd Wright's Taliesin (Fig. 9.41), Tower Hill State Park, the House on the Rock, and the American Players Theater make Spring Green a focus of cultural activities in southwestern Wisconsin.

The Spring Green master plan (Fig. 9.42) (prepared at the request of the village board) demonstrates the role that an interdisciplinary team of experts can play in developing a comprehensive design for restoration, enhancement, and continued health of a small rural community.

Our interdisciplinary team, including land-use planners, attorneys, agricultural economists,

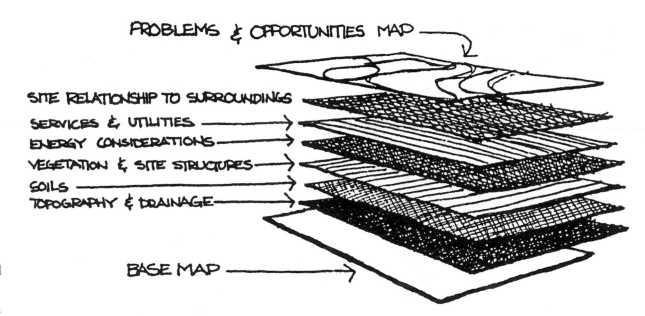

landscape architects, and 13 students, produced a master design and plan that made recommendations for land use, community design, downtown restoration, and subdivision and zoning practices. Of particular importance was the conservation of extraterritorial land, the perimeter of open space surrounding the village. Although business, industrial, and residential uses were present, the extraterritorial area

was rich in natural, cultural, and recreational diversity, primarily agricultural in use. There is a high proportion of "prime" and "good" soils in the area, and they make agriculture a valuable and permanent part of the local economy if properly managed. The comprehensive plan included an extraterritorial land-use plan to preserve prime agricultural land around the community.

Figure 9.39 Potential land-use conflicts

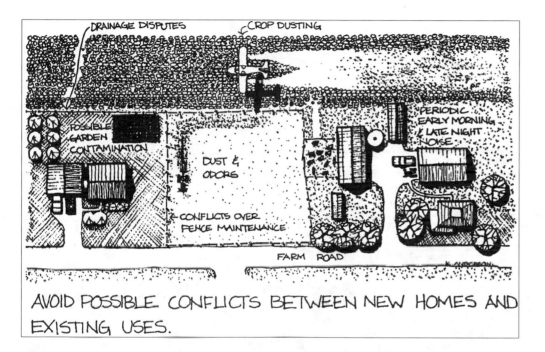

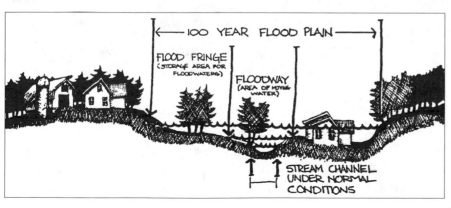

The goals of the extraterritorial land-use plan were to:

- Recognize and respect the natural, environmental, and historical features as irreplaceable resources and assure their value for future generations.
- Preserve the productive farmland in the extraterritorial area for long-term use and maintain agriculture as a major economic activity and way of life.

An evaluation of the local residents' response to the Spring Green master plan was conducted in 1983. The audience involved in the evaluation consisted of the original project participants. Among the many questions asked of the appraisal audience was: "To what extent do you believe the extraterritorial zone around the village was the right decision?" In reply, 74 percent said to a great extent, and 26 percent said to a fair extent. As evidence of this substantial early support the protection of the extraterritorial zone stood until May 1994, when all lots within the city limits had been built upon and a new subdivision between Spring Green and the

Figure 9.40 Topography in the Wyoming Valley south of Spring Green

Figure 9.41 Taliesin ("Shining Brow"), the house designed and built near Spring Green by Frank Lloyd Wright, a master of site design built on the edge of a gentle slope

state highway was approved. Further applications and refinements of the Regional Design Process occurred during studies done in Iowa County immediately to the south of Spring Green.

UPPER IOWA COUNTY STUDIES (1984–1990)

Between 1984 and 1990 two major landowners in this area contracted with the Environmental Awareness Center to analyze their holdings and propose sustainable concepts for guiding the development and management of them in the same context as the Land Users' *Handbook,* one with about 3000 acres in the area of Frank Lloyd

Figure 9.42 Village of Spring
Green master plan

Wright's Taliesin and another with 1500 acres.
Both properties are within a few miles of each
other and both are near the Wisconsin Idea
Guideway.

On the smaller of the two areas, in the Upper
Wyoming Valley (Fig. 9.43) a teaching application of the Regional Design Process by the Environmental Awareness Center at the
undergraduate level was funded jointly by the
University of Wisconsin Center for Biological
Education and the landowner. This substantial
budget allowed 23 advanced undergraduate students with a wide range of backgrounds to take
part. The intent was threefold. The first part was
to complete resource inventories of the valley
including pre- and postsettlement vegetation,
geography, wildlife, hydrogeology, soils, climate,
human settlement, sociological character, economic and political dynamics, aesthetic assessment, and landscape design characteristics. (Fig.
9.44) The second part involved interpreting the
inventories and making management recommendations based on the findings.

Once organized, the student team (Fig. 9.45)
spent much time developing a common vocabulary so that the information and processes of different disciplines would be understood by all

Village of Spring Green
MASTER PLAN

VILLAGE LAND USE PLAN
EXTRATERRITORIAL LAND USE PLAN
COMMUNITY DESIGN

DOWNTOWN REVITALIZATION PROGRAM
SUBDIVISION ORDINANCE
ZONING ORDINANCE

Figure 9.43 Upper
Wyoming Valley project

Figure 9.44 Upper Iowa
County study areas:
Wyoming valley topography
indicated on map

members of the team. They discussed laying out their work as a group, decided individually on the appropriate tools and procedures, and met again to determine the total interdisciplinary approach.

The Upper Wyoming Valley Project allowed students to work independently as representatives of their fields of study, and together to broaden their educational experience to learn to work on a common goal from many different directions. Their studies covered the wetland, forest, regional context, and changes that have occurred since the time of settlement. By working with each other, asking and being asked questions, and making conclusions as to the action that should be taken, they produced a proposal. The final product was a series of display panels to inform the local people of the data, method, and results. The analysis and proposal for restoration of a major wetland on the property has been the first successful proposal to be acted upon by the landowner. With help from the U.S. Fish and Wildlife Service, a portion of the wetland has been restored, and almost immediately, sandhill cranes have returned in the spring of 1994 to their historical wetland habitat. They showed that advanced undergraduates can effectively complete first-approximation studies to identify criti-

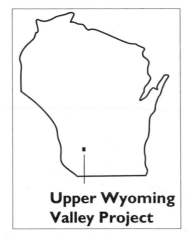

Upper Wyoming Valley Project

cal areas of focus for specialists to do more detailed studies.

The students felt that because as undergraduates they were not yet firmly set within the boundaries of their chosen fields that they were able to work together as an interdisciplinary team. They wrote in their report that this project "has set precedent in broadening undergraduate education and providing greater access to university research through applied extensional activities [and] the common detractors of academic bias, ego, and arrogance were not ingrained among our undergraduate team. These taboos are thought to result from over-specialization and occlusion of

broader, open and more generalized approaches to problem solving. Thus because we have not yet become too specialized as undergraduates, we feel we have a unique advantage over some faculty in the quest for interdisciplinarity."

Figure 9.45 Wyoming Valley
team organizational structure

BOSCOBEL (1992)

Boscobel is a retail and agribusiness center of
2662 serving the farm and rural areas of Crawford, Grant, and Richland counties. Today, it is at
a significant juncture in its development as its
role as a farm service community changes with
the decline of the region's farm economy. In
addition to enhancing its retail business opportunities in the downtown and improving potential
industrial land uses, there are now opportunities
in the regional expansion of tourism. Well situated in the driftless area along the Wisconsin
River, the inherent aesthetic and natural amenities of Boscobel can provide a base on which to
build new facilities and improved services. Farming of the hilltops and narrow valleys is slowly
giving way to recreational use by some of the 17
million people of Circle City.

In 1980, the Environmental Awareness Center was asked by the city of Boscobel to develop
a master plan (Fig. 9.46) reflecting these existing
and potential land uses. To develop the plan,
under the immediate direction of Thomas
Lamm, the EAC assembled a team of land-use
planners, extension agents, economists, social
workers, historians, and designers to work with

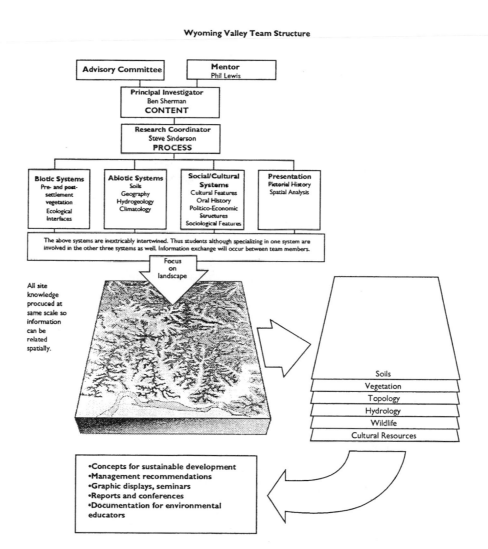

Wyoming Valley Team Structure

Figure 9.46 City of Boscobel master plan

the city over a 10-month period. Students from agricultural economics, landscape architecture, and sociology also participated. The primary purpose of this project was to demonstrate and test a variety of community development, planning, and design principles through the development of a comprehensive plan.

The planning project involved four citizen subcommittees, and a 337-person public opinion survey was conducted. In the final document, a land-use plan (providing for utility, street, park, industrial, and downtown development over a 20-year period) was presented. An intensive survey of historic architecture was conducted by the historian member of the interdisciplinary team.

Fifty-eight buildings were found to be potentially eligible for the National Register of Historic Places, and the master plan made recommendations for the creation of an historic district on Wisconsin Avenue (Fig. 9.47).

This documentation has encouraged the restoration of a number of buildings, including the transformation of a historical school building into an attractive apartment building. The most recent restoration has been the significant work to turn the railroad station (on the Wisconsin Idea Guideway) into an interpretation center for

the city of Boscobel. The EAC plans supported the successful proposal to the State Transportation Department for ISTEA (Intermodal Surface Transportation Act) funds that will allow completion of all restoration work.

KICKAPOO RIVER VALLEY PLANNING (1975) (FIG. 9.48)

Located in the heart of southwestern Wisconsin's driftless area, the valley contains some of the state's most rugged and scenic terrain; with a drainage area of 766 square miles, it is also flood-prone. Bound together by common experiences, including the tragedy of flooding, a regional identity has developed among the residents of the valley. For over a century, to be a "Kickapoogian" has symbolized self-reliance, independence, and resourcefulness.

About 42 percent of the Kickapoo River Valley is forested. (Fig. 9.49) These forestlands are important but often underutilized because landowners have neither the training nor the funding to manage the resource adequately either as a timber crop or for beauty and recreation. They could play an important role in the eco-

City of Boscobel
MASTER PLAN

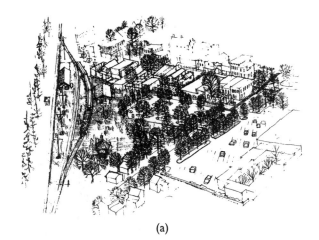

(a)

Figure 9.47 (a) The triangle area holds many opportunities for revitalizing downtown Boscobel; (b) two options for Wisconsin Avenue in Boscobel.

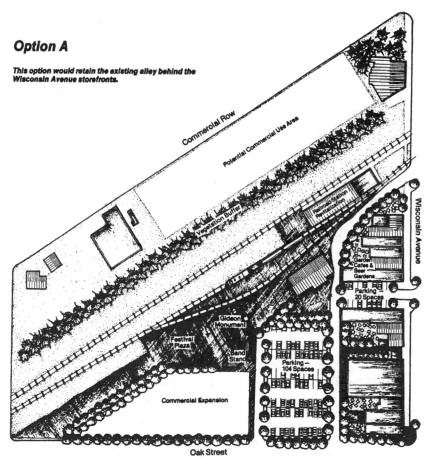

Option A

This option would retain the existing alley behind the Wisconsin Avenue storefronts.

Commercial Row

Potential Commercial Use Area

Vegetation Buffer

Wisconsin Avenue

Garden Cafes & Beer Gardens

Parking — 20 Spaces

Gideon Monument

Festival Plaza

Band Stand

Parking — 104 Spaces

Commercial Expansion

N

Oak Street

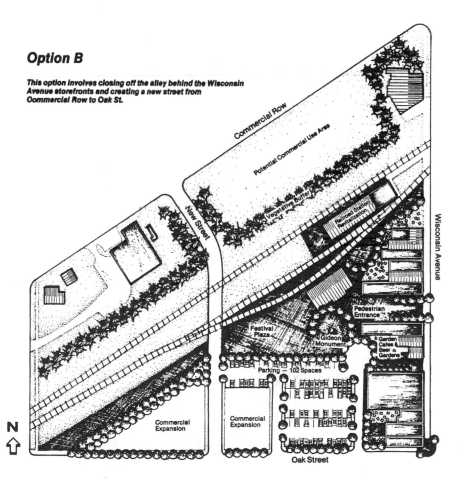

Option B

This option involves closing off the alley behind the Wisconsin Avenue storefronts and creating a new street from Commercial Row to Oak St.

Commercial Row

Potential Commercial Use Area

New Street

Vegetation Buffer

Revitalized Storefronts

Wisconsin Avenue

Pedestrian Entrance

Festival Plaza

Gideon Monument

Garden Cafes & Beer Gardens

Parking — 102 Spaces

Commercial Expansion

Commercial Expansion

N

Oak Street

(b)

Figure 9.47 (*continued*)
(c) design details of traditional commercial buildings.

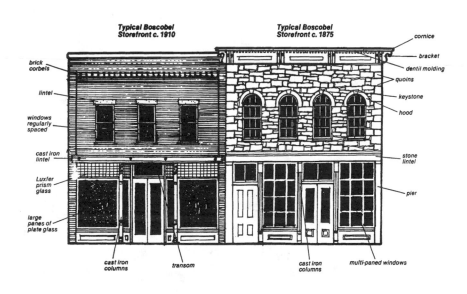

**Design Details of Traditional
Commercial Buildings**

*Typical Boscobel
Storefront c. 1910*

*Typical Boscobel
Storefront c. 1875*

brick
corbels

lintel

windows
regularly
spaced

cast iron
lintel

Luxfer
prism
glass

large
panes of
plate glass

cast iron
columns

transom

cast iron
columns

multi-paned windows

cornice

bracket

dentil molding

quoins

keystone

hood

stone
lintel

pier

(c)

nomic, energy, and environmental future of the valley. The Environmental Awareness Center prepared the *Forest Resources Report* for local property owners to assess forestry and related resource issues in the valley.

Based on a field study conducted in the town of Haney (Fig. 9.50) in Crawford County and augmented by other data, the report[4] collected information and presented perspectives necessary to advance the proper utilization of the valley's resource base. Discussion of forest ecology, forest aesthetics, and forestry-related public programs were included.

Recognizing that recreation and tourism are also an important part of the total valleywide development picture. *The Recreation and Tourism Resources Report* provided a perspective on the potential of tourism near the Kickapoo River, well situated in the heart of Circle City. These early studies by the Environmental Awareness Center were the basis for a current study of the valley by the Cooperative Extension Program of the University of Wisconsin in conjunction with well-informed citizen committees.

Figure 9.48 Kickapoo Valley

Figure 9.49 Issues and opportunities in the Kickapoo Valley

SOLDIERS GROVE (1976)

In 1976 the small village of Soldiers Grove faced a critical problem. Located on the flood-prone Kickapoo River, the community enacted a floodplain zoning ordinance. The ordinance prohibited future development in the floodplain, including the village's commercial center, putting the future of 40 businesses and 22 residences in jeopardy.

The U.S. Army Corps of Engineers had proposed that levees be built to protect Soldiers Grove from the recurring floodwaters. However, other options were discussed within the community, including partial community relocation. The community relocation idea became a graduate design project for students at the Environmental Awareness Center. With a grant from the Mississippi Regional Planning Commission, the EAC studied the feasibility of moving Soldiers Grove out of the way of the Kickapoo River and its floodplain.

Following Regional Design Process procedures, students inventoried and mapped the floodway, valley slopes, vegetation, historical buildings, weather patterns, and exposure to sunlight for possible solar energy capture. In

Wisconsin

Kickapoo River
● Soldiers Grove
● Madison

addition, all streets, businesses, and parklands were identified and mapped. Then it was clear which lands in the floodplain were available for building-relocated facilities. A scale model for the arrangement of buildings considered most attractive and useful was constructed to visualize the new downtown for the prospective owners. The business leaders were able to rearrange construction paper squares representing their buildings. After the squares were pushed around

FORESTED LAND COVER

KICKAPOO RIVER VALLEY

kindergarten fashion and located in resting spots, the result was a first conceptual plan for the new downtown. Some wanted to be located on the main highway, some near the bank or post office, and some near parking areas at a location accessible to delivery trucks. The biases

Figure 9.50 Detailed study
of one township in the
Kickapoo Valley: forest ownership size units

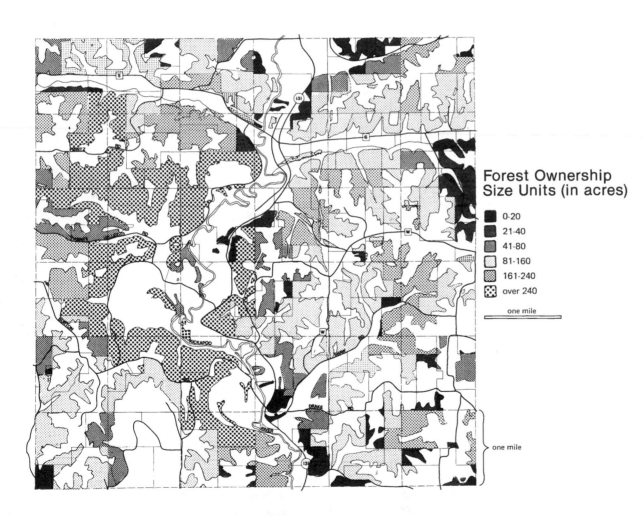

Forest Ownership
Size Units (in acres)

■ 0-20
▨ 21-40
▨ 41-80
□ 81-160
▨ 161-240
▨ over 240

one mile

and needs of business people were discovered
and they learned about taking everyone's needs
into account, and a workable central business
district resulted. The complexity of the jigsaw
puzzle of new development made the participants more inclined to cooperate and compromise during the master design process. The
resulting arrangement was approved by those
moving from the floodplain to higher ground.
Business professor James Graaskamp, home
management professor Keith Moyer, and the
EAC analyzed relocation costs, social problems
related to relocation, and community design
and development opportunities. The study con-
cluded that relocation was a good choice, providing an economic boost for the local
economy and the opportunity to create a park
on the floodplain.

Once informed of practical design options,
the residents of Soldiers Grove made a decision
to relocate utilizing federal funds for 60 percent
of the cost, to remove themselves permanently
from the path of flooding by river waters.[5] The
relocated village of Soldiers Grove is the first
solar village in the United States, with each business deriving at least 50 percent of its energy for
heating from the sun.

Figure 9.51 City of Prairie
du Chien master plan

PRAIRIE DU CHIEN (1981)

Explored by Marquette and Joliet in 1673 and settled in 1813 as Fort Shelby, Prairie du Chien is Wisconsin's second oldest city. In 1981 the Environmental Awareness Center received a request from the mayor of Prairie du Chien for a flower garden plan to welcome visitors as they crossed the new Mississippi River Bridge from the west. In addition to responding to this specific request, the EAC proposed a comprehensive plan (Fig. 9.51) for this historic community in Wisconsin at the juncture of the Wisconsin and Mississippi rivers. The mayor, city council members, and leading citizens were invited to Madison for a meeting. After viewing about 400 running feet of exhibits on regional design prepared by students and staff, an agreement was made for Prairie du Chien and the EAC to make a joint proposal for Federal Title Five Rural Development Grant funds to be matched by an equal sum from Prairie du Chien to finance the study. The money was granted and the EAC staff, professional planners and student employees produced a comprehensive study which included a city land-use plan, design and development proposals, and a St. Feriole Island re-use plan to

project community needs. One important focus was the proposed transformation of St. Feriole Island into a center of cultural and economic variety. Working with the Committee for the Re-Use of St. Feriole Island, a group representing a wide spectrum of citizens, the plan (Fig. 9.52) developed by the Environmental Awareness Center Staff and graduate student Monika Thompson recognized the significance of the island to the history of the state. St. Feriole Island, in the Mississippi River, is adjacent to Prairie du Chien, just north of the historical junction of the Wisconsin and Mississippi rivers.

The Wisconsin and Fox river corridor links Prairie du Chien with Green Bay, Wisconsin's oldest city. It is surprising to many that the midwest city of Green Bay was settled only 13 years after Plymouth Rock.

Prairie du Chien and St. Feriole Island are surrounded by an array of impressive sites where early historical events took place. On the high bluffs of Iowa on the west side of the Mississippi River are the Effigy Mound National Monument and the Pike's Peak (Iowa) State Park. Both possess dramatic views up and down the Mississippi River. The high bluffs to the south of the Wisconsin River have been protected and made accessible as

City of Prairie du Chien
MASTER PLAN

Wyalusing (Wisconsin) State Park. The Villa Louis on St. Feriole Island has been maintained by the Wisconsin State Historical Society. Other historical buildings of interest are scattered throughout Prairie du Chien. Wisconsin's first railroad, the Milwaukee Road, which runs from Milwaukee and Lake Michigan to Prairie du Chien and the Mississippi River, terminates on St. Feriole Island just north of the Villa Louis. This railroad serves as the spine of the Wisconsin Idea Guideway. Clusters of effigy mounds on the island, the Dousman River Boat Hotel, and the train depot are included in the comprehensive design/plan for the area. (Fig. 9.53)

Figure 9.52 St. Feriole
Island re-use plan

St. Feriole Island Re-Use Plan

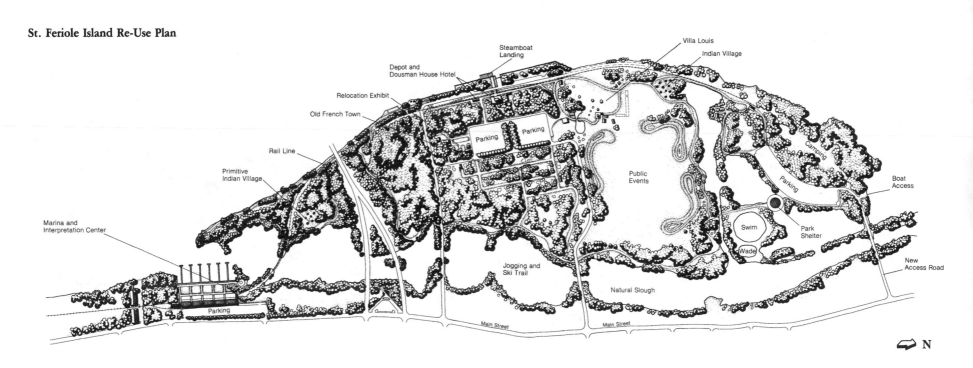

After a typical Regional Design Process inventory of all the assets, the Environmental Awareness staff prepared specific design concepts for the island and Prairie du Chien. More recently I have suggested to Prairie du Chien that the entire nationally significant junction area be considered as a national park. The design report prepared for Prairie du Chien has been instru-mental in obtaining major grants from the Wisconsin Transportation Department's ISTEA funding for design implementation. A local developer has purchased both the Dousman Hotel and the rail depot. Restoration of the hotel began early in 1995. A new, more attractive landing for the river boat *Delta Queen* (Fig. 9.54) and other recreational craft on the island has been funded for rail/riverboat travel connections in the Wisconsin Idea Guideway. Another significant result of the design was the execution of a street tree planting program to enhance the approach to Prairie du Chien from the east.

The design projects along the Wisconsin Idea Guideway have made possible development and refinement of interdisciplinary planning using the

Figure 9.54 Proposed sketch plan for the restoration of the *Delta Queen* landing at the Wisconsin Idea Guideway Rail line terminal. At the right is the historic Dousman Hotel.

Regional Design Process. In the rural regional studies of the eastern rail corridor and the driftless area it was apparent that many outstanding natural and cultural resources are still present and can be protected and enhanced with the necessary public awareness, funding, and professional assistance.

The Madison, Beloit, Schenectady, and Harambe urban projects revealed that like the rural regions, urban corridors of great diversity can be identified and linked with rural regional corridors of considerable diversity offering both urban and rural benefits in an integrated corridor system. Such systems have been shown to offer beneficial quality of life, tourism, and educational potentials.

The Wisconsin Idea Guideway project studies also confirmed the original concept of the Wisconsin Idea, that both the university and state government can work together with local communities in an interdisciplinary way to create progressive ideas. In such studies we must not ignore the long history of such work, but take advantage of the vast base of skill and knowledge of university and government together with the wisdom of local citizens when regional and local design plans are being made.

Figure 9.53 City amenity network.

City Amenity Network

1. Bridge Entrance from Iowa
2. Tourist Information Center
3. Regional Awareness Center and Marina
4. Milwaukee Road Entrance
5. St. Feriole Island
6. Historical Business District
7. Civic District and Courthouse
8. Shopping Center Infill Potential
9. Streets with Historical Houses
10. Medical Museum and Wyalusing Academy
11. Walking Tour
12. Martin Luther Prep School
13. Entrance
14. Marquette Road Enhancement
15. High School and Rehabilitated Flood Basin
16. La Riviere Farm

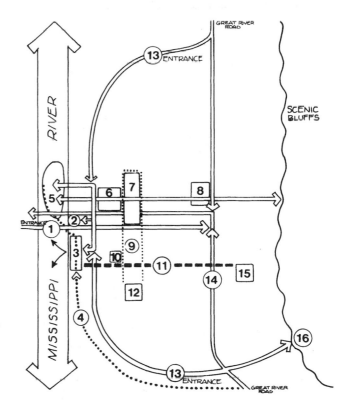

Finally, the Upper Wyoming Valley project demonstrated that interdisciplinary success lies in a team whose members are also generalists, open-minded enough to work with representatives of various disciplines. These conclusions ought to be universal in their application in the same way that successful crop production is achieved by the joining of expertise in soil science, meteorology, agronomy, marketing, and skilful farmers. A successful, sustainable living environment is achievable by a similarly interdisciplinary approach. In Chapter 10 the importance of such interdisciplinary teams in national, regional, and local analysis and design using the Regional Design Process is examined, together with the range of expertise and the facilities required for their operation.

Notes

[1] Ben Niemann, Bruce Murray, and Philip Lewis, who at the time were in the Department of Landscape Architecture; consultant Charles Holzbog, and staff members Tom Lamm, Bob Hartman, and Lester Doré, among others

[2] As reported by Jeffrey Adams of Beloit College.

[3] The publication is the result of a joint effort of the University of Wisconsin Environmental Awareness Center, the Dane County Regional Planning Commission, and the town of Vermont in Dane County. Funds were provided by Title I of the Higher Education Act of 1965 and Title V of the Rural Development Act of 1972.

[4] Funding for Kickapoo Valley studies has been provided by the Ralph Nuzum Fund, held by the University Foundation.

[5] William Becker, *The Making of a Solar Village* and *Come Rain or Come Shine,* Bureau of Water Regulation and Zoning, Wisconsin Department of Natural Resources, P.O. Box 7921, Madison, WI.

CHAPTER 10

THE INTERDISCI-PLINARY REGIONAL DESIGN PROCESS

A review of the evolution of the Regional Design Process shows that the process depends on the incorporation of many fields of knowledge and inquiry in an interdisciplinary process. It is interdisciplinary in its derivation and application. This implies coordination of a wide range of information and insight under overall ethical guidelines, synthesis of the results into a unified analysis, and formation of conclusions in the form of a design, local, regional, or national in scale. It is a holistic approach to design and planning for sustainable land use. Years of experimentation have yielded some guidelines on how to make the interdisciplinary approach effective.

The studies of changing land uses in Circle City and along the Wisconsin Idea Guideway have required the efforts of individuals in various disciplines working with local residents. It has been observed over the course of these studies that university faculty and consultants who have *experience and interest in team effort* offer important contribution to an interdisciplinary planning process.

These efforts have been made with the contributions of staff and students from the university system. A fully funded broadscale effort would require considerably more staff and support in personnel, equipment, and working space.

On the national level the United States concentrates on defense from military and economic threats to our security and well-being, ignoring in large part other threats. Security is largely defined as being assured of safety by the strength of arms, firmness of alliances, and economic health. Other threats to humanity exist in the form of contaminated water and air, ozone-layer destruction, acid rain, changes in weather and perhaps climate, and the destruction of habitat types and biotic diversity within those habitats. Famine, wars of the "conventional" kind, unguided urban sprawl, vast areas of unhealthy living conditions, and ghettos are serious threats to the political stability of an increasing number of nations. The use and misuse of national resources is a source of internal conflict and friction between neighboring states and countries.

In 1989 the U.S. National Security Council formed a committee on oceans, environment, and science that is a recognition among policymakers in Washington and around the world that the traditional definition of national security is incomplete without recognition of environmental and biological factors.

Aspirations for this wisp of an anchor for a broadened policy of national interest to grow into a comprehensive and adequately funded program are slender at the present time of national budget cuts and plans for reduced environmental standards and regulation rollbacks. Yet in view of our true national assets and sense of continuing destiny, it is not a question of whether we can afford such a program but a question of how we can afford not to have it.

We have always been willing to finance measures to counteract military threats and maintain a formidable military force. In 1941 and 1942 we constructed the world's largest office building, the Pentagon, to house the Department of Defense. It encompasses 3,700,000 square feet of usable air-conditioned floor space, parking for 8000 cars, cost $83 million in 1942, and provides for at least 30,000 personnel on government payrolls. At about the same time we built the research and development headquarters for the U.S. atomic energy program at Oak Ridge, Tennessee on a 58,000-acre site behind security fences. The maximum wartime employment here was 82,000 people. In the 1950s the Atomic Energy Commission field office was located here with two huge uranium processing plants and the Oak Ridge National Laboratory, at a cost of many millions of dollars. Among other major

investigatory and technical complexes are the Argonne National Laboratory, Sandia Laboratories, and the skunk works that we are told produced the Stealth bomber, touted as being highly successful in the Gulf War. We have been committed to formally training military officers since the founding of West Point in 1802, and subsequently, the U.S. Naval Academy, the U.S. Coast Guard Academy, the U.S. Merchant Marine Academy, and the Air Force Academy. The buildings, curriculum, and teaching method at West Point were developed under Colonel Sylvanus Thayer (1817–1933), and civil engineers trained as military technicians designed the improvements accompanying America's westward expansion. There have been joint civil/military efforts throughout our history.

Unmeasured sacrifices were made to pose the world's mightiest military force. What are we willing and able to do to build the staff and facilities to sustain a defense and offense against the global deterioration of our life-support system and the conditions of human life?

Neither the national military enterprise and its economic sphere nor regional analysis and design are cottage industries. Both are of national importance. There are many reasons for military

efforts being controlled by government, yet there is much involvement of the private sector and civilian personnel and organizations.

The time is certainly ripe (for reasons of our true economic self-interest and redirection of goals to universal survival) for the establishment of at least one academy for the training of professionals in regional analysis and design for sustainability and regeneration who can deal with reconciling urban expansion with our magnificent landscape resources. Those presently involved in these activities come from various disciplines not centered primarily on this sort of regional design, who are trained by experience and following their interests and intellectual proclivities.

Whether such education is provided with government or private funding and direction or both together is not important to this debate—it is more crucial that such professionals are employed by government and private agencies to do their work. Applying the focus and activities of a curriculum to at least one particular urban constellation and its subsidiary rural regional resources could be funded, at least in part, by government or a federation of environmental organizations. Private money is currently expected to bear a huge burden in accomplishing public purposes without the promise of any immediate return. This is an endeavor that should bear recognizable results in a relatively short time. The evaluation and promulgation of such a program promise to be of great value and should also bring about opportunities for private-sector involvement that would provide new sorts of skills and employment at many levels (processing and presenting information, mapping, all phases of design and development).

This sort of beginning could also involve professional and governmental offices in the design and planning fields. They already do much of the early training of design professionals after they leave school. An academy requires first and foremost a set of teams working together to achieve a holistic goal. A site, specially designed facilities, and appropriate resource materials (a library of books, maps, models, communications equipment, computers, design tools, and so on) are necessary.

INTERDISCIPLINARY TEAMS

Land and People Inventory Teams

The Regional Design Process applied in the classroom or in the field requires interdisciplinary teams of two kinds at the resource inventory stage: a land team and a people team. The first step for both is a literature, mapping, and database search to determine available information and define the best method of using it. Then information that is needed can be defined and the means to provide it devised. Raw data can be made use of in many ways by those with insight into its implications to the questions at hand. From the beginning, guidance is necessary to provide the ethical, moral, and philosophical underpinnings for the options offered by the Regional Design Team. (Fig. 10.1) It should be stated clearly, rather than merely understood, at the outset that the goal of the process is to be beneficial to the long-term health of people and their environment. Our errors to date are due to devotion to the short-term goals of individuals or small groups (usually in a monetary way), lack of acknowledgment at various levels of the private and public sectors of the basic factors involved (clean air, water, food supply) and continued ecological balance of our ecosystem (the earth and its place in the universe), willingness to compromise ("it's just a little more pollution, destruction of productivity, or you-name-it"), inability to allocate our resources to preservation

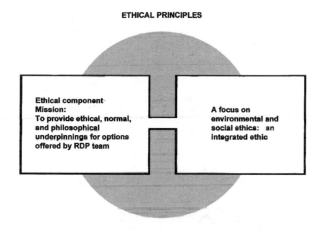

Figure 10.1 The ethical component

ETHICAL PRINCIPLES

Ethical component
Mission:
To provide ethical, normal, and philosophical underpinnings for options offered by RDP team

A focus on environmental and social ethics: an integrated ethic

of life for ourselves and our descendants, and ignorance of the actual results of our planning and design efforts. We must be wise enough and openminded enough to discuss and expose the ethical consequences of our actions. Even when we try our best to do the right thing we make mistakes, so an effort to make changes in our environment beneficial is a great deal more than "political correctness." It is the lifeblood of our continued existence in a state of hopefulness rather than despair. From time to time it may be necessary for corrections to be made by ethical advisors not likely to reap windfall profits of any sort from the Regional Design Process.

Figure 10.2 The land team

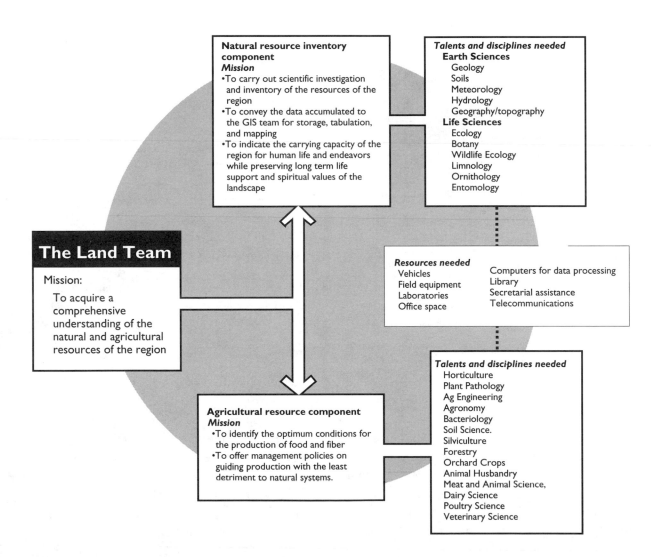

The land team's mission (Fig. 10.2) is to assemble a comprehensive understanding of the landscape resources in the region by inventorying both natural and agricultural resources of the region. Disciplines that should be involved in the natural resource inventory include geology, soils, meteorology, hydrology, geography, ecology, botany, wildlife ecology, limnology, zoology, and entomology. Those required for putting together the agricultural resource inventory include horticulture, plant pathology, agricultural engineering, agronomy, bacteriology, soil science, silviculture, forestry, growing of orchard crops, animal husbandry, meat and animal science, dairy science, poultry science, and veterinary science. These can identify existing data concerning the native biota as well as the area's natural history and domestic plants and animals: their environment, history, economic characteristics, environmental importance, pests, diseases, and other important factors.

The people team's mission (Fig. 10.3) is to acquire a comprehensive understanding of the basic needs and expectations of the people of the region. Like the land team, the people team is divided into two components. The first compo-

Figure 10.3 The people team

nent includes the behavioral sciences, which are concerned with information about human needs. Those with a knowledge of sociology, psychology, physiology, anthropology, family resources, social work, public health, food science, nutrition, ergonomics, economics, and political science can supply this inventory. They have the training necessary to provide information on social structure and needs, human history and development, the dynamics of the marketplace, food supply and demand and the adequacy of various aspects of that system, the political structure of an area, demographic dynamics, and many other things that impinge on the effectiveness of a regional design, its acceptability, and its implementation. The other component of the people team is the resource analysis and maintenance group responsible for inventorying the cultural resources of the region. Disciplines required for this inventory include history, anthropology, folklore, art history, architecture, landscape architecture, archaeology, and library science. Those conversant with these areas can provide information in their fields on the specific area being studied and put it in context both in time and geographically.

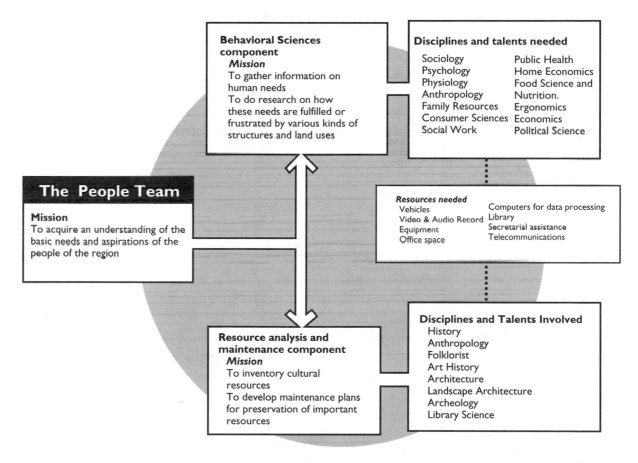

Behavioral Sciences component
Mission
To gather information on human needs
To do research on how these needs are fulfilled or frustrated by various kinds of structures and land uses

Disciplines and talents needed

Sociology	Public Health
Psychology	Home Economics
Physiology	Food Science and
Anthropology	Nutrition.
Family Resources	Ergonomics
Consumer Sciences	Economics
Social Work	Political Science

The People Team

Mission
To acquire an understanding of the basic needs and aspirations of the people of the region

Resources needed

Vehicles	Computers for data processing
Video & Audio Record	Library
Equipment	Secretarial assistance
Office space	Telecommunications

Resource analysis and maintenance component
Mission
To inventory cultural resources
To develop maintenance plans for preservation of important resources

Disciplines and Talents Involved
History
Anthropology
Folklorist
Art History
Architecture
Landscape Architecture
Archeology
Library Science

Figure 10.4 Regional awareness centers have the
potential of portraying all of
the natural and cultural values of a region as well as

options for the future to
guide growth in harmony
with these many life-
enhancing and life-sustaining
resources.

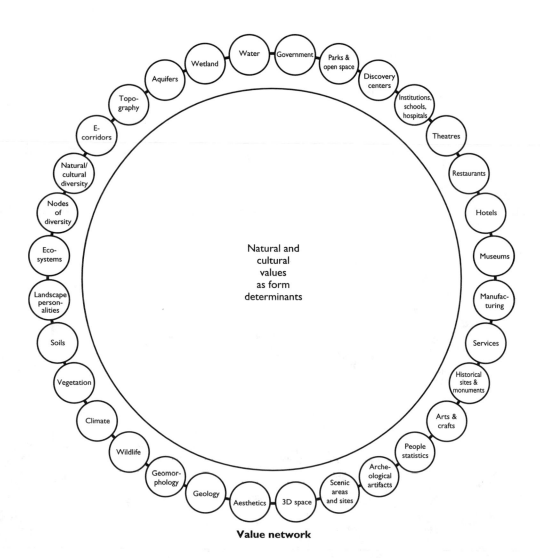

Value network

It is not necessary to have all of these people
available full-time for any particular design problem, but their services or studies should be represented to obtain a true assessment of regional
resources. Clearly, access to other resources by
team members and breadth of experience are
necessary attributes.

In the studies done at the Environmental
Awareness Center at the University of Wisconsin
and under governmental auspices and with private firms, these inventories were performed
with the maximum staff afforded by the budget
at hand and the use of data in the public domain
(maps, surveys such as those of crops, economic
data, climate, biota, vegetation and so on, population, geography, tourism, education, and related
subjects) (Fig. 10.4). Informal and formal estima-
tions of the needs of the design area and population are provided by local officials and agents,
citizen participants, and occasional surveys.
Regional design requires a consistently comprehensive array of analytic and design capabilities in
both teaching and practice.

The inventories of the land and people teams
need to be mapped as a single data set. To do this,
the data should either be plotted on overlay maps

or be entered into a GIS (geographical information system) program. The purpose of mapping resources is to abstract them to reveal patterns. It is important to note that depending on the level of abstraction, different patterns will be apparent. This process involves using a common scale for all information—it is found at varying geographical scales and varying degrees of accuracy. Computer technology provides an ideal tool for adjusting the scale of maps and other data.

The less expensive method is the overlay map. Mylar overlay maps are used to plot each resource; the separate sheets can then be overlaid to show how the different resources relate to each other. Although overlay maps are cheaper to produce, GIS, which is essentially a computer version of the overlay maps, is much more flexible than physical overlay maps for updating and manipulating inventory information. Originally, mapping systems stored inventory information by 1-kilometer-square grid cells. This was useful but restricted analysis to a fairly rough level of specificity. To alleviate this restriction, programmers have since developed a polygon system that allows a resource's exact shape and location to be stored in the computer, making GIS systems a far more powerful inventory tool. Its uses are many and far from fully explored.

After inventory information has been entered into the computer, GIS provides flexibility for manipulating the data and organizing it in an almost endless variety of combinations. Flexibility is a benefit for developing design options, but GIS systems are expensive specialized programs that require training to operate. Both GIS and overlays are valuable tools, but the money and skills that are available for a given project will determine which method is appropriate. Overlays have the additional benefit of being useful in themselves as a tool to communicate the results of the inventory to the clients, usually members of the affected public who are familiar with their surroundings and are able to recognize the relationships being shown.

Analysis Team (Fig. 10.5)

The process used to interpret inventories greatly influences the conclusions drawn from the data collected. The interpretation process most useful for guiding growth to minimize impact on the land involves identifying resource patterns, recognizing what changes have occurred in the past from historical data and maps, and identifying what forces are presently at work making further changes. The rural and urban resource icons used in the inventory process to identify the location of particular items (such as historic buildings, vistas, museums, schools, etc.) on maps, diagrams, schemes, or charts provide a first level of abstraction to help identify connections among system elements. Identifying resource patterns is the key to the next level of abstraction, providing a mechanism to comprehend how individual resources fit into the big picture and operate as components in a larger system. Depending on the inventory's scale and depth, different critical patterns can be identified. The largest of these patterns, constellations, identifies the broad, regional patterns of urbanization. On a regional scale, landscape personality and environmental corridor patterns can be identified. Significant patterns at a more local scale include spatial patterns and nodes of diversity. Once these patterns are identified, they can be used as form determinants to guide growth in order to minimize impact on the land.

Figure 10.5 The analysis
team

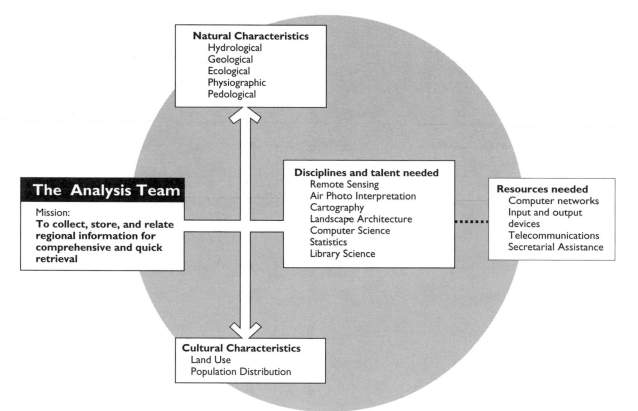

Natural Characteristics
Hydrological
Geological
Ecological
Physiographic
Pedological

The Analysis Team

Mission:
**To collect, store, and relate
regional information for
comprehensive and quick
retrieval**

Disciplines and talent needed
Remote Sensing
Air Photo Interpretation
Cartography
Landscape Architecture
Computer Science
Statistics
Library Science

Resources needed
Computer networks
Input and output
devices
Telecommunications
Secretarial Assistance

Cultural Characteristics
Land Use
Population Distribution

The real significance of using pattern interpretations to analyze inventory data lies in providing a systematic mechanism for establishing priorities for future efforts. They make it possible to quickly identify particularly fragile biomes, niches, and areas most threatened by human impact. Where small damages (e.g., the death of a miner's canary from poisonous gases) and changes of small but measurable extent occur (e.g., small changes in the pH of surface water), we obtain clues about damage and threats of damage to the total ecosystem and ourselves. Once threats are identified through resource pattern interpretation and other site-specific data, they are established as priority areas for detailed inventories, design of options, and education efforts.

As with resource inventories, resource pattern interpretation benefits from the multiple perspectives of an interdisciplinary approach. In the Regional Design Process, comprehensive natural and cultural regional data are collected, stored, and evaluated for quick retrieval and manipulation. Fields of study that should be brought together in this team include remote sensing, air photo interpretation, cartography, landscape architecture, computer science, statistics, and library science. This is the stage at which value judgments about the suitability of land and other resources for the suggested use must be made. Preservation and restoration judgments begin at this point in the process.

THE REGIONAL DESIGN PROCESS

Options for the Future: Making Land-Use and Regional Design Decisions

Much of human history records efforts to discover and establish their relationships to the natural environment. Early on, most human effort has been dedicated to sustaining and protecting human life, either in a struggle with the forces of nature itself or with others over the allocation of the environmental resources. Only later in the development of civilizations are there time and resources for more long-term efforts and the application of more advanced thought and art.

Our present complex society involves decisions that have a complex and interwoven set of consequences.

An acre of land is no longer simply another acre to be drained, stripped of plants and trees, fertilized, plowed, and planted for food crops. We see that the same acre of land might be more effectively utilized as wildlife habitat, a nature preserve, or as a natural or cultivated green corridor to provide relief from the visual cacophony of the urban landscape. Some of these functions can be included with broadened agricultural use by minor modifications. It is this multiplicity of possible uses that is the basis for the options of choice on which democracy depends. Land uses that preclude a wide range of future uses are the least desirable (an extreme example is a toxic waste dump—in England, land considered the least redeemable is classified as derelict land) and need to be restricted to the utmost possible degree. Land with the widest range of potential uses is the remaining remnant acreage of vast undisturbed prairie. Such prairie survives only because it has been protected. The remaining protected tracts of prairie that are accessible by roads and other transportation are known, visited, photographed, studied, managed, and used as seed sources.

Multiple uses of land are prevalent because there truly is no part of the world that is undis-

turbed by human influence. Compatible multiple recreational and commercial uses are common in national forests. In rural agricultural land hedgerows can be managed to foster wildlife as well as protect from wind damage. In urban areas residential and commercial uses are often mixed. Devising further application of multiple use could result in greatly increased use of air rights over transportation corridors for residential, commercial, and industrial uses; and more subterranean facilities can be devised.

Present population and resource consumption pressures complicate determination of appropriate uses for our natural and cultural resources. Decisions based on a very narrow perspective take into account too few critical factors that influence sustainability and future flexibility. Vast and far-reaching decisions are often made with less than a full range of necessary information because hitherto it has been nearly impossible to process, categorize, or utilize such a range of data. Often, greed on the part of a few takes precedence over the long-range interests of all.

The goal of the Regional Design Process is a systematic, inclusive approach to our relationship with the land. The inventory and pattern interpretation part of the process directs efforts and energy toward understanding the landscape continuum. Combining this information with principles of natural and social ethics, regional insight, and resource patterns facilitates designing comprehensive sustainable options for the future.

However, when development and other decisions are made under pressure of budget, time, natural disaster, and so on, good judgment and a firm set of operating principles are called for. Advice by Paul Cawood Hellmund on decision-making and data in the recent book *The Ecology of Greenways* is:

> The ability to make decisions with limited information is vital because in many situations there will be no means of getting other than rudimentary data about a place. Being able to move forward in the design process with less than complete data is a key characteristic. This capability, however, should not be used as an excuse to avoid thorough inventorying when it is possible and needed.[1]

When we have the necessary broadscale warnings, and action is required, delays to collect more data can also be a serious mistake.

Overall appraisal is necessary before detailed inventories are undertaken, and further study is sometimes a substitute for necessary action. When conventional superhighways are proposed and even built in densely populated areas disrupting every urban system, physical and human, detailed inventories would not be necessary to reveal the folly of such construction. A new transportation system more economical of space and operation must be devised for urban centers. In general, we should take advantage of and use as many data and as much expert interpretation and utilization of that data as possible. When limited in scope, the best possible decisions are dictated by tested, well-founded principles.

Design Team (Fig. 10.6)

Integrating knowledge from natural and cultural resource inventories is a task requiring interdisciplinary effort. The form-giving design team is the key to combining resource inventory and pattern information to create aesthetic and functional designs for the future. Design professionals (landscape architects, architects, engineers, industrial designers, and physical planners) are the core

members. They can visualize creative options for the future by combining imagination, intuition, lessons from history, and the ability to manipulate form and function. Another interdisciplinary component of the design team is to express the designers' concepts graphically. Artists and computer-aided-design (CAD) technicians can do this.

Feasibility Team (Fig. 10.7)

The feasibility of a design depends first on the quality of the design. It must be workable, of high quality aesthetically, and satisfy the needs of the client and the public. During the design process, those in charge of the original data search and mapping need to be aware of the design development so that omissions and corrections in basic assumptions can be made (e.g., effects such as the area of a 100-year flood zone need to be corrected to include the effect of the project being designed and other watershed changes, such as further paving and building, changes in vegetational cover such as crop and forest variations, and increases in drainage and canalization). Note can be taken of changes in wetland and other vegetation that signal other environmental

Figure 10.6 The design team

changes. Changes in transportation, such as highway construction and improvement, may have a profound effect on an evolving design. A staff that includes nondesigner members or consultants, such as lawyers, economists, urban and regional planners, and social scientists, will be far superior to one that does not include these considerations. A single project may not constitute full-time employment for many of these professionals whose knowledge and skills may be required, but some way must be found to included their services as needed.

The economic plan for implementing a design plan must make the best possible use of the available funds and the timing for expenditures spelled out. Exploration of all possible funding sources for design functions carried out is helpful, as often some funds can be used as leverage to secure other moneys, as matching grants or loans.

Review of the function of the design by the administering body will show where corrections are necessary and where funds can be most effective. The devil can be in the details. Unless construction and other details are of first quality, even the most visionary and inclusive design is

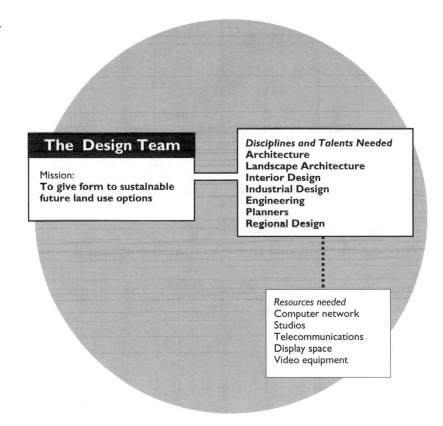

The Design Team

Mission:
To give form to sustainable future land use options

Disciplines and Talents Needed
**Architecture
Landscape Architecture
Interior Design
Industrial Design
Engineering
Planners
Regional Design**

Resources needed
Computer network
Studios
Telecommunications
Display space
Video equipment

Figure 10.7 The feasibility
team

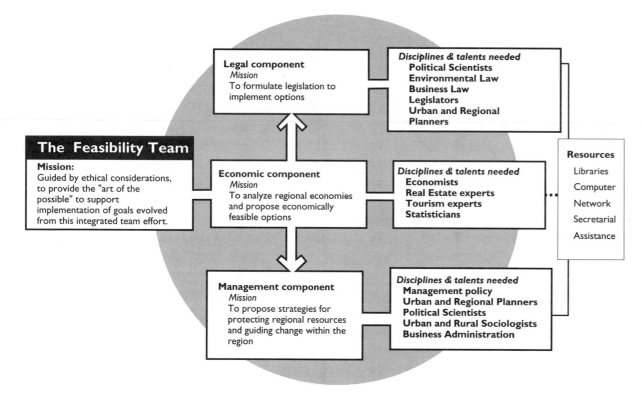

likely to fail. Members taking part in the process must be available for additional consultation in the final stage, and each must be vigilant in reviewing and overseeing the entire composite procedure.

Communication and Education (Fig. 10.8)

Portrayal of environmental options, problems, potentials, and causal relationships using every available means can ensure that they are disseminated and become part of the common stock of environmental planning knowledge. Once a clear image of a particular set of options is established, the way the Futurama exhibit at the 1939 New York World's fair became known, it can be considered in all of its ramifications and seems possible to the viewer. When information to several senses is combined, using sight, sound, motion, and different views and interpretations, a clearer image is established. The more often it is experienced, the more likely it is to be retained. The image becomes part of our common knowledge. The examples discussed in this book have involved small segments of our total U.S. population in planning discrete local projects. Larger regional studies have been undertaken by university and governmental agencies. Such projects have been undertaken as teaching and learning exercises. The Regional Design Process, or something like it, is required to short-circuit the waste and environmental degradation that is presently under way.

Communication is the key to environmental option awareness for planning and design processes, for until the public distinguish between the values of various alternatives, until they can exercise their discriminatory powers, only then will they become a society exercising freedom of true choice and select wiser options through the sifting and winnowing process.

Such communication occurred in the Harambe project (see Chapter 9) when graphic representations of resources and design solutions were presented to residents of the area utilizing 360° projections. It is generally conceded that if environmental quality is to be achieved, public reeducation to new sustainable design options is essential. Public participation in community classes, seminars, and demonstration projects is needed, as is an overview of resource opportunities for planning generalists who oversee the work of specialists. Environmental quality (including the environment of people as part of the environmental system) is the basic long-term

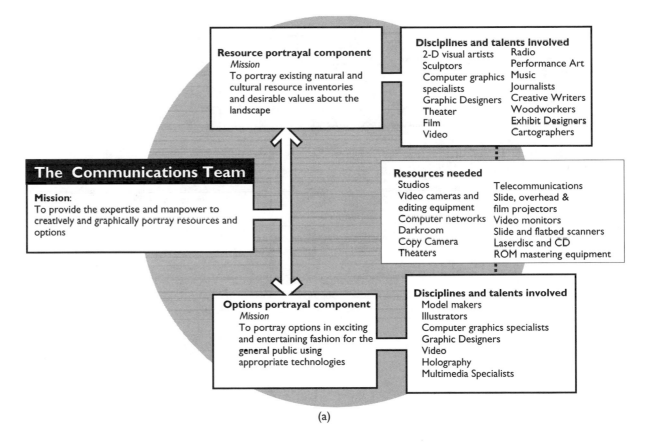

Figure 10.8 (a) The communications team

(a)

Figure 10.8 (*continued*)
(b) the educational team

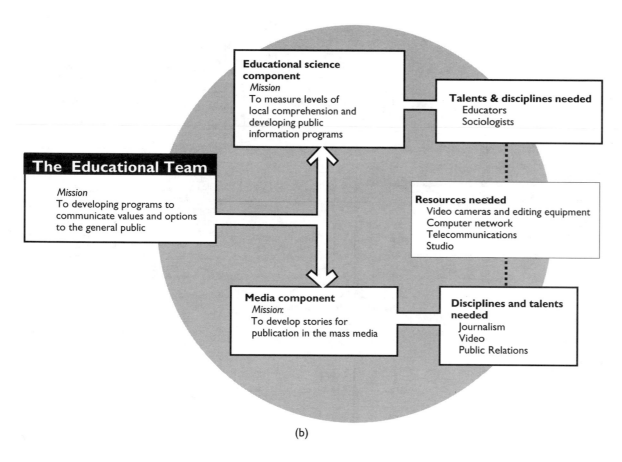

(b)

goal and criterion of regional design; it is not a minor hurdle or passing expedient.

Reassessing values and priorities is a national and international struggle to overcome environmental and social degradation, a task requiring mobilization of every resource. The teaching and communications techniques developed for World War II and other conflicts can be turned to current use to recruit and train environmental soldiers quickly. As military recruits were trained with films, Link trainers, and field laboratories, vivid teaching techniques can be turned to train designers. Air cadet training in World War II introduced many 18-year-old recruits to trainers that simulated flight. On the wall a scoreboard recorded hits scored by simulated weapons. Such tools have never been available for my students in the past 43 years that could show them the immediate results of their design efforts, even though such technology is widely used for amusement purposes. We could simulate the effects of changing transit systems, population redistributions, farmland protection, vegetation changes, weather effects on proposed development, and so on.

Thousands of hands-on training devices have in the past taught how to defeat and kill an enemy while surviving the physical hardships of

Figure 10.9 360-Degree
theater: maps and models

war. In wartime, time, money, creative effort, and the lives of men, women, and children are recklessly consumed.

The addition of 95 million new beings to our fragile earth each year will force us to accept unprecedented diminution of our life-support system if we do not invoke similar retraining efforts to deal with the onslaught of ever-larger coming generations, to show the effect of intensified human use of the earth, and to aid in the design process. Careful, even parsimonious expenditure of resources demands a careful and complete planning effort.

Perhaps even more than other regional design components, communication must be interdisciplinary. It must inform by creatively and graphically portraying a region's natural and cultural resources and options for the future (Fig. 10.9 a, b). The products of model makers, illustrators, computer graphics specialists, graphic designers, videographers, holography experts, creators of virtual reality, and multimedia specialists can all present alternatives in an exciting and entertaining fashion, separately and in various combinations (Fig. 10.10).

The whole panoply of artists (sculptors, computer graphics specialists, graphic designers, the-

ater artists, writers and performers in various media, woodworkers, exhibit designers, and cartographers) can help demonstrate information about natural and cultural resource inventories. Educators and sociologists can develop public information about natural and cultural resource inventories. Educators and sociologists can develop public information programs and collect data and interpret public comprehension of those programs. The communications media (Fig. 10.11) can be utilized to disseminate information in many ways.

An educational philosophy in use at the University of Wisconsin, the Wisconsin Idea, is a conceptual tool. It is strongly supported in the state as well as beyond its boundaries. The Wisconsin Idea centers around university research and the necessity for putting it in the hands of the public by means of an active partnership among the university, government, and the public to disseminate information and receive public reactions.

The success of interdisciplinary projects directed by the Environmental Awareness Center is doubtless due, at least in part, to the long history of interdisciplinary endeavors on the University of Wisconsin campus spawned by the

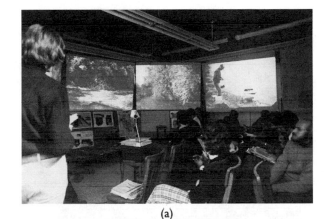

(a)

(b)

Figure 10.10 Environmental Awareness Center presentation at the St. Croix Conference in St. Paul, Minnesota utilized three- dimensional props, music, slides, and the talents of actor/communicator Graham Greene.

Figure 10.11 Computer graphic simulations can use data from two-dimensional maps to create a simulated three-dimensional image.

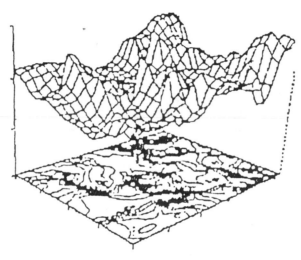

Wisconsin Idea Era, which provided a fertile ground for such an effort. The public participation and governmental involvement components also owe a debt to the Wisconsin Idea philosophy.

It is true that such a cooperative effort is not commonly assembled in normal times. At a critical time ways must be found to meet the needs. Uncommon action is required to meet extraordinary needs such as we presently have. Turmoil and disorder will overcome us other- wise. Change will be wrought somehow; the only question is how that change will be determined. The way of life that we cherished is becoming unsustainable, so by extracting the essentials we must determine how best to use our resources to preserve them. New methods of demonstrated effectiveness soon become ordinary methods.

Individual priorities differ, but our joint freedom, educational opportunities, economic wealth, and the beauty that surrounds us—our mental, spiritual, and physical health—must be put first. By bringing together an interdisciplinary staff to teach, research, and carry out prototype studies and designs, a concerted effort can be made to carry out a comprehensive educational effort. Such a broad-based effort can include research and teaching in other institutions because they will have the expertise and the time to incorporate the results of an even-wider range of thought and practice.

Fundamentals of Interdisciplinary Cooperation

At an interdisciplinary seminar entitled "Man and His Environment" held at the University of Wis-

Figure 10.12 A simple diagram defining the basic components of the Regional Design Process and what task each component is expected to accomplish

consin in the 1960s, obstacles to achieving an unruffled and freely flowing discourse were noted. The following observations are generally applicable to interdisciplinary efforts.

1. Interdisciplinary efforts are hampered when the work of team members has evolved an extensive set of specialized vocabularies, methods, and ideas that they use in debate.
2. It is helpful if participants are proficient in at least two professional areas.
3. Discussions on design for sustainability are found to proceed more effectively when they are focused on a particular area, site, or region. For example, centering our efforts on Iowa County in the driftless region we found common ground in a set of physical realities. Sharing findings based on a geological region facilitated crossing disciplinary borders and modified team conclusions. The way that team members thought changed fundamentally. They began to produce holistic, interdisciplinary syntheses in addition to the conclusions drawn within their respective disciplines.

It is this interchange and development of joint efforts that is of fundamental importance to the Regional Design Process.

Through the years staff and students have graphically portrayed this process in a variety of ways to illustrate its critical components and the sequence of their application in ways that appeal to the intuitive understanding of the viewer (Figs. 10.12, 10.13).

4. No interdisciplinary team can succeed unless interdisciplinary blinders are removed—that is, unless it is recognized that the work of each member is related to the work of the others. Experts must work as generalists as well. This is a view espoused by Buckminster Fuller, who noted that both specialists and generalists can dive deep into a discipline, but the major difference between them is that while the specialist focuses only on in-depth knowledge of a single discipline, the generalist comes up for air and also focuses on how specific knowledge fits into a bigger frame of reference. Since an overall "theory of everything" is still far

Basic Component of Process and Training	
1. Regional Inventories	Acquiring comprehensive understanding of region
2. Computer Capabilities	To store, retrieve and update regional data
3. Design-Engineering	Creating new options for society
4. Arts/Media	Enhancing inventories, values and new visions
5. Simulation Center	Presenting options for public involvement and reaction
6. Administration	Implementing process and new visions

from our reach, even for the physical world, the art of combining insights to form new syntheses is valuable indeed.

5. It was noted that earlier lectures by Walter Gropius stressing that collaborative teams work best when they recognize the value and nature of interdisciplinarity as opposed to single-purpose efforts. He also rightly advocated a reward structure that took in all team members. All the best experts in all the right fields can be brought together as a team, but if they are not adequately funded or open-minded enough about learning from the perspec-

Figure 10.13 Regional Design Process: integration of information gathering, interpretation, design, education, and public interaction. The components in a slightly different form, explaining the role of the Academy for Sustainable Design. The diagram then suggests that E-Way trail systems would connect the Academy to Regional Discovery Centers with their sense-of-place museums, simulation center, and sense-of-place market, where regional values and visions would be displayed for tourism and education. The diagram concludes that an environmental CCC Corps might be located next to the discovery center to provide a workforce of young and old to carry out the physical plans advocated in the center.

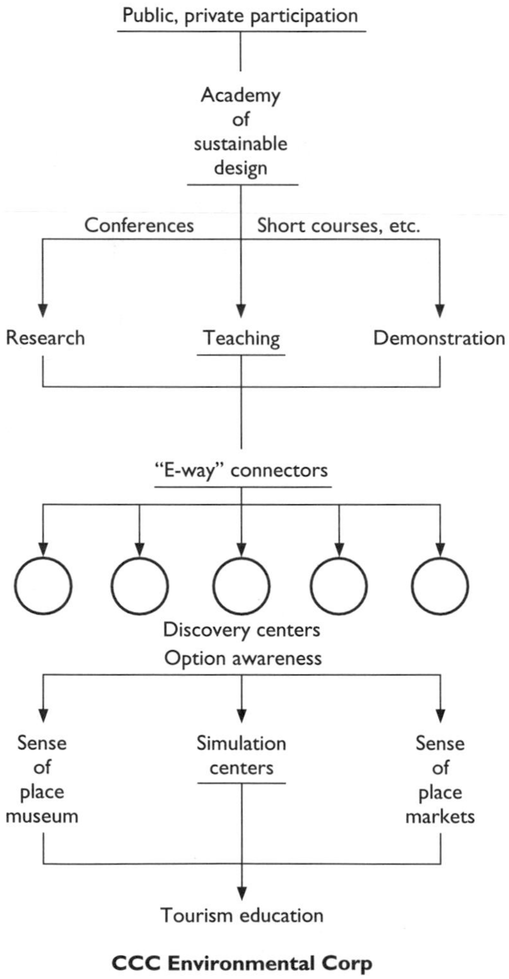

Public, private participation

Academy
of
sustainable
design

Conferences   Short courses, etc.

Research   Teaching   Demonstration

"E-way" connectors

Discovery centers
Option awareness

Sense
of
place
museum   Simulation
centers   Sense
of
place
markets

Tourism education

CCC Environmental Corp

tives of other disciplines, the team will not succeed. Rewards can come in different forms. For instance, during the undergraduate study of the Engle properties in Iowa County, gatherings were held at the homes of different team members and a jointly financed lobster dinner was achieved by one member arranging shipping from Maine to augment the rewards of a modest pay scale.

An historical and successful interdisciplinary endeavor was reported recently by Kermit C. Parsons in the Autumn 1994 *Journal of the American Planning Association* (pp. 462–482). He documents the organization of the Regional Planning Association of America, led by Clarence Stein from 1923 to 1933 with a core of a dozen or so New York intellectuals. They were close friends with shared values and complementary interests which motivated the creative thinking and project development of the group. Stein managed the agenda, and Benton MacKaye developed its first project, the Appalachian Trail. Lewis Mumford, Stein, MacKaye, and Henry Wright conceptualized its "regional city idea." Stein and Wright designed its prototype communities, including Sunnyside Homes and Radburn; Alexander Bing provided the organizational and financial structure for building its experimental communities. The RPAA collaborated for a decade to formulate, build, and write about a vision of future urban communities and regions that continues to infuse Western city and regional planning thought.

Clarence Stein's personal leadership and his skill ensured that the RPAA members' spirits were high by making their gatherings enjoyable social occasions as well as intellectual events. They took meals together at the New York City Club or his apartment, with its accomplished cook and its large living spaces overlooking Central Park. They enjoyed each other's company at the theater and on short working vacations in the New Jersey countryside, where they cooked up new ideas and improved project strategies.

Any Regional Design Process program depends on an interdisciplinary creative intellectual team supported by congenial surroundings, remuneration, and professional recognition of their efforts. Balancing the scientific, artistic, and humanistic perspectives may seem daunting, but the experience of the Environmental Awareness Center suggests that there is no other good option but to persist in the effort. The bright side is that outstanding practitioners in any field are frequently widely read and experienced and open to new ideas. Many already realize the value of pooling efforts to produce a whole that is truly more than the sum of its parts.

A number of opportunities to participate in a variety of interdisciplinary groups and to benefit from the use of this concept by various institutions have come to me. The Regional Design Process has been used in working toward various goals. For example, in the 1970s a large group of staff members at Sandia Laboratories heard me broach the idea of developing a broad effort to mend the earth. The goal proposed was to overcome the threat posed to our survival by environmental degradation and depletion by using the same team approach that was used in developing the atomic bomb. The difference between weapons technology development and environmental problem solving is to reverse the modus operandi, that is, to harness and redirect the efforts from destruction to benefiting human existence.

An eminently successful interdisciplinary effort is documented in the development and application of the Wisconsin Idea, which is strongly backed in Wisconsin and beyond its borders. The Wisconsin Idea is attributed to Senator Robert M. LaFolette, University of Wisconsin President Charles Van Hise, and Charles McCarthy (first Chief, and founder of the Wisconsin Legislative Reference Library; author of the book *The Wisconsin Idea,* published in 1912; and advocate of university extension, adult, and vocational education) at the turn of the century. They argued that universities and government can meet joint needs and still maintain their separate structures. They can collaborate to make informed policy decisions, evaluate policies objectively, and do teaching and research. Urban and rural support of landscape and design studies have borne out the validity of the Wisconsin Idea in those fields.

The Wisconsin Idea concept led to the establishment of the internationally recognized Wisconsin Extension Service and is also credited with fostering progressive legislation, including child labor laws. The Wisconsin Idea philosophy and the interdisciplinary cooperation that it

embodies are components of a process that will guide human growth to minimize human impact on the land.

OVERVIEW CORPORATION

A private interdisciplinary endeavor in which I was involved, known as the Overview Corporation, founded in 1969, was an example of the sort of interdisciplinary effort being discussed. It was to be an international environmental consulting organization. Stewart L. Udall, who served as Secretary of the Interior for the Kennedy and Johnson administrations, founded it with the belief that solving the environmental crisis would require a broad systems approach, including interdisciplinary teams. He chose as his team members people who were on the leading edge of creativity in their respective fields but who also saw themselves as generalists. They were talented, had social concerns, and showed a disposition for pioneering projects and multidisciplinary syntheses.

Central to the Overview group's success was its philosophical dedication to an interdisciplinary approach which first identified the problem and its parameters. Key personnel and appropriate techniques were then identified so that project team members were assigned to solving the specific problem. The final stage included budgeting, scheduling, and execution, all of which were done only after the completion of the first two stages. The method was first to define the scope of the problem under consideration and then allocate budget and staff as appropriately as possible to avoid the pitfall of having priorities be determined by budgetary restraints.

The Overview group's interdisciplinary approach emphasized the public relations and communications skills necessary to obtain participation and support of all affected members of the public. The focus of the group was not to do plans *for* clients. Rather, the clients were part of the interdisciplinary team, so that the group did projects *with* the client. Local talent was always part of the team, so that local insights and conditions would be reflected.

In 1970 and 1971 I had two rewarding experiences with members of this group and have often thought how valuable such a consulting team would be today for advising the highest environmental authorities in the country. The

first encounter with the creative think-tank was in New York City, where key members were brought together in an Overview Seminar to discuss a proposed international airport north of the Everglades in southern Florida. My prior experience with the Everglades proved useful in the discussion of future options, a gratifying example of applying academic training to immediate problems. Analysis led to a recommendation to separate airport visitors from environmental hazards. To date, no airport has been built in that location.

The second encounter involved a contract with Overview to provide a landscape analysis of the service area of Southern California Edison. Landscapes Limited (my design firm) mapped and analyzed the characteristics of the geographical area comprising the greater service area of Southern California Edison, and a more detailed study of Orange County was made with the goal of improving power transmission alignment and design. Attention focused on the carrying capacity of the landscape to support power transmission, as well as developing three-dimensional graphic illustrations of proper design considerations. These Overview experiences led to another Landscapes Limited contract with Bon-

neville Power, to formulate guidelines for power distribution in the northwestern United States. The transmission alignment process used is discussed in Chapter 6. In these interdisciplinary endeavors natural and cultural patterns were used as form determinants to locate facilities.

ENVIRONMENTAL AWARENESS CENTER (FIG. 10.14)

While chairing the Landscape Architecture Department at the University of Wisconsin (1964–1972), the opportunity arose for an interdisciplinary endeavor within the university. A newly formed executive committee to establish the Institute of Environmental Studies, of which I was a member, had given little importance to design as their endeavors proceeded over several years. As an alternative, the Environmental Awareness Center (EAC) was founded in 1967 under my direction. It was established as part of the School of Natural Resources and the College of Agriculture and Life Sciences at the stroke of a pen by the late Steven Smith, dean of the school.

The center has provided an opportunity to carry on the design work begun in the Outdoor

Figure 10.14 Environmental
Awareness Center logo

Recreation Plan of the State of Wisconsin in the Department of Resource Development. The goal of the EAC has always been to further develop the regional design process that allows interdisciplinary teams (staff and students from the University of Wisconsin), working with local and regional citizen groups and agencies, to identify, protect, and enhance natural and cultural amenities of cities, towns, and rural landscapes.

The Regional Design Process developed at the EAC recognizes the importance of regional diversity and communicating statewide options that assure freedom of choice. The center has been supported through the years by a modest yearly grant from the University of Wisconsin Cooperative Extension program. In addition, contracts with various state agencies, counties, cities, towns, and villages have been negotiated and significant grants from nonprofit organizations and individuals have been received. These sources have funded many undergraduate and graduate students working on real-world problems and opportunities in Wisconsin and the midwest.

In addition to interdisciplinary endeavors, students at the Environmental Awareness Center working on small-scale research projects have been encouraged to undertake their work in the context of large-scale regional characteristics prior to detailed site-specific solutions. A case in point was an undertaking by one landscape architecture student to identify the appropriate range of plant materials that would assist in stabilizing erosion on a slope of mineral mining tailings. At the EAC she was encouraged to do a study that located all mineral mining areas in North America, to define the scale of the problem. She was then asked to identify first-priority applications of her stabilization techniques: Which areas required attention first; mining areas isolated from major urban areas, or mining areas near concentrations of people? Are mining areas upwind from major concentrations of people most important? Are all of the above most important? By answering these questions for a specific site, conclusions as to how to set priorities for a particular activity were made— where it is most important to stabilize mining debris, and how best to do it.

Too often students are isolated from broad-scale applications of the information and skills that they are developing. At the Environmental Awareness Center students have been required to defend their regional and local concepts and proposals to county boards, city councils, and state agency personnel. The center has shown leader-ship in assuring these opportunities for students and has provided many opportunities for advanced landscape architecture students to work and experiment on interdisciplinary teams with students and staff from a variety of other disciplines and fields.

In addition to the applied research in the Environmental Awareness Center, students and staff have developed design concepts and consulted on awareness center facilities that could be developed in each global landscape depicting the uniqueness of landscape and townscape features and the universal basics of needs and resources out of the awareness center models and simulating new sustainable technologies for development in its particular region.

Of the awareness center conceptual models about to be discussed, four [the Environmental Awareness Center at the University of Wisconsin, Madison; the Gordon Bubolz Center (Fig. 10.15) near Appleton, Wisconsin; the Havenwoods Awareness Center (Fig. 10.16) at Milwaukee, Wisconsin; and the Iron Range Interpretive Center (Fig. 10.17 and 10.18) at Chisholm, Minnesota] are presently in operation in the United States, and two more are designed with fundraising under way [the Heritage Center, Madison, Wisconsin (illustrated in Chapter 11), and the Northern Great Lakes Regional Visitor Center (Fig. 10.19 and 10.20)]. One designed under the direction of Albert Tsao (a former student of mine whose graduate work was done at the University of Wisconsin) has just opened in Taipei, Taiwan.

ACADEMY FOR SUSTAINABLE DESIGN, DEVELOPMENT, AND REGENERATION

An **Academy for Sustainable Design** would be an institution to teach and work in this way that would have an institutional structure and continuing future. Any existing or new institution could use this model. Utilizing the regional design process components (inventories, pattern interpretation, developing design options, and communication) is a clearly complex endeavor requiring a sustained, centrally coordinated effort. The process necessitates cooperation among those from many diverse fields. Experience with the Environmental Awareness Center suggests that a strategically located physical facility, an **Academy for Sustainable Design, Development, and Restoration,** is the key to successful coordinated implementation of the regional design process. Such an *Academy* would be a facility designed to house research and laboratory space to accommodate and relate the work of the regional design process teams. Adequate administrative and secretarial staff would be included. Such prototype centers for sustainable design would be most effective if located in environmentally exciting places where the professionals found in state governmental and university centers congregate.

The most important space in the academy would probably be devoted to verbally and visually communicating the Regional Design Process, in the form of sketches, charts, and graphs as future academy studies would proceed. Such a visual laboratory for teaching would explain and

Figure 10.17 Iron Range Interpretive Center. Perhaps one of the most dramatic awareness centers in the upper midwest is the Iron Range Interpretive Center in Chisholm, Minnesota. In the 1970s, when I was a consultant to the local planner, Charles Aguar, I visited a sterile site devastated by iron ore extraction and was asked what I could recommend that might attract tourists. Aside from illustrating the effect of human beings on a beautiful north-woods landscape, I suggested portraying the destinations of the iron ore shipped out from the site, to build America, building and construction products molded from its ore, ethnic groups brought into the region to mine the ore, together with documentation of their crafts, foods, recipes, architecture, customs, and so on. Today, about 20 years later, the entire concept has been realized.

Figure 10.18 Iron Range Interpretive Center

Compliments of Professor Roger Miller

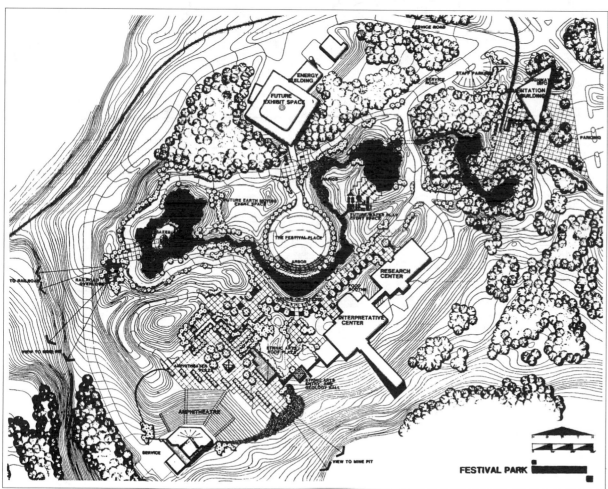

Figure 10.19 Northern Great Lakes Visitor Center. A more recent Wisconsin extension endeavor chaired by Harold Jordahl developed conceptual plans for a new Northern Great Lakes Regional Visitor Center. The preliminary design is now complete, and the site, located strategically in the Lake Superior region, has been purchased.

Figure 10.20 Northern Great Lakes Visitor Center.

Southwest Elevation

Reception/Orientation Area

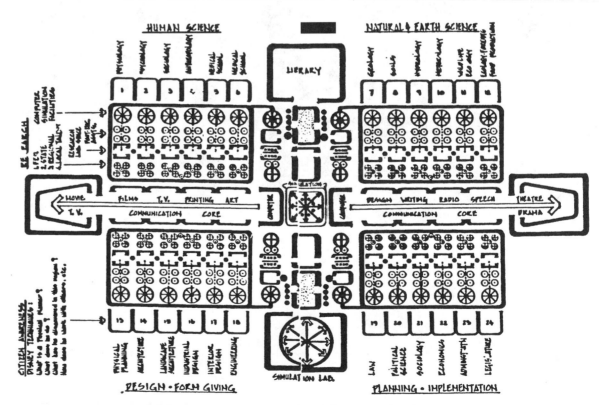

Figure 10.21 Diagram of an Academy for Sustainable Design.

Figure 10.22 A three-dimensional conceptual building plan for an

Academy for Sustainable Design

demonstrate the Regional Design Process that identifies and communicates two- and three-dimensional design options for a community or region while respecting guidelines provided by the biological, physical, and social sciences.

Using these basic concepts, staff and students of the Environmental Awareness Center as well as those of the University of Illinois Chicago Circle campus developed sketches of such an academy (Figs. 10.21, 10.22). They illustrate the Regional Design Process and how it relates to some preliminary concepts for a facility for an Academy of Sustainable Design to house the interdisciplinary team and communicate the results of their Regional Design inquiries and research. They reflect one concept that such an academy should be highly mobile, utilizing inflatable structures that could be shipped by air or truck to any location and erected quickly to do regional analyses.

It is one thing to develop a comprehensive Regional Design Process and quite another to write of its complex and varied structure. The sketches and diagrams on the next few pages have been helpful in communicating the evolving Design Process, staffing and facility requirements.

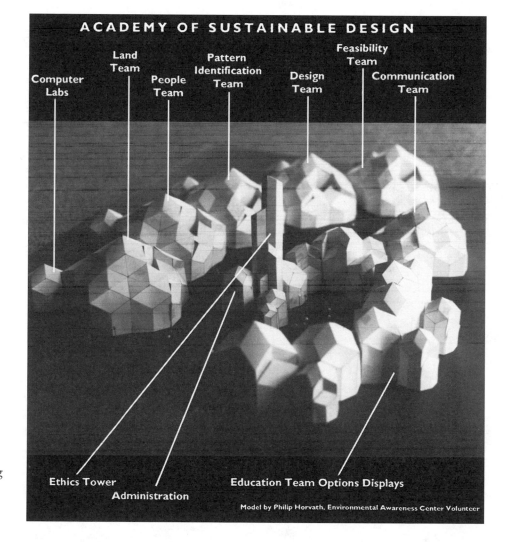

ACADEMY OF SUSTAINABLE DESIGN

Computer Labs

Land Team

People Team

Pattern Identification Team

Design Team

Feasibility Team

Communication Team

Ethics Tower

Administration

Education Team Options Displays

Model by Philip Horvath, Environmental Awareness Center Volunteer

Figure 10.23 Sustainability
and profit

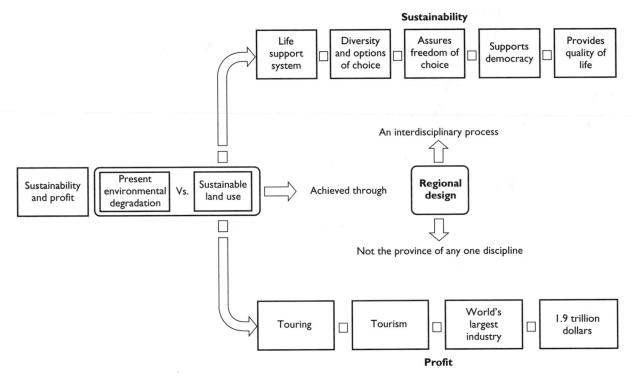

Once thoroughly informed, environmental students, under the direction of an interdisciplinary staff, would proceed to apply the process to the region in which the academy is located. These various studies and resulting design options would then be added to the Academy laboratory and regional design centers located in the domain of each regional personality or bioregional area as education/tourism centers.

Opportunities for funding the management costs for tourism/education centers surely exist among tourism and educational development funds of cities, towns and counties, states, and regions (Fig. 10.23). Each center would personify the singular composition and personality of its region or locality. Associated "sense-of-place" markets (Fig. 10.24) and museums would display products, artifacts, and exhibits as well as presenting cultural and civic activities to publicize what is available to be enjoyed and used. Regional E-Ways, the life-support museum, the sense-of-place market, and possibly a simulation lab would all be related to the Academy of Sustainable Design, to present sustainable regional options to the public (Fig. 10.25). Avoiding standard design solutions and utilizing native forms, materials,

Figure 10.24 A Sense-of-Place Market (as a component of regional awareness centers) offers opportunities to generate funding for center operation.

and construction will also develop regional and local identity.

FUTURE OF REGIONAL DESIGN IN WISCONSIN

While a sustainable land-use program for the state is the subject of study by at least 10 groups of considerable public standing, it is interesting to note that most of them recognize the need for some form of integrating council for such a program and also a planning and design process. They also feel that we need a real-world laboratory for sustainable land-use demonstrations as a focus for integrated regional design endeavors. At this time of uncertainty about land-use policy and the consequences of current practices, there is a great opportunity to put into effect a proven process for putting available data to good and immediate use.

Chapter 11 shows the educational process with two examples of regional design exercises carried out by students in my design studio at the University of Wisconsin. Both focused on local growth strategies within the context of Circle

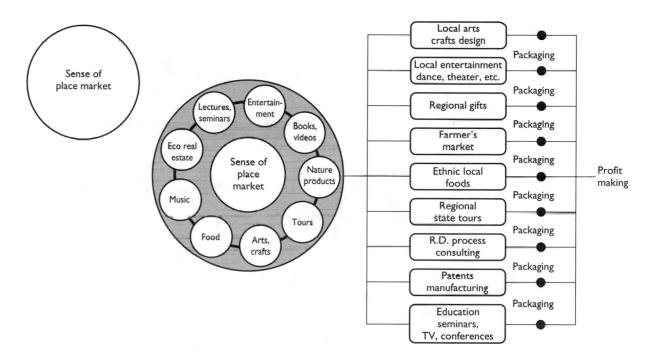

Figure 10.25 A diagrammatic model of an academy that could be expressed in any one of many different architectural styles, most likely one selected to harmonize with styles and landscape characteristics of the region in which it is built. Any Academy should reflect the best of the region it characterizes and demonstrate new technology in structure and environmental sustainability, such as use of solar energy.

Process and academy

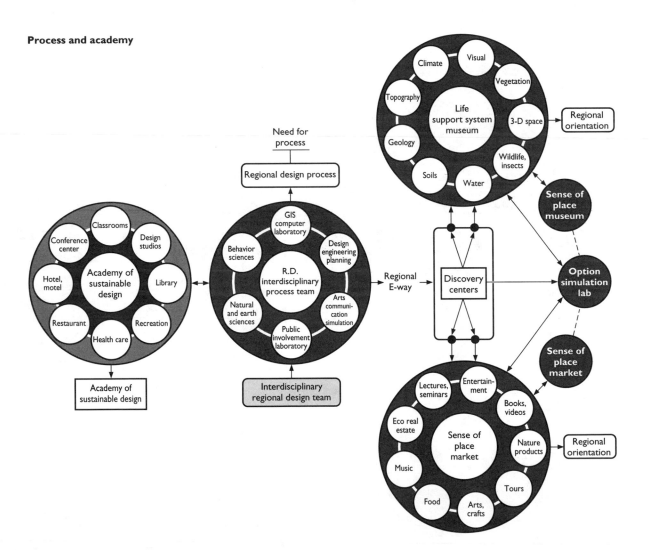

City, Dane County, and Madison, Wisconsin, in an expanded Wisconsin Idea Guideway. The students simultaneously learn about the process and carry it out.

Note

[1]Paul Cawood Hellmund, "A Method for Ecological Design," in *The Ecology of Greenways,* University of Minnesota Press, Duluth, Minn., 1993.

C H A P T E R   1 1

THE REGIONAL
DESIGN PROCESS
AS APPLIED IN THE
CLASSROOM

Figure 11.1 Midwestern recreation, tourism, and education Network

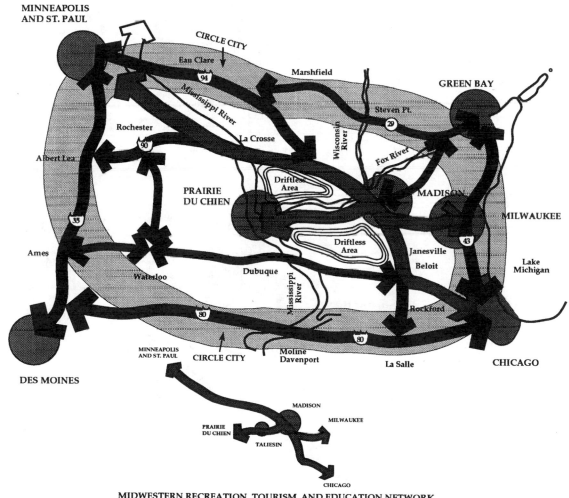

MIDWESTERN RECREATION, TOURISM, AND EDUCATION NETWORK

Figure 11.2 Wisconsin Rail
Park; recreation, tourism,
educational trail network

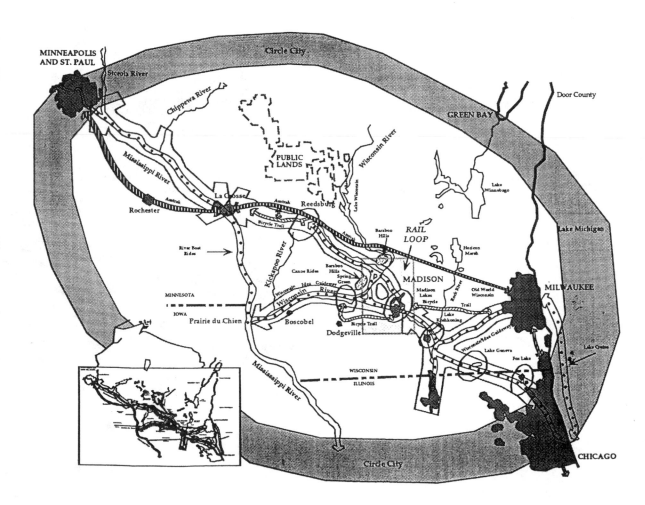

In recent undergraduate and graduate design studios in landscape architecture, students were first introduced to the regional design philosophy and materials in this book. The concepts of urban constellations, Circle City, and the Wisconsin Idea Guideway fall within this national and regional frame of reference. In addition, they were introduced to an expanded version of the Wisconsin Idea Guideway (Fig. 11.1, 11.2) and various growth strategies (Fig. 11.3). We were able to develop both the undergraduate and graduate studios around a design project centered on a *local* design strategy. Dane County, located in the center of Circle City and in the center of the Wisconsin Idea Guideway, was selected as a focus for both student studies.

Since Dane County (Fig. 11.4) contains the capitol city, Madison, and the University of Wisconsin, ample resource information as well as a wide range of assistance from other departments in the university, state, county, and city government is accessible by professionals, students, and the general public.

To reduce the design project to a manageable size, the students were presented with the concept of building higher livable densities along the magnificent county rail network that was put

Figure 11.3 Growth strategies

into place when land values were low and the region relatively undeveloped. The rail lines were envisioned by the railroad builders as the means and mainstay of development (Fig. 11.5). They have been that for over 100 years, and in Dane County almost all cities, towns, and villages (and thus most of the population) are located on the rail corridors (Fig. 11.6). There is no budget available that could assemble such a system at the present time and the political will for such projects is clearly lacking, but we are not using it to the full extent of its capacity by any means. Freight is being transported on it, but not a single passenger is presently being carried on this system. Building other means of transit involves land acquisition costs just as large.

These factors make the rail corridors economically attractive as the location for additional population and commuter rail development. Out of the present spider web of rail corridors, the undergraduate class selected a rail loop (similar to Circle City) that served the northwest quadrant of Dane County and the adjoining counties of Sauk and Columbia (Fig. 11.7).

Both class projects were based on the assumption that all arteries of growth, transit, utilities, and communication lines were in place within

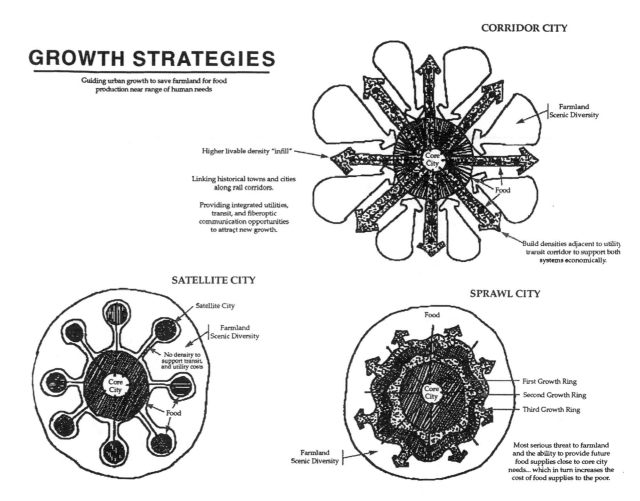

GROWTH STRATEGIES

Guiding urban growth to save farmland for food
production near range of human needs

CORRIDOR CITY

Farmland
Scenic Diversity

Higher livable density "infill"

Linking historical towns and cities
along rail corridors.

Providing integrated utilities,
transit, and fiberoptic
communication opportunities
to attract new growth.

Core City

Food

Build densities adjacent to utility
transit corridor to support both
systems economically.

SATELLITE CITY

Satellite City

Farmland
Scenic Diversity

No density to
support transit
and utility costs

Core City

Food

SPRAWL CITY

Food

First Growth Ring
Second Growth Ring
Third Growth Ring

Core City

Farmland
Scenic Diversity

Most serious threat to farmland
and the ability to provide future
food supplies close to core city
needs... which in turn increases the
cost of food supplies to the poor.

Figure 11.4 Dane County
and Madison, within the
original and the expanded
Wisconsin Idea Guideway

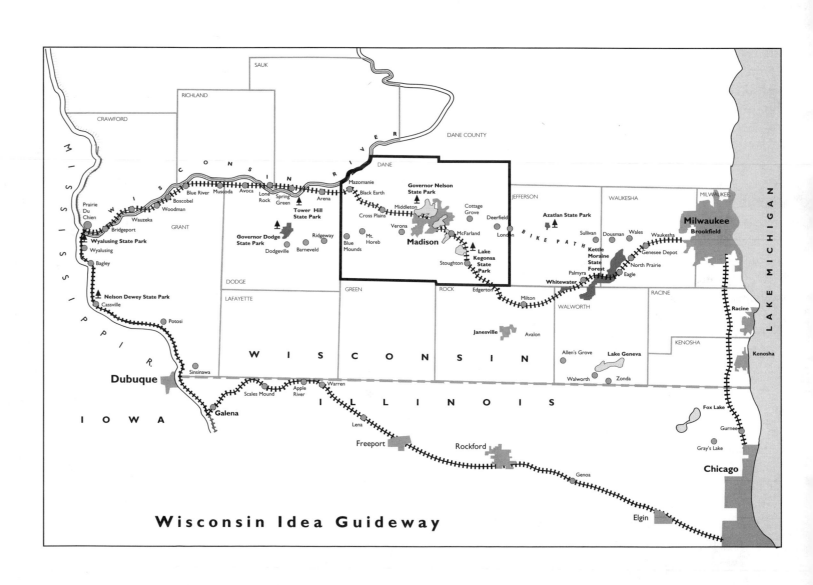

Figure 11.5 (a) Dane County Rail Corridors; (b) presently, most Dane County cities and villages are located within the two-mile-wide rail corridor system in Dane County.

Figure 11.6 Historically, most high population density patterns in Dane County are located within the two-mile-wide rail corridor system.

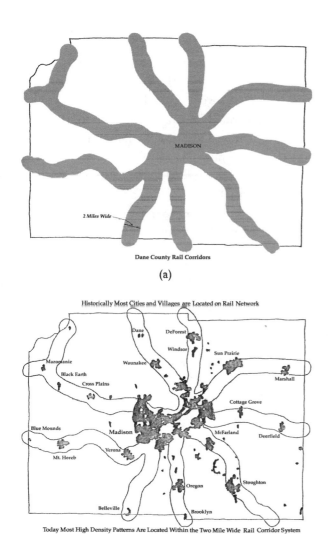

Dane County Rail Corridors

(a)

Historically Most Cities and Villages are Located on Rail Network

Today Most High Density Patterns Are Located Within the Two Mile Wide Rail Corridor System

Dane County
Highest Density Areas
(Over 320,000 Persons/Square Km)

(b)

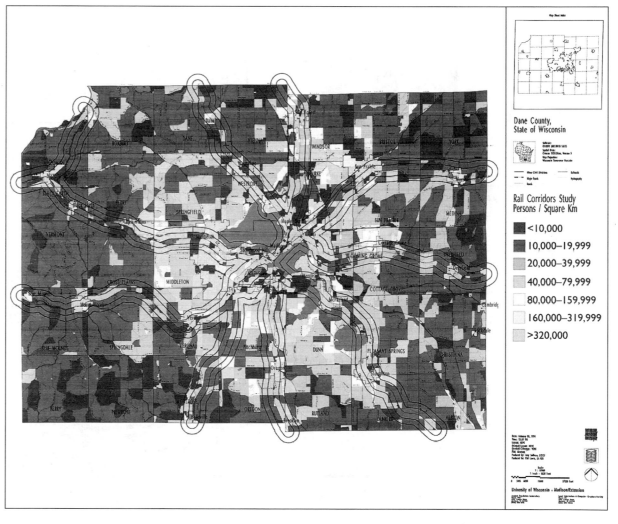

Dane County,
State of Wisconsin

Rail Corridors Study
Persons / Square Km

<10,000
10,000–19,999
20,000–39,999
40,000–79,999
80,000–159,999
160,000–319,999
>320,000

University of Wisconsin - Madison/Extension

Figure 11.7 The rail loop
study area

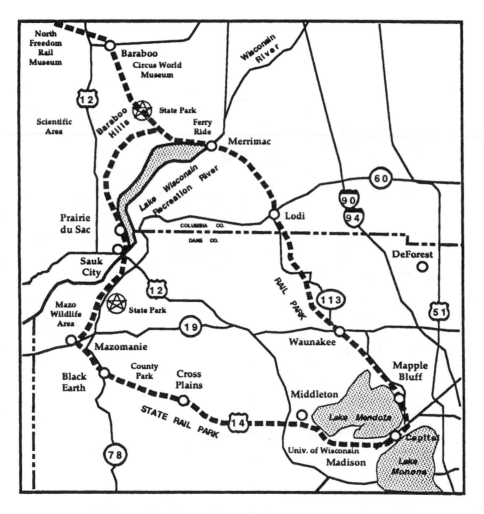

RAIL LOOP PROPOSAL

the rail corridors, serving as an urban service magnet for future growth. The undergraduate class was to inventory, in eight weeks, the basic natural and cultural resources of the designated area and demonstrate how the rail loop might serve as a commuter service for rural inhabitants to travel to Madison for jobs, education, shopping, and entertainment, while permitting the inhabitants of Madison to escape to the rural resources identified in the exercise.

One major concept considered in the exercise was to explore the possibilities of encouraging new growth and increased densities along and within an urban service area boundary parallel to the rail spokes radiating out from Madison, leaving wedges of open space, scenic diversity, and rich farmlands in between them. Following Regional Design Process guidelines, all water, wetland, and steep topography of 12.5 percent or greater were identified and plotted on sheets of Mylar (Fig. 11.8). Once this was done, the students combined these patterns in an environmental corridor overlay (Fig. 11.9). The third overlay presented a pattern of vegetation types in the area as well as public ownership of land and large corporate farm areas (Fig. 11.10). The county land regulation and deeds staff and former student Eva Serra provided

Figure 11.8 All water, wetlands and steep topography
of 12.5 or greater were
plotted on a sheet of mylar
(computer methods were
not available for this eight-
week exercise).

Figure 11.9 Combining
water, wetlands, and steep
topography of 12.5% or
greater defined the environmental corridor network of
the area.

Figure 11.10 On the third
overlay of the study area, all
vegetation, publicly owned
land, and large corporate
farm areas were plotted.

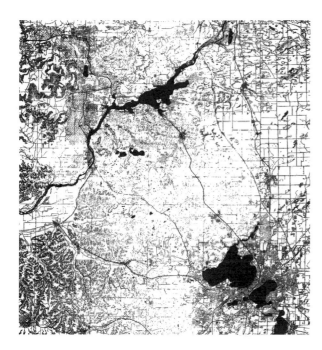

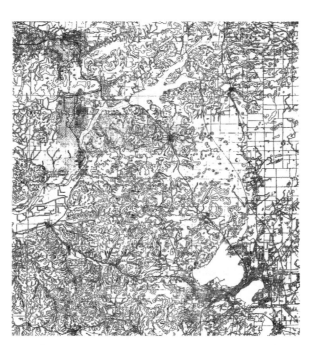

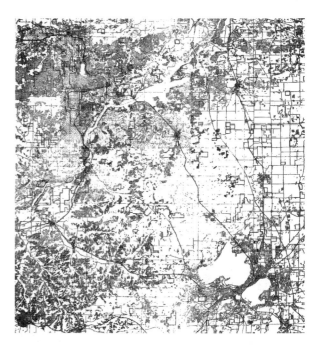

the class with a color computer printout of all class
A farmland in the Dane County portion of the
study area. A sixth map, not available for public
viewing, plotted extensive patterns of known
archeological sites and historical buildings.

The studio project was highly successful in
demonstrating to the class the many outstanding
features that a commuter rail service could link

into an outstanding recreation and educational
system for Madison and the 40,000 inhabitants
living within the small towns along the loop. A
field trip that included a drive along the rail loop
covered all of the exciting potential of the system not only for recreation and education but
for our state's current $6.4 billion tourism
industry. In summary, the commuter loop con-

nected two state parks, numerous county parks,
the Wisconsin River, and Lake Wisconsin with
the lakes of Madison. In addition to these
important natural features were cultural features,
including the North Freedom Rail Museum, the
Circus World Museum at Baraboo, and of
course the many museums and attractions in
Madison.

Comparing for the students and for the public the proposed impact of a reconstructed four-lane State Route 12, a highway serving the area, to use of the rail loop already in place and largely owned by the state of Wisconsin was an added value of the study. When the resource information was assembled it was possible to see how the small communities along the rail line could be expanded to enhance ridership and lower transportation costs for users. This strategy also has the virtue of lessening the deleterious impact on the local life-support system of its natural resources. The studio project also confirmed the practicality of similar regional design applications at the Circle City scale.

While the method for implementing sustainable land use was being developed, I felt that an appropriate subject for my graduate design class would be a preliminary land use/growth strategy demonstration project involving a segment of the rail loop studied by the undergraduate class. From the spider web of rail corridors the graduate design class selected a section of the rail loop and Wisconsin Idea Guideway that stretches from Cross Plains through Middleton, the University of Wisconsin campus, the fringe of downtown Madison, the Dane County Expo

facilities, the Nine-Springs E-Way, to McFarland (Fig. 11.11).

As our Dane County E-Way has been successful in demonstrating the importance of protecting both natural and cultural values in our legislature and state university, it was reasonable to expect that a sustainable land design for the capitol county would provide a similar teaching opportunity midpoint on the Wisconsin Idea Guideway. Today we still adhere to many of yesterday's design concepts and standards. This exercise was an effort to offer an opportunity for an interdisciplinary team with a holistic point of view to utilize the Regional Design Process to achieve a new range of urban forms for living, working, and playing. By accepting a long-term ethic, and through the use of materials and technologies devised for sustainability, we can envision new systems, structures, and models to provide for a wide range of options for optimum human benefit in harmony with our life-sustaining landscape along the rail spokes.

Like the undergraduate study, the graduate class project was based on the assumption that all arterial growth, transit, utilities, and communication lines were in place within the rail corridor, serving as an urban service magnet for future

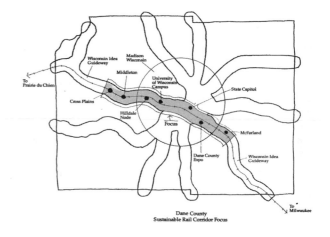

Dane County
Sustainable Rail Corridor Focus

Figure 11.12 Schematic representation of the delineation of corridor sections to be protected for purposes of maintaining productivity of land and resource protection areas; and those areas suitable for development. These land use categories as well as where trains are to stop must be firmly established and protected before passenger and intensified freight service is provided.

growth. In principle, they were to encourage higher livable densities adjacent to the arteries of growth, leaving wedges of open space, scenic diversity, and rich farmlands in the land wedges remaining between the rail lines (Fig. 11.12).

This was to be the last class I would teach as a full-time faculty member prior to retirement after a 42-year career, and I looked forward to the task as an opportunity to apply the principles, methods, and ideas of the Regional Design Process locally. The students were to proceed from their own skills, knowledge, and interests to a collaborative design, with all the supporting material, present it to a jury, and defend their proposals, the underlying principles, and their methods.

Their basic assignments were to:

1. Learn new sustainable technologies, including the most innovative new transit systems possible.
2. Inventory the many natural and cultural features found in the selected corridor within the distance of one mile on each side of its centerline, and from these inventories determine where not to build, and review from the historical standpoint

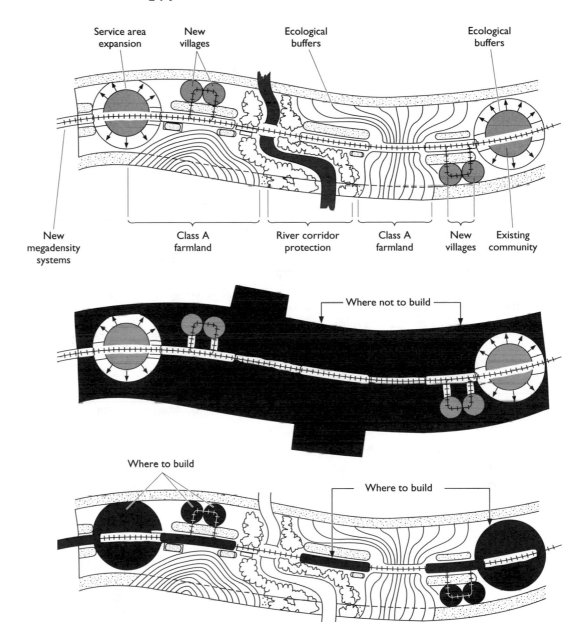

various building densities, undertake historical research, and consider restoration.

3. Based on the inventories, select one high-density node along the corridor, where through creative design, higher-livable-density design options would be sketched.

The project was designed to serve as a regional design model, demonstrating that such an approach could be applied to any rail corridor connecting the range of city sizes found in urban constellations. In the introduction to the students' final report, the students observed that:

> The regional design class is intended to teach graduate students to work together using the expertise that each brings from his or her academic and professional background. The team then addresses regional design issues and seeks to develop better alternatives to present-day environmentally unsound urban sprawl. The graduate students in the Landscape Architecture Department at the University of Wisconsin come from a wide variety of disciplines, including architecture, landscape architecture, biology, horticulture, wildlife management, economics, literature, and social sciences. This diverse knowledge base creates

a dynamic, challenging, and exciting class. The problems of inner-city decline and suburban sprawl have been widely discussed. Solutions abound, and every year new literature is available emphasizing sustainable building techniques, alternative energy sources, sustainable food production, more efficient transportation systems, and other innovations and improvements.

In a final jury of their work, the students reported that:

> the problem is not that we lack solutions, but rather we are unwilling to make the apparent sacrifices necessary to bring about changes. . . . We are addicted to the very thing that will ultimately destroy us. We make excuses and deny there is really a problem. We make excuses as to why we cannot change. This class is an attempt to raise the consciousness of those that may, in the future, make decisions regarding planning and designing the landscape of the United States and abroad. Yet, we must admit that we are a part of the problem. The main objective for the design team was to utilize our expertise in designing solutions for urban sprawl. Focus-

ing on this issue emphasized awareness of the problem's complexity and urgency.

HISTORICAL CHANGE

The class noted the development decisions and changes from the time of early settlement in the mid-nineteenth century brought about locally by the Industrial Revolution, particularly the location of towns on transportation routes (roads and railroads rather than paths and rivers); the advent of the automobile society and central heating and the resultant increase in energy consumption and air pollution; sprawl, urban decay, loss of farmland, proliferation of agricultural, commercial, industrial, and personal use of hitherto unknown herbicides, pesticides, and other environmentally damaging substances; and mixed-use land development patterns.

As an alternative they noted:

> Part of sustainable design and development involves increasing building densities . . . accompanied by mixed use zoning that encourages concentrated development in the urban core or adjacent to

existing transportation, utility, and communication systems . . . compact and diverse so that services, recreational, retail and cultural activities are within walking distance. [To achieve this goal] progressive legislation and zoning are essential. . . .

Policies that help people work and live in close proximity should be subsidized . . . infrastructure costs can be cut [and] less environmental damage [will be sustained].

Energy, monetary, and resource savings (short and long term) were deemed necessary and desirable. They cited references in Register, Calthorpe, and Stenhouse for guidance in urban design. The notable design failures of megastructures were noted and corrections suggested.

ORGANIZING FOR CLASSROOM ACTION

To understand new approaches to these vexing problems and to the policies within which we now operate, and to consider new goals and policies, the work of the design studio was organized into four phases. The first phase was examination of sustainable technologies in design and design processes by gathering information, reporting it to the class, and suggesting how it might apply to the corridor. The second phase was an inventory and analysis of the site characteristics done by placing natural, cultural, and historic features on site maps. The third phase was to identify areas of intense human activity, called development nodes, along the rail system. The fourth phase involved a detailed design for one node, the Hilldale node. For each phase the class conducted charettes and brainstorming sessions, and revisions and changes were made on a weekly basis to each stage according to consensus among the class as they learned and corrected errors and made changes in the course of the design process to accommodate the work of each team member. The final stage was presentation and defense of the resulting design and its details and supporting material.

Phase One: Technology Review (Fig. 11.13)

Some examples of the technological ideas discussed in phase one included a schematic arrangement of the facilities that could be integrated in one travel/utility/communication corridor structure, ways of harnessing solar and wind energy on-site for individual or community use, the Taxi 2000 PRT System[1] (a prototype of which is to be built at Rosemont in Chicago in 1996–1997 as an elevated, comparatively low cost transit loop), and the evolution of complex dwelling structures according to the requirements of their inhabitants and the site on which they are built.

In classroom reviews of change on the global scale, it is truly apparent that nothing is permanent but change itself. Through the ages we have documented vast alterations in the way we build structures. Population densities, single-home sprawl, and costs of labor and materials have, in this century, given rise to a developing demand for totally new structural systems consistent with environmental preservation.

Moshe Safdie and Richard Rogers are two of a growing number of architects designing and building such new architectural systems. In his book *Richard Rogers + Architects*[2] Richard Rogers expresses his opinion about such new directions:

The benefits of industrialization and its method of expression have had a profound influence on architecture. It is a process which when correctly used, gives cost, time

Figure 11.13 (a) A review of
sustainable technology for
the future; (b) evolution of
building systems

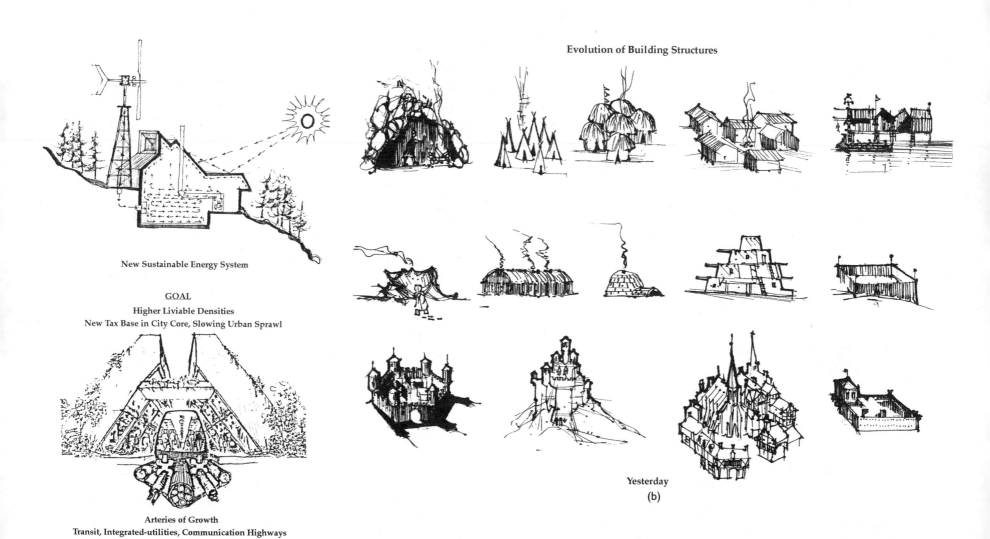

New Sustainable Energy System

GOAL
Higher Liviable Densities
New Tax Base in City Core, Slowing Urban Sprawl

Arteries of Growth
Transit, Integrated-utilities, Communication Highways

(a)

Evolution of Building Structures

Yesterday

(b)

(c)

Figure 11.13 *(continued)* (c) and (d) historical and contemporary building systems and; (e) linear structures integrating transit, utilities, and solar collectors with earth mounding to block northern winter winds

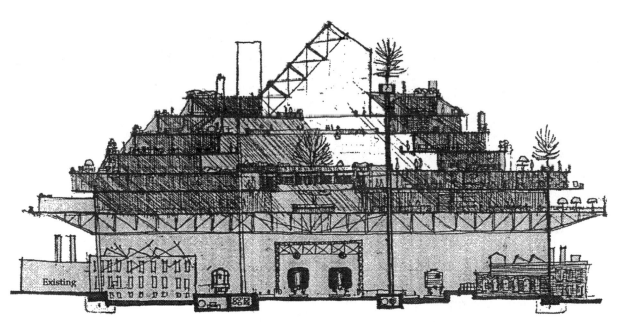

New Structure to Utilize Rail Corridor Air Rights

Existing

Tomorrow Designs?
Future High Density Systems?
(d)

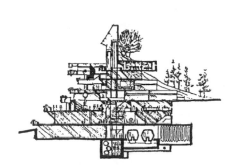

Integrated Utilities, Transit System, Solar Collectors, and Earth Mounding to
Block Northern Winter Wind.

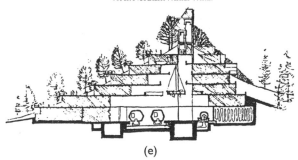

(e)

and qualitative benefits and must be maximized if we are to meet the needs of a world whose population doubles every 33 years. I believe in the rich potential of a modern industrial society. Aesthetically one can do what one likes with technology for it is a tool, not an end in itself, but we ignore it at our peril. To our practice its natural functionalism has an intrinsic beauty. The aesthetic relationship between science and art has been poetically described by Horatio Greenough as: "Beauty is the promise of function made sensuously pleasing." It is science to the aid of the imagination.

Phase Two: Natural and Cultural Inventory and Analysis

In the inventory phase, the students mapped the water, wetland, steep topography (that of 12.5 percent or greater slope), class A farmland, and vegetation in the corridor. In the analysis phase they related and integrated these individual patterns to determine the location of an environmental corridor within the rail corridor (where not to build) (Fig. 11.14).

By protecting and enhancing this natural/cultural corridor, the students could assure that natural areas and open space could be maintained for human use, existing natural vegetation and animal habitat could be protected and wildlife movement corridors provided, and by managing vegetation, stabilization of the steep slopes enclosing the rail corridor could be assured, offering continued availability of a scenic corridor. Protected and enhanced, environmental corridor diversity would provide a recognizable demarcation between urban and rural, preserving the small towns and an agricultural sense of place, buffer zones of vegetation between development and high-quality natural areas (unbroken environmental corridors: waterways, lakes, shorelines, wetlands, and steep topography). Opportunities for people to take part in restoration, creation, enhancement, and management of natural areas as well as for scientific study were envisioned as a means of education and recreation as well as labor cost savings. A range of open space is to be provided for by various measures both public and private, including areas of high environmental quality possessing a high degree of biodiversity (or containing rare or valuable species) for conservation, restoration, and study, and small or lower-quality (more degraded) areas for urban parks or recreation areas. Restoration

or mitigation (e.g., in applying for and using highway or public open space funds) could be invoked in already built-up locations where disruption of soils and topography has occurred in areas essential to open space or urban site improvement. Connection of open spaces by means of trails for recreational use was a design criterion. Agricultural stabilization and cost-sharing for conservation practices were suggested as a source of some of the necessary funds.

Phase Three: Identification of Development Nodes

Development nodes are places already recognized as community centers by the respect they already hold, their architectural resources of style, workmanship, and expression of local values, as well as the beauty and charm of their settings. They are enhanced by the way they were designed, built, and maintained and by the natural characteristics of the setting. Such nodes are compact in size—defined as encompassing an area described by about a half-mile radius from the center or 10 or 15 minutes of walking time (easy walking distance) (Fig. 11.15).

They have a diversity of uses and have elements such as a variety of residential types,

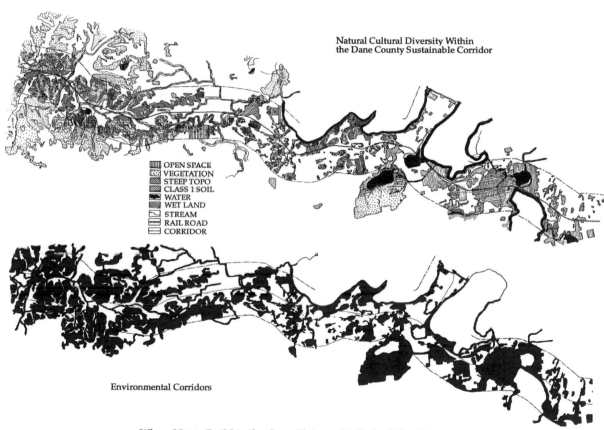

Figure 11.14 Where not to build in the Cross Plains-McFarland corridor

Natural Cultural Diversity Within the Dane County Sustainable Corridor

OPEN SPACE
VEGETATION
STEEP TOPO
CLASS 1 SOIL
WATER
WET LAND
STREAM
RAIL ROAD
CORRIDOR

Environmental Corridors

Where Not to Build in the Cross Plains to McFarland Corridor

retail/commercial establishments (grocery, barber shop, cafe, tavern, restaurants) with employment opportunities within the area, civic structures (medical centers, schools, post offices, police/fire stations, civic centers), cultural structures (churches, theaters, and museums), passive and active recreation opportunities, economic services (banks, offices, delivery services), and social gathering areas such as social clubs or centers of recreational activity and bus stops, or other transportation transfer locations. Fragile (easily destroyed, possibly already infringed upon by construction or other activities) environmental and cultural areas were identified by analysis of maps, photographs, inspection, and research of the literature and the information used in defining the nodes so as to protect fragile areas.

Phase Four: Design Proposal for a Node Prototype

The Hilldale node was chosen as a prototype node, to receive a detailed design (Figs. 11.16 and 11.17). It possesses a wide spectrum of housing densities, income levels, and age levels. There is a mixture of banks, grocery stores, drugstores, restaurants, book and other retail stores (Hilldale shopping mall), employment opportunities in

Figure 11.15 Existing development nodes within the rail corridor

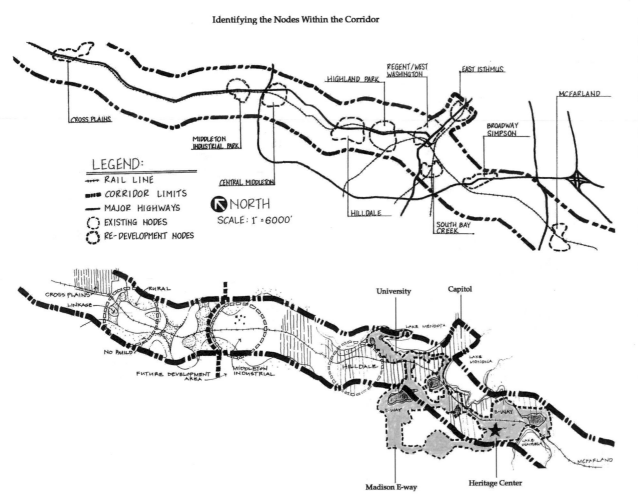

Identifying the Nodes Within the Corridor

LEGEND:
- RAIL LINE
- CORRIDOR LIMITS
- MAJOR HIGHWAYS
- EXISTING NODES
- RE-DEVELOPMENT NODES

NORTH
SCALE: 1" = 6000'

CROSS PLAINS

MIDDLETON INDUSTRIAL PARK

CENTRAL MIDDLETON

HIGHLAND PARK

REGENT/WEST WASHINGTON

EAST ISTHMUS

MCFARLAND

BROADWAY SIMPSON

HILLDALE

SOUTH BAY CREEK

CROSS PLAINS
RURAL
LINKAGE

NO BUILD

FUTURE DEVELOPMENT AREA

MIDDLETON INDUSTRIAL

HILLDALE

University

Capitol

LAKE MENDOTA

LAKE MONONA

E-WAY

E-WAY

LAKE WAUBESA

MCFARLAND

Madison E-way

Heritage Center

state and private offices and medical offices, schools and a fire station, churches and theaters, and parks and a golf course. By comparison with other community centers and the distance to some much-used facilities, desirable additions for a stronger sense of community are considered to be library and social center facilities, linkages between open spaces, and location of a transit center at the Hilldale node to link the rail, bus, automobile, bicycle, and potential new transit methods at this point where a junction of rail, road (automobile and bus), and bicycle modes of transit already exists. Their desirability is determined because of the benefits afforded to the community by permitting increased density while maintaining or improving amenities. Putting buildings with a "Main Street" character in parking lots (assuming that construction of alternative transit and/or underground parking will make this space available) and along the street edges of the mall is suggested in the design, as is a commercial and residential strip between University Avenue and the railroad. The open area near the state of Wisconsin office building is suggested to be used as allotment gardens; and rooftop gardens, small neighborhood parks, and

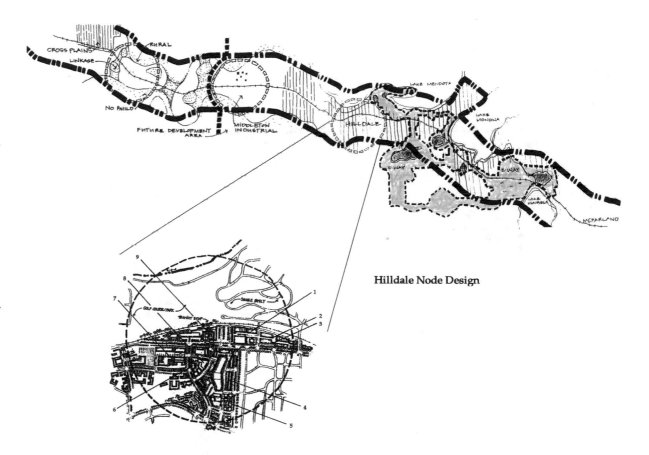

Figure 11.16 The Hilldale node within the rail corridor was selected for a prototype design focus.

streetscape enhancement are advocated. The use of solar-powered energy-conserving building materials and more sustainable use of space are detailed design criteria: southwest-to-southeast orientation for buildings to capture sunlight for solar windows and walls, and sunspaces with blocking of winter winds by tree plantings. Exterior building materials such as glass, stone, brick, and wood are suggested for exteriors and structural members, and plaster, wood, and tile for interiors are recommended because of their lower than normal environmental impact in both construction and eventual disposal as well as for their surface attractiveness. Additional types of housing are suggested. An overpass for pedestrians over University Avenue is proposed as part of the circulation pattern.

Transportation

Since the rail corridor is the system which linked the settlements that existed when it was built, and on which subsequent urbanization occurred until the suburbanization of the 1960s and 1970s, it is the source of our present pattern of urbanization and the only available place in which it is economically feasible to place new mass transit.

Hilldale Node Design

Figure 11.17 (a) Proposed Hilldale Design Node and (b) Hilldale recommendations.

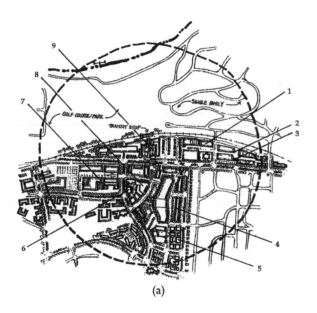

(a)

Improved, comfortable, convenient, and affordable transportation must be made available if the present trend toward road building and increased consumption of petroleum products is to be changed. Savings in time and money for individuals and increased amenities in our surroundings are further incentives for addition of new transportation facilities.

In conjunction with phase four, the class deemed a well-designed multimodal system to be

---

Hilldale Recommendations

1. A day care center with outdoor play areas along "Main Street."

2. An arcade along pedestrian mall provides protection from the elements.

3. An urban plaza located along the pedestrian "Main Street." This is a smaller, more intimate space than the plaza recommended in 9.

4. Two rows of proposed townhouses (3 floors).

5. A commercial/retail area on the ground floor with a central plaza (proposed) and an additional second floor of residential (proposed).

6. A commercial area with proposed interior courtyard and the addition of housing on second floor.

7. A proposed residential building with southern exposure, rooftop gardens, and a courtyard (3, 5, and 7 floors).

8. An infill development proposed within the block. Townhouses have been added to create a better diversity of housing types. An enclosed space was created between existing apartment buildings and the proposed townhouses. This space is proposed to be a higher livable density lot. A mixture of office (proposed second floor) and commercial (ground floor) is also found on this block. A plaza has been created for these uses.

9. An active plaza area surrounded by commercial, retail, and offices. This area also provides a strong pedestrian link from the transit stop, through the plaza, across University Ave (via the proposed pedestrian overbridge) to the shopping mall and office buildings.

(b)

---

the key to success of the entire corridor design. It connects all nodes in the corridor and is the spine of the system that is available to the areas bordering and surrounding the corridor on either side.

The first level in the transportation hierarchy in order of complexity and expense is pedestrian circulation. The two major impediments to walking are automobile traffic and cold, snow, and ice in winter. Pedestrian connections made by closing one arm of an intersection; by dead-ending streets (and providing pedestrian connections between them); and by building plazas over parking lots, overpasses over major roads, elevated skywalks, and enclosed grade-level sidewalks are recommended amenities.

New linear development adjacent to the rail transportation line would provide protected walking opportunities in both winter and summer (Fig. 11.18) The second level of transportation is human-powered transport: bicycles, in-line skates, cross-country skis, "sparks" or push-sleds, skateboards, and wheelchairs. Bicycle and skating lanes can be made along existing road shoulders or on their own rights-of-way, possibly in enclosed tubes separated from the grade levels of other traffic to eliminate stops at crossings.

Figure 11.18 From small
intimate spaces to large
public spaces, all within the
corridor system

Overpasses and underpasses can also provide pedestrian and wheelchair access to walks.

The third level is public transit, municipal or private. A PRT (personal rapid transit) guideway network linking nodes, with additional loops linking adjoining neighborhoods to the main line, is part of the final design. Energy-saving technologies such as photovoltaic cells and windmills can be incorporated into the overall energy system, and the use of battery-powered or biomass-fueled vehicles developed as part of the transportation system.

Applying the Regional Design Process to the Dane County Rail Corridor Study (Cross Plains to McFarland segment) demonstrates that it can be used to develop sustainable options for higher population densities that are more amenable to pleasant daily living and bring about financial and resource savings through less expensive transportation, less energy use, higher living densities, and the other strategies described previously. The process is applicable to any constellation corridor, particularly those in urban cores or urbanizing areas. Replacing dirty, noisy locomotive behemoths with quiet, clean PRT and light rail systems that can coexist with communications

From the Small Intimate Spaces to Large Public Spaces All Within the Corridor System

facilities and with bicycle and walking trails offers the opportunity to rehabilitate rail corridors with residential and commercial development. Such intensification and diversification of the use of these corridors can enhance the urban tax base

and make urban sprawl economically and aesthetically unattractive by comparison. An elevated PRT system eliminates grade crossings, is much less expensive than motorways and individual engine-driven vehicles, and greatly reduces the need for parking facilities. Halting successive waves of development of the countryside will preserve access to open areas and bring them into closer contact with urbanization by planned, continuously connected open space corridors connecting parks, recreational trails, waterways and water bodies, conservation areas, and agricultural land with public access at appropriate places.

Earlier Environmental Awareness Center studies of the University of Wisconsin node and the rail corridor through the University of Wisconsin campus reviewed the historical development of the corridor. It was proposed to utilize PRT 2000 and concentration of structural systems along its route to utilize the air rights over the rail corridor. This strategy takes advantage of the existing buildable space at an attractive distance from centers of employment and recreation and concomitant savings in transportation costs and environmental (including human) protection.

STUDENT DESIGN FOR THE CORRIDOR

The final plan incorporated the factors mentioned (amenity, economy, environmental protection,

convenience, aesthetic value, recreational areas and open space protection, provision of urban utilities and services, protection of agricultural land, water quality protection, and good infill standards). The recommended policies to achieve the design goals were incorporated to modify or reverse the extension of present trends to achieve a different overall pattern of urbanization, with less homogenization of the landscape, more urban amenities in the populated areas, and more natural features in both urban and rural parts of the corridor.

The plan also encompassed flexibility (building so that changes in use can be accommodated and making rules and procedures open to improvement by public participation and advances in technology) and foresees a process of continual revision, so that future needs can be met. A process of public information and review for new policies is part of the legal and governmental procedures. Presentation of graphic representations, models, and other information are some of the tools by which public participation can occur.

This project provided students with an opportunity to understand and apply the Regional Design Process and coordinate the skills found in their group to maximize their efforts and talents. They have produced a plan

and design with the potential to steer development in Dane County by providing graphic evidence of how some of their suggestions might look, together with the resource material to be used to guide particular proposed development.

CONCLUSIONS

The chief realization resulting from the work of the class was that even with the finest plans derived from the best of processes, if we fail to communicate the options to the public there is little likelihood that they will ever be implemented. The impetus of support from the public through the perception of what public needs and desires should be met is the necessary source of change.

By reviewing the successful efforts of the Environmental Awareness Center in creation of E-Ways and interpretation centers (Discovery Centers or Heritage Centers) students learned an appreciation for their capacity to educate, inform, and provide recreational opportunities. In addition, development of an Academy of Sustainable Design capable of housing a regional design team, supporting its efforts, and providing for public participation is the best tool yet

Figure 11.19 The Heritage Center, a regional awareness center for the Nine-Springs E-Way in Dane County has been designed and fundraising for it is under way.

devised to provide both analysis and design facilities and an opportunity for public involvement in the process as well as a central agency for resource information. The location of such a center for local values, visions, and ventures in a future Madison metropolitan megastructure is a logical integral part of the development envisioned by the graduate class.

At this time a Heritage Center for the Nine-Springs E-Way in Madison and Dane County has been designed and a program to fund it is well under way. The facility is to be maintained and operated with public funds. It will be located a short distance from the Dane County rail corridor discussed in this chapter (Figs. 11.19 and 11.20).

Tomorrow offers opportunities and cause for optimism for constructive changes utilizing the Regional Design Process. There are many instances of its success, and any degree of reflection on our current situation will reveal the possibilities for its use. It can be used from the scope of a single property to an entire nation or continent. Plans for educating its practitioners have been laid out and put into practice at a modest scale at the University of Wisconsin. Because of the number of students who have been trained, the dissemination of the concept through partici-

Figure 11.20 A birds-eye view of Madison relating the locations of the University, the Capitol, Olbrich Botanical Gardens, the Dane County E-Way, and the proposed Heritage Center facility in the E-Way

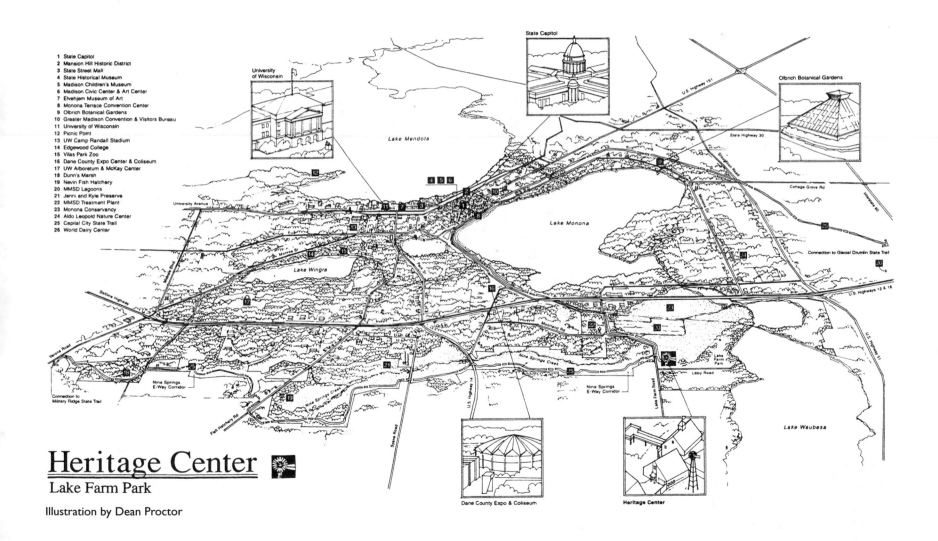

1 State Capitol
2 Mansion Hill Historic District
3 State Street Mall
4 State Historical Museum
5 Madison Children's Museum
6 Madison Civic Center & Art Center
7 Elvehjem Museum of Art
8 Monona Terrace Convention Center
9 Olbrich Botanical Gardens
10 Greater Madison Convention & Visitors Bureau
11 University of Wisconsin
12 Picnic Point
13 UW Camp Randall Stadium
14 Edgewood College
15 Vilas Park Zoo
16 Dane County Expo Center & Coliseum
17 UW Arboretum & McKay Center
18 Dunn's Marsh
19 Nevin Fish Hatchery
20 MMSD Lagoons
21 Jenni and Kyle Preserve
22 MMSD Treatment Plant
23 Monona Conservancy
24 Aldo Leopold Nature Center
25 Capital City State Trail
26 World Dairy Center

Heritage Center
Lake Farm Park

Illustration by Dean Proctor

pation by professional and lay people, the readers of articles and books, television viewers, and participants in seminars and meetings, the idea is already being acted upon and developed. The training, abilities, and imaginations of students and professionals will determine the usefulness of the ideas presented in this book.

Notes

[1]Edward Anderson, "A New Transit System Serves as a Catalyst for the Circle City Concept," *Focus Newsletter 2,* January 1985, Environmental Awareness Center, University of Wisconsin, Madison, Wisc.

[2]Richard Rogers, in *Richard Rogers + Architects,* Frank Russell, editor, Architectural Monographs, Academy editions, Dr. Andreas Popadakis, London, and St. Martin's Press, New York, 1985.

EPILOGUE

Today, more than two years after first beginning this book and after reviewing many planning, architecture, ecology, art, and landscape architecture books in my own library, I am pleasantly reminded that in the 46 years since receiving my undergraduate degree at the University of Illinois, we have made substantial improvements in the way we think about our global landscape.

Despite the fact that we still offer more constructive advice on the single components of a holistic process than on a broad environmental scope, we are at least developing the building blocks that are necessary for an integrated approach. This book is an effort to encourage an integrated way of including the many single and related components of that holistic process.

As Aldo Leopold, our Wisconsin mentor, stated in his book on wildlife management, examples of how to think, observe, deduce, and experiment rather than specifications of what to do are the goal. *Tomorrow by Design* may go far afield in presenting specifications on what to do, but it does so with the realization that creative people scanning the chapters will reinterpret, complement, and disagree but in the end modify and integrate these many thoughts into their own design and action vocabulary. In the spirit of the University of Wisconsin, there is a lot of winnowing and sifting to be done.

Nonetheless, a short list of principles can be stated to underscore the importance of implementing the Regional Design Process.

1. Given the present rate of population growth, we must accept that the only sensible alternative to unregulated growth is a rational global growth strategy and design and planning guidelines that will be enforced.
2. To reduce the expense and waste of building additional infrastructure and to reduce the further loss of rural land, we must accept the specification of higher livable densities to preserve the life-sustaining treasures of our global landscape.
3. We must understand that there exists an ever-increasing set of tools for inventorying and defining critical resources that are to be preserved, including urban constellations, environmental corridors, landscape personalities, and nodes of diversity.

4. We must view both the land and social ethic as an integrated holistic ethic that in addition to well-conceived legislation is essential for constructive action.

5. We must apply a simpler process than detailed, time-consuming, and expensive ecological surveys of the landscape by which outstanding resource patterns can be both identified and prioritized according to threatened human impact. Time is of the essence if we are to save resources from current destructive pressures.

6. We must exploit the vast array of resource studies and recommendations that have been made through the years to protect our life-sustaining landscape, which may, in the past, have lacked the support to be implemented. There is much to be learned, and much effort to be saved, by making use of findings from work previously completed.

7. We must recognize that the resources we seek to protect are the same resources on which the $1.9 trillion global tourism industry depends. By careful design these resources can be linked to develop the tourism/education circuits that we term E-Ways, Heritage necklaces, and National Parkways, which can enable people to enjoy these resources without destroying them.

8. We must understand that the necessary design efforts will demand the contributions of a wide-ranging interdisciplinary team. The Wisconsin Idea offers one model of how these talents can be integrated in a university-wide extension program. Recognizing the scale of environmental degradation as a threat to national security, we might recognize the need to provide academies of sustainable design that could house such interdisciplinary teams and support services in every major region and constellation.

9. As Jefferson recommended, we must inform the public's discretion so that the best choices for the future can be made. Even the best designs cannot proceed without public support, and the effective communication of future design options is essential to their success. The display of such options at Discovery Centers located strategically along E-Ways and Heritage Necklaces, involving the creative contribution of the arts community, would strengthen the educational opportunities needed to inform an enlightened public.

10. We must recognize that these efforts will require the full moral and financial support of leaders at every level of government, industry, and academia, as well as among private citizens. When 20 percent of the eligible voters determine who shall be our government, the wealth of our nation's talent is not properly utilized. Every vote counts in evaluating candidates, and at every level of government, we elect candidates who run. More of us must be willing to serve at all levels and take responsibility for government by taking part in it.

Landscape and townscape patterns are of great personal and public value. By knowing them, governors and the governed can choose appropriate implementation tools for the protection of our resources and our future.

From national overview to
local Wisconsin Awareness
Center

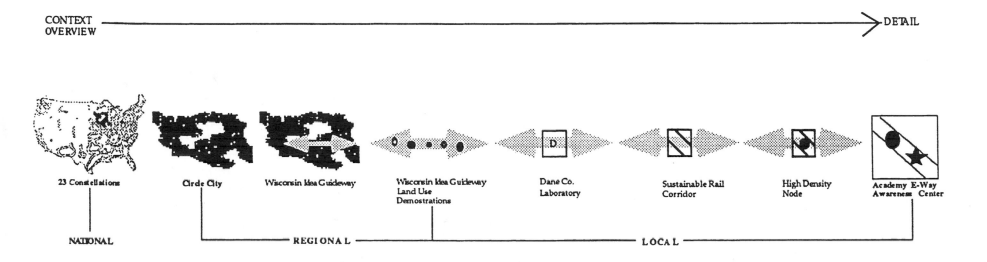

From National Overview to Local Wisconsin Awareness Center

In the past we have mobilized our resources for wasteful wars. It is time we organize to design for tomorrow. In this book I offer a possible process for meeting this responsibility. I choose to call it the Regional Design Process, and I advocate its adoption in whatever form is suitable for the place in which it is employed. The most important action is to evaluate the results of broad-scale analysis and implement the use of our resources in the least destructive and most rewarding way possible to our beloved human race.

GLOSSARY

Definitions of words and concepts that have special meaning in the Regional Design Process, as they are used in this book.

academy for sustainable design   for the purposes of this book, the ideal place in which the requirements of carrying out the Regional Design Process will be met with respect to working conditions, staff, and equipment.

aquifer recharge pattern   areas in which water enters the groundwater part of the hydrologic system from the atmosphere and surface of the earth.

awareness center   facility where local values and visions can be displayed for education and public participation in decision making.

carrying capacity   the ability of a site to support a given land use or population without undue deterioration—that is, without irreversible, irreplaceable changes occurring whose sacrifice is an important loss to future generations.

density, livable   a concentration of population such that the individual person has privacy, indoor and outdoor living space suitable for his or her needs, and indoor and outdoor spaces designed so that necessities and desired amenities are available.

driftless area   that area of the upper midwest untouched by the various recent episodes of glaciation that flattened the surrounding areas, leaving a hilly terrain dissected by a dendritic drainage pattern.

education and tourism   combining exploration of places away from home with planned opportunities to learn about those places and about resources, design, history, land use, and related subjects, as well as teaching simply by making available the opportunity to experience and observe places of extraordinary interest.

environment   the "ecos" or home of the human species; the earth and all of its physical parts, the forces to which they are subject, and the total relationship of all its parts and their workings.

environmental corridors   the linear pattern of occurrence of any or all of the combined features of water, wetlands, and steep topography of 12.5 percent or greater.

erosion   the gradual wearing away of any resource, notably soil, but also soil nutrients, rock, other physical resources, and even social resources.

E-Way   an ecological, educational, environmental, aesthetic, exercise way: a corridor with a trail or pathway accommodating pedestrians, bicyclists, cross-country skiers, and other nonmotorized use (with the possible exception of motorized wheelchairs).

guideway   a linear route for human travel that includes a multiple series of guides exemplifying wise and sustainable design.

heritage necklace   a particular connecting rail loop from Chicago, then to Milwaukee, to Prairie du Chien, to Rockford, and back to Chicago, connecting outstanding resource features.

hydrologic system   the interconnected system of water in the solid, liquid, or gaseous forms that exist in the earth's atmosphere, surface, and interior.

icon   (as in "resource icon") a graphic symbol representing a particular resource, useful in mapping resource inventories, or a spatial icon, referring to kinds of outdoor space (enclosed ore

defined by various elements of vegetation, topography, or other barriers).

integrated ethic   an ethic that combines social and land/resource ethical considerations.

interdisciplinary imperative   for an understanding of a region, the necessity for the integrated efforts of professionals with training in various applicable disciplines.

life-support system   the earth and all its resources that support life—that of humans and all other species; total earthly ecosystem, air, water, and land; life in all its forms and their relationships to each other and the place in which they live, reproduce, and evolve.

pattern   the spatial distribution (for our purposes, generally on the surface of the earth represented by a map) of the occurrence of a given set of data representing features such as topography (elevation of surface above or below sea level); water and wetlands; populations of people, animals, or plants; climate and weather effects and ranges; resources such as minerals, ores, and subsurface waters; characteristics of such resources, such as density, quantity, rarity, or quality; age-class distribution; land uses such as forest, agricul-

tural crops, residential, transportation commercial, industrial, and so on. Qualities such as color, textures, and spatial characteristics can be indicated.

personal rapid transit (PRT)   a transit system that moves large numbers of people in small groups (say one to five), separated from pedestrian, auto, and bicycle traffic, according to destination and the time of arrival at the system access point.

pollution, non-point-source   water or other pollution emanating from a source covering a wide area, such as runoff from a hillside loaded with fertilizer and silt.

pollution, point-source   water or other pollution, such as that contained in the plume from a single smokestack loaded with carbon dioxide, sulfur oxides, and nitrogen oxides.

population density   the concentration of people per acre; to be livable, human density must be viewed in relation to the physical, social, political, aesthetic, and other conditions of living spaces and their surroundings.

population explosion   a steep increase in the number of people in the world.

quality of life   our degree of satisfaction with our surroundings; the extent to which we are provided with the necessities and amenities of life.

Regional Design Process   to guide human development in such a way as to have the least impact possible on the dynamic balance between ourselves and the natural and cultural resources vital to our continued existence; a systematic, flexible, comprehensive approach to analyzing the landscape and guiding human growth to minimize impact on the land; communication through explanation, demonstration, and persuasive education; includes the components of resource inventory, analysis design, and communication (education and publicity).

resource depletion   destruction or consumption (often at a rapid rate) of a resource.

resource inventories   identifying, locating, and quantifying specific resources by kind and description resource patterns; the two-dimensional outline of the occurrence of a given resource on the surface of the earth.

restoration   to rehabilitate and put in as near original condition as possible a deteriorated natural or cultural resource.

sense of place   our appreciation of the design elements, style, and materials that encompass the particular characteristics of a given locality, in scale from that of a tree or house to a region, a nation, or the globe.

sustainable   capable of sustainability (q.v.).

sustainability   the degree to which our methods of using the life-support system will provide our descendants with as good a life as ours, or better; preserving or restoring the environment in which they live so as to be stable in the relationships of all parts of the system. We have set in motion processes that have not worked themselves out to an endpoint, which are perceived to be significantly and/or massively producing changes in the nature of the resources and the dynamics of the system, for better or worse (probably worse). Sustainability is used in the broad sense of preserving the means of our present way of life as well as the options for changes, improvements, and adjustments in human affairs.

urban sprawl   the spread of urbanization or sub-urbanization in an unmanageable and unplanned way that diminishes the value of both the urbanized and rural area involved.

wise use   intelligent utilization of resources in the way least destructive to the existence of the resource in question. Wise use involves not using finite resources when resource that can be replenished will serve, recycling materials where possible, not wasting useful materials and energy.

BIBLIOGRAPHY

Alexander, Christopher, *A Pattern Language,* Oxford University Press, New York, NY, 1977.

Alexander, et al., *The Oregon Experiment,* Oxford University Press, New York, NY, 1975.

American Heritage (eds.), *American Album,* Simon and Schuster, New York, NY, 1968.

Appleyard, Donald, *Livable Streets,* University of California Press, Berkeley, CA, 1981.

Arnheim, Rudolf, *Visual Thinking,* University of California Press, Berkeley, CA, 1969.

Bachelard, Gaston, *The Poetics of Space,* Orion Press, 1964. Translated by Jolas, Maria. Reprinted, Beacon Press, Boston, MA, 1994.

Badger, R. Reid, *The Great American Fair,* Nelson-Hall, Chicago, IL, 1979.

Baker, Richard St. Barbe, *Sahara Challenge,* Lutterworth Press, Cambridge, England, 1954.

Banham, Reyner, *Megastructure: Urban Futures of the Recent Past,* Harper and Row, London, 1976.

Bates, Marston, *Man in Nature,* Prentice-Hall, 1964.

Beard, Richard R., *Walt Disney's Epcot: Creating the New World of Tomorrow,* Harry N. Abrams, NY, 1982.

Beardsley, John, *Art in Public Places,* Partners for Livable Places, 1981.

Becker, William, *The Making of a Solar Village,* Wisconsin Energy Extension Service, Madison, WI.

Becker, William, *Come Rain or Come Shine,* Bureau of Water Regulation and Zoning, Wisconsin Department of Natural Resources, Madison, WI, 1983.

Berry, Dick, *The Wisconsin Idea . . . Then and Now,* Center for the Study of Public Policy and Administration, University of Wisconsin Extension, Madison, WI, 1972.

Berry, Jack, and Roger Podwell, *Man in the Urban Environment,* Waveland Press, Prospect Hts., IL 1975.

Bracken, John R., *Planting Design,* Pennsylvania State University Press, University Park, PA, 1953.

Breines, Simon, and William Dean, *The Pedestrian Revolution: Streets Without Cars,* Vintage Books, NY, 1974.

Bush-Brown, Louise, *Garden Blocks for Urban America,* Scribner's, 1969.

Calthorpe, Peter, and Sim Van der Ryn, *Sustainable Communities: A New Design Synthesis For*

Cities, Suburbs, and Towns, Sierra Club Books, San Francisco, 1986.

Carty, Donald, *The New City,* Urban America Inc., Praeger, 1969.

Chang, Amos Ih Tiao, *The Tao of Architecture,* Princeton University Press, Princeton, NJ, 1956.

Ching, Francis D.K., *Architecture: Form, Space, and Order* Van Nostrand Reinhold, New York, NY, 1979.

Clegg, Peter, *Energy for the Home,* Garden Way, 1975.

Crane, Jacob L. Jr., *Report on the Iowa 25 year Conservation Plan,* The Iowa Board of Conservation and the Iowa Fish and Game Commission, Wallace-Homestead, Des Moines, Iowa, 1933.

Creese, Walter, *Eight Great Spaces and Their Buildings,* Princeton University Press, Princeton, NJ, 1985.

Crowe, Sylvia, *Landscape of Power,* Architectural Press, London, England, 1960.

Crowe, Sylvia, *The Landscape of Roads,* Architectural Press, London, England, 1960.

Cullin, Gordon, *Townscape,* Reinhold, New York, 1961.

Cutler, Phoebe, *The Public Landscape of the New Deal,* Yale University Press, New Haven, CT, 1985.

Davidson, Frank P., *Macro-Engineering and the Future,* William Morrow and Co., New York, NY, 1983.

Davis, Sam, *The Form of Housing,* Van Nostrand, Van Nostrand Reinhold, Div. of International Thomas Publishing Prof./Ref. Div., New York, NY, 1977.

Day, Richard, *Vincennes,* G. Bradley Publishing, St. Louis, MO, 1988.

Dini, Massimo, *Renzo Piano: Projects and Buildings 1964–1983,* Rizzoli, New York, 1984.

Duany, Andres, and Elizabeth Plater-Zybeck, *Towns and Town-Making Principles,* Rizzoli, New York, NY, 1991.

Dyckman, John, and Joseph R. Passonneau, *Planning For a Nation of Cities,* MIT Press, Cambridge, 1961.

Environmental Awareness Center, *City of Prairie du Chien Master Plan,* University of Wisconsin, Madison, WI, 1981.

Environmental Awareness Center, *Future Development Alternatives for Circle City,* University of Wisconsin, Madison, WI, 1982.

Environmental Awareness Center, *Town of Dunn Open Space Preservation Handbook,* University of Wisconsin, Madison, WI, 1979.

Environmental Awareness Center, *The Madison E-Way System,* University of Wisconsin, Madison, WI, 1971.

Environmental Awareness Center, *Village of Spring Green Master Plan,* University of Wisconsin, Madison, WI, 1980.

Feininger, Andreas, *Leaves,* Dover, New York, NY, 1977.

Feininger, Andreas, *Trees,* Penguin, New York, NY, 1968.

Fitch, James Marsten, *American Building,* Houghton Mifflin, Boston, MA, 1947.

Fowler, Edmund P., *Building Cities that Work,* McGill University, Queen's University Press, Montreal, 1992.

Friebe, Wolfgang, *Buildings of the World Expositions,* Druckerei Volksstimme Magdeburg, 1985.

Friends of the Earth, *Progress as if Survival Mattered: A Handbook for a Conserver Society,* Friends of the Earth, San Francisco, 1981.

Fuller, Buckminster, *Utopia or Oblivion, Prospects for Humanity,* Bantam Books, Div. of: Bantam, Doubleday Dell, New York, NY, 1981.

Garreau, Joel, *Nine Nations of North America,* Houghton Mifflin, Boston, MA, 1981.

Gary, Dennis A. (ed.), *Personal Rapid Transit III,* University of Minnesota Press, Minneapolis, MN, 1976.

Gavois, Jean, *Going Up,* Otis Elevator Co., Farmington, CT, 1983.

Gerster, Georg, *Flights of Discovery,* Paddington Press, Ltd., New York and London, 1978.

Gibberd, Frederick, *Town Design,* Architectural Press, London, England, 1953.

Giedion, Sigfried, *A Decade of New Architecture,* Editions Girsberger, Zurich, 1951.

Giedion, Sigfried, *Space, Time, and Architecture,* Harvard University Press, Cambridge, MA, 1946.

Goc, Michael J., *Where the Waters Flow,* New Past Press, Friendship, WI, 1991.

Golany, Gideon, and Daniel Walden, *The Contemporary New Communities Movement in the United States,* University of Illinois Press, Champaign, IL, 1974.

Gottman, Jean, *Megalopolis,* Massachusetts Institute of Technology Press, Cambridge, MA, 1961.

Hardin, Garett, *Nature and Man's Fate,* Mentor, Woodland Hills, CA, 1959.

Hellmund, Paul Cawood, *The Ecology of Greenways,* University of Minnesota Press, Minneapolis, MN, 1993.

Hills, G. Angus, The Classification of Lands in Northern Ontario According to their Potential for Agricultural Production (Soil Report No. 1) Toronto: Research Division, Ontario Department of Lands and Forests, 1949.

Hills, G. Angus, The Classification of Lands in Ontario According to Their Potential for Agricultural Production in an Economy of Multiple Land-Use. Maple: Ontario Department of Lands and Forests, 1956.

Hills, G. Angus, Comparison of Forest Ecosystems (Vegetation and Soil) in Different Climate Zones. Forest Ecosystem Symposium, IXth International Botanical Congress, Montreal, 1959.

Hills, G. Angus, A Consideration of the Time Factors Which Determine the Satisfactory Use of Renewable Land Resources (paper presented at a seminar on Land-Use Problems in Ontario) sponsored by the Conservation Coucil of Ontario, Nov. 26–28, 1958, Vineland, Ontario.

Hills, G. Angus, Definitions: Ecological Basis of Land-Use Planning (unpublished mimeo for class use) October, 1966.

Hills, G. Angus, *Developing a Better Environment,* Ontario Economic Council, Toronto, August, 1970.

Hills, Angus, *The Ecological Basis for Land-Use Planning* (Research Report No. 46), Toronto: Ontario Department of Land and Forests, 1961.

Hills, G. Angus, *Field Methods for Investigating Site* (Site Research Manual 4), Toronto: Ontario Department of Lands and Forests, 1954 (revised 1957).

Hills, G. Angus, *Forest Site Evaluation in Ontario* (Research Report No. 42), Toronto: Ontario Department of Lands and Forests, 1960.

Hills, G. Angus, and R. Portlance, *The Glackmeyer Report of Multiple Land-Use Planning,* Toronto: Ontario Department of Lands and Forests, 1960.

Hills, G. Angus, *Ranking the Recreational Potential of Land Units by Gradient Analysis; a Physiographic Classification of Land for Recreational Use,* Ottawa: Proceedings—National Meeting on Land Capability Classification for Outdoor Recreation, February 24, 1966.

Hills, G. Angus, *Regional Site Research,* Forestry Chronicle (pp. 401–423), December 1960.

Hills, G. Angus, The Use of Aerial Photography in Mapping Soil Sites, *Forestry Chronicle,* Vol 26: Ottawa, Canada, 4-37.

Hills, G. Angus, The Use of Land-Type Maps in Land-Use Planning (Section Report [site] no.

31), Maple: Ontario Department of Lands and Forests, 1960.

Hiss, Tony, *The Experience of Place: A Completely New Way of Looking at and Dealing with our Radically Changing Cities and Countryside,* Knopf, New York, 1990.

Holland, *Who Designs America?,* Doubleday, New York, NY, 1966.

Horowitz, Alan J. (ed.), *Land-Use Impacts of Highway Projects,* University of Wisconsin Press, Madison, WI, 1984.

Holloway, Dennis (project director) and Corl, Huldah (ed.) (based on student work; Energy Design Studio, School of Architecture and Landscape Architecture). Winona (Towards an Energy Conserving Community), University of Minnesota School of Architecture, Minneapolis, MN, 1975.

Hough, Michael, *City Form and Natural Process,* Routlege, Div. of Routlege, Chapmart Hall, Inc., New York, NY, 1984.

Hough, Michael, *Out of Place,* Yale University Press, New Haven, CT, 1960.

Hunt, Mary and Don, *Hunt's Highlights of Michigan,* Malloy, 1991.

Hyams, Edward, *Soil and Civilization,* Thames and Hudson, New York, NY, 1952.

Jacobs, Allan B., *Great Streets,* MIT, Cambridge, MA, 1993.

Jacobs, Timothy, *The History of the Baltimore and Ohio,* Crescent Books, Random House Value, Div. of Random House, Inc., Avenal, NJ, 1989.

Jakle, John A. and David Wilson, *Derelict Landscapes: The Wasting of America's Built Environment,* Rowman and Littlefield, Savage, MD, 1992.

Kansas State University American Society of Landscape Architects, CAT Studio Report, The Kansas City Metropolitan Greenway, 1991.

Knevitt, Charles, *Space on Earth,* Thames-Methuen, London, England, 1985.

Knowles, Ralph L., *Sun, Rhythm Form,* University of Massachusetts Press, Amherst, MA, 1981.

Lamm, Thomas and Brian Vandewalle, *The Land Users Handbook For the Ridge and Valley Lands of Southwest Wisconsin,* Environmental Awareness Center and UW Extension, University of Wisconsin, 1979.

Lasdun, Denys, *Architecture in an Age of Scepticism,* Oxford University Press, New York, NY, 1984.

Laseau, Paul, and James Tice, *Frank Lloyd Wright, Between Principle and Form,* Van Nostrand Reinhold, Div. of International Thomson Publishing Prof./Ref. New York, NY, 1992.

Leopold, Aldo, *A Sand County Almanac,* Oxford University Press, New York, NY, 1949.

Lewis, Philip H., Aesthetic and Cultural Values, in Upper Mississippi River Comprehensive Basin Study, UMRCBS Coordinating Committee, 1970.

Lewis, Philip H., Jr., with L. B. Wetmore, J. A. Russell and others, The Challenge of Opportunity, unpublished report to the Wabash Valley Association by the Research Advisory Committee, Part I, The Plan for Research, Part II, The Plan for Research, Appendices, Stipes Publishing, Champaign, IL, January 14, 1960.

Lewis, Philip H., Jr. (ed.), *The Changing Landscape,* Department of Landscape Architecture, University of Illinois, Champaign, IL, 1957.

Lewis, Philip H., with W. T. Lamm, City of Boscobel Master Plan, Environmental Awareness Center, University of Wisconsin, Madison, WI, 1982.

Lewis, Philip H., The Door County, Wisconsin Comprehensive Plan pp. 109–179, Recreational Portrait of Door County, State of Wisconsin Department of Resource Development, Recreation Resource Section, 1964.

Lewis, Philip H., Environmental Design Concepts for Open Space Planning in Minneapolis and its Environs, in Parks and Recreation in Minneapolis, Vol. III, Minneapolis Board of Park Commissioners, December, 1965.

Lewis, Philip H. Jr., Environmental Values in the Paths of Progress, paper in proceedings of the Texas conference on Our Environmental Crisis, pp. 64–68, 1966.

Lewis, Philip H. Jr., The Havenwoods Awareness Center, Environmental Awareness Center, University of Wisconsin, Madison, WI, 1974.

Lewis, Philip H. Jr., The Highway Corridor as a Concept of Design and Planning, pp. 1–8, Bulletin 166 of The Highway Research Board, National Academy of Science, Washington, D.C., 1958.

Lewis, Philip H., et. al. Housing and Wood Products Assessment for Office of Technological Assessment, U.S. Congress, Environmental Awareness Center, University of Wisconsin, Madison, WI, 1982.

Lewis, Philip H. Jr., Landscape Awareness, in *The Thirtieth Star,* The State Historical Society of Wisconsin, pp. 8–14 May, 1964.

Lewis, Philip H. Jr., Landscape Inventory and Design of Everglades National Park, Florida Masters thesis, Harvard University, Cambridge, MA, 1953.

Lewis, Philip H. Jr., Fine, I. V., and Hovind, Ralph B., The Lake Superior Region Recreational Potential, preliminary report, 66 pp., Wisconsin Department of Development, Madison, WI, 1962.

Lewis, Philip H. Jr., Landscape Analysis I: Lake Superior South Shore Area, Wisconsin Department of Resource Development, Madison, WI, 1963.

Lewis, Philip H. Jr., Landscape Inventory and Design of Everglades National Park, Florida, Masters thesis, Harvard University, Cambridge, MA, 1953.

Lewis, Philip H. Jr., *Landscape Planning, Soil and Water Conservation Journal,* Ankeny, Iowa, 1964.

Lewis, Philip H. Jr., Landscape Resources, *Wisconsin Blue Book* (annual), Madison, WI, 1964.

Lewis, Philip H. Jr., Open Space Study and Analysis in the State of Illinois, Regional Landscape Planning Conference proceedings pp. 80–92, Department of Landscape Architecture, University of Illinois, 1961.

Lewis, Philip H. Jr. (participating author), Open Space in Northeastern Illinois, Technical Report No. 2, Northeastern Illinois Metropolitan Area Planning Commission, 132 pp., circa 1960.

Lewis, Philip H. Jr., Regional Design for Human Impact, privately published (Thomas Publishing Co.), Madison, WI, 146 pp., 1969.

Lewis, Philip H. Jr., Resource Inventory and Analysis, The Outdoor Recreation Plan (Wisconsin Development Series), State of Wisconsin Department of Resource Development, Madison, WI, 1963.

Lewis, Philip H., Recreation and Open Space in Illinois, University of Illinois Department of Landscape Architecture and Bureau of Community Planning, University of Illinois, Urbana, IL, 1961.

Lewis, Philip H., The Rural Environment, *Crops and Soils,* WI Society of Agronomy, Madison, WI, 1964.

Lewis, Philip H., Quality Corridors For Wisconsin, *Landscape Architecture Quarterly,* January, 1964, pp. 100–107.

Lewis, Philip H. Jr. and Bruce Murray, *Southern California Edison Transmission Alignment Study,* Landscapes Ltd., Madison, WI, 1971.

Lewis, Philip H. Jr., L.B. Wetmore, and Patrick Horsbrugh, A Visual Approach to Highway Planning and Design, The Highway Research Board Bulletin 190: 2924, National Academy of Science, 1958.

Lewis, Philip H. Jr., University of Illinois Annual List, publications of the faculty, published semi-annually, a source of articles and reports.

Limerick, Jeffrey, Nancy Ferguson, and Richard Oliver, America's Grand Resort Hotels, Random House, Avenal, NJ, 1979.

Little, Charles E., Greenways For America, Johns Hopkins University Press, Baltimore, MD, 1990.

Little, Charles, *The Dying of the Trees,* Viking, Div. of Penguin USA, Viking Penguin, New York, NY, 1995.

Litton, Tetlow, Sorensen, and Beatty, *Water and Landscape,* Water Information Center, Div. of Geraghty & Miller, Inc., Denver, CO, 1974.

Londenberg, Kurt, *Papier und Form,* Scherpe Verlag, Krefeld, Germany, 1972.

Lyle, John Tillman, *Design for Human Ecosystems,* Van Nostrand Reinhold, Div. of International Thomson Publishing Prof./Ref. Div, New York, NY, 1985.

Lyle, John T., *Regenerative Design for Sustainable Development,* Wiley, 1994.

Lynch, Kevin, Richard Unterman, and Robert Small, *Site Planning,* MIT Press, Cambridge, MA, 1962.

Lynch, Kevin, *Site Planning for Cluster Housing,* MIT Press, Cambridge, MA, 1962.

Lynes, Russell, *The Tastemakers,* Universal Library, 1949 (1980 reprint, Dover, New York, NY).

MacKaye, Benton, *The New Exploration: A Philosophy of Regional Planning,* University of Illinois Press, Urbana, IL, 1962.

Mandelker, Daniel R., *Green Belts and Urban Growth,* University of Wisconsin Press, Madison, WI, 1962.

Martin, Lawrance, *The Physical Geography of Wisconsin,* University of Wisconsin Press, Madison, WI 1965 (1st Ed. 1916).

McHarg, Ian L., *Design With Nature,* Natural History Press, Garden City, New York, 1969.

McHarg, Ian, with W. Robinson Fisher, Ann Spirn and Narendra Juneja Pardisan, Plan for an Environmental Park in Tehran, the Mandala Collaborative: Wallace, McHarg, Roberts, and Todd, Winchell Press, 1975.

Marsh, William M., *Environmental Analysis,* McGraw-Hill, New York, NY, 1978.

Marsh, William M., *Landscape Planning Environment Applications,* Wilcy, NY, 1983.

Meredith, Robert W. Jr., and Laurie S.Z. Greenberg, Global Sustainability: A Selected, Annotated Bibliography, Report 137, Institute for Environmental Studies, University of Wisconsin, Madison, WI, 1992.

Minneapolis Planning and Development Urban Design Studio, *Downtown Edges,* Minneapolis, MN, 1975.

Mumford, Lewis, *The Culture of Cities,* Harcourt, Brace, subsidiary of Harcourt General Corp., Orlando FL, 1938.

Mumford, Lewis, *The Urban Prospect,* Harcourt, Brace, NY, 1968.

National Academy of Science, *Productive Agriculture and a Quality Environment,* Washington, DC, 1974.

New Jersey State Planning Commission, *Communities of Place,* Trenton, N.J., 1992.

Newnan, Oscar, *Defensible Space,* Macmillan, New York, NY, 1972.

Oliver, Paul (editor), *Shelter and Society,* Praeger, 1969.

Olmstead, Frederick Law, *Landscape into Cityscape* Cornell University Press, Ithaca, NY 1968, c1967.

Ophuls, William, *Ecology and the Politics of Scarcity,* W. H. Freeman, San Francisco, 1977.

Pell, Claiborne (Senator), *Megalopolis Unbound, the Supercity and the Transportation of Tomorrow,* Praeger, NY, 1966.

Piano, Renzo, *Projects and Buildings 1964–1983, Architectural Documents,* Rizzoli, subsidiary of Rizzoli Editore Corp., New York, NY, 1984.

Process Architecture 100, *Renzo Piano Building Workshop: In Search of a Balance,* A+U Publishing, Tokyo, 1989.

Process Architecture 101, *Jerde Partnership, reinventing the communal experience, a problem of place.* Process Architecture, Tokyo, 1992.

Process Architecture, *Plazas of Southern Europe,* Kato Akinori (ed.), Process Architecture, Tokyo, 1985.

President's Council on Recreation and Natural Beauty, *From Sea to Shining Sea,* United State Government Printing Office, 1968.

Rapuano, Michael, *The Freeway in the City,* United States Printing Office, 1968.

Real Estate Research Corporation, *The Costs of Sprawl: Environmental and Economic Costs of Alternative Residential Development Patterns at the Urban Fringe,* U.S. Government Printing Office, 1974.

Redstone, Louis G., *The New Downtowns,* McGraw-Hill, New York, NY, 1976.

Register, Richard, *Ecocity Berkely: Building Cities For a Healthy Future,* North Atlantic Books, Berkely, CA, 1987.

Reilly, William K., *The Use of Land: A Citizen's Policy Guide to Urban Growth,* Crowell, 1973.

Risebero, Bill, *Fantastic Form,* New Amsterdam Bks., Franklin, NY, 1992.

Rogers, Richard, *Richard Rogers and Architects,* (Frank Russell, ed.), Architectural Monographs, Academy editions, London, in U.S., St Martin's, NY.

Safdie, Moshe, *Beyond Habitat,* MIT Press, Cambridge, MA, 1970.

Safdie, Moshe, *Form and Purpose,* Houghton Mifflin, Boston, MA, 1982.

Schumacher, E. F., *Small is Beautiful,* Harper and Row, NY, 1973.

Scully, Vincent, *American Architecture and Urbanism,* Henry Holt, New York, NY, 1969.

Sharp, Thomas, *Exeter Phoenix: A plan for rebuilding,* Architectural Press, London, 1946.

Sharp, Thomas, *Oxford Replanned,* Architectural Press, London, 1948.

Smith, Herbert, *The Citizen's Guide to Planning,* Chandler-Davis, West Trenton, N.J., 1962.

Spirn, Anne Whiston, *The Granite Garden: Urban Nature and Human Design,* Basic Books, NY, 1984.

Steichen, Edward, *The Family of Man,* Museum of Modern Art, New York, NY, 1955.

Stein, Clarence S., *Toward New Towns for America,* Reinhold, New York, NY, 1957.

Stenhouse, David, *Understanding Towns,* Hove, Wayland, Madison, WI, 1977.

Stokes, Samuel N., A. Elizabeth Watson, Genevieve P. Keller, and J. Timothy Keller, *Saving America's Countryside: A Guide to Rural Conservation,* Johns Hopkins Press, Baltimore, MD, 1989.

Storer, John H., *The Web of Life,* Signet Books, New York, NY, 1953.

Tate, H. Clay, *Building a Better Home Town,* HarperCollins, New York, NY, 1954.

Taylor, Lisa (ed.), *The Phenomenon of Change,* Rizzoli, Subsidiary of Rizzoli Editore Corp., New York, NY, 1984.

Thomas, William L., Jr., *Man's Role in Changing the Face of the Earth,* University of Chicago Press, Chicago, IL, 1956.

Tubbs, Ralph, *The Englishman Builds,* Penguin, New York, NY, 1945.

Tunnard, Christopher, and Henry H. Reed, *American Skyline,* Mentor Books, 1956.

United States Department of Housing and Urban Development, Earth Sheltered Housing, 1980.

U.S. Green Building Council, *Local Governments Sustainable Buildings Guidebook* (prepared for Public Technology, Inc., Washington, DC 20004).

United States Department of Agriculture, Our National Landscape, (a conference on Applied Techniques for Analysis and Management of the Visual Resources), 1979.

United States Department of Transportation, Scenic Byways, 1988.

United States Government Printing Office, Beauty for America, 1965.

United States Government Printing, The Rebirth of the American City, Part I, 1976.

Unterman, Richard, and Robert Small, *Site Planning for Cluster Housing,* VanNostrand-Reinhold, New York, NY, 1974.

Urban Design Studio, Downtown Edges, Minneapolis Planning and Development, 1974.

Vander Ryn, Sim, and Peter Calthorpe, *Sustainable Communities,* Sierra Club, Santa Fe, NM, 1986.

VanMatre, Steve, and Bill Weiler, The Earth Speaks, Institute for Earth Education, 1983.

Von Eckardt, Wolf, *The Challenge of Megalopolis,* MacMillan, NY, 1964.

Walker, Lester, *American Shelter,* Overlook Press, New York, NY, 1981.

Watts, May Theilgard, *Reading the Landscape of Europe,* Harper and Row, New York, NY, 1971.

Whyte, William H., *City,* Doubleday, New York, NY, 1988.

Whyte, William H., *The Last Landscape,* Doubleday, Garden City, NY, 1968.

Wisconsin Blue Book, *Natural Resources of Wisconsin,* State of Wisconsin, 1964.

Wong, Wucius, *Principles of Three-Dimensional Design,* Van Nostrand-Reinhold, New York, NY, 1977.

Wood, Denis, *The Power of Maps,* Guilford Press, New York, NY, 1992.

Worldwatch Institute, *State of the World,* Norton, NY, 1993.

Wrenn, Tony P., and Elizabeth D. Mulloy, *America's Forgotten Architecture,* Random House, New York, NY, 1976.

Wu, J. and Loucks, Orie, *Balance-of-Nature and Modern Ecological Theory: A Shift in Ecological Thinking,* in Sino-EDC (ed), *Development and Trends in Modern Ecology,* University Science and Technology Press, Hefei.

Zevi, Bruno, *Architecture as Space,* Horizon Press, Tucson, AZ, 1957.

INDEX